Is Jihād a Just War?
War, Peace, and Human Rights Under Islamic and Public International Law

IS JIHĀD A JUST WAR?
WAR, PEACE, AND HUMAN RIGHTS UNDER ISLAMIC AND PUBLIC INTERNATIONAL LAW

Hilmi M. Zawati

The Edwin Mellen Press
Lewiston•Queenston•Lampeter

Library of Congress Cataloging-in-Publication Data

Zawati, Hilmi.
Is Jihād a just war? : war, peace, and human rights under Islamic and public international law / Hilmi M. Zawati.
p. cm. --
Includes bibliographical references and index.

1. Just war doctrine. 2. Jihād. I. Title.
ISBN 0-7734-0804-5

KZ6396 .Z39 2001
297.7'2--dc21

2001044081

hors série.

A CIP catalog record for this book is available from the British Library.

The Edwin Mellen Press
Box 450
Lewiston, New York
USA 14092-0450

The Edwin Mellen Press
Box 67
Queenston, Ontario
CANADA L0S 1L0

The Edwin Mellen Press, Ltd.
Lampeter, Ceredigion, Wales
UNITED KINGDOM SA48 8LT

Printed in the United States of America

To the memory of my late parents,
may Allah bestow on them
His mercy and
be pleased with them

Contents

Transliterations

ا a	س s	ل l
ب b	ش sh	م m
ت t	ص ṣ	ن n
ث th	ض ḍ	ه h
ج j	ط ṭ	و w
ح ḥ	ظ ẓ	ي y
خ kh	ع ‘	
د d	غ gh	
ذ dh	ف f	
ر r	ق q	
ز z	ك k	

Short vowels:
Damma = u
Fatha = a
Kasra = i

Long vowels:
Madd bil-wāw = ū
Madd bil-alif = ā
Madd bil-yā’ = ī

Diphthongs:

أي = ay

أو = aw

PREFACE

This book by Hilmi M. Zawati is a welcome contribution to the indispensable reflection on, and struggle for, peace and human rights. The author examines fundamental issues of war, peace and human rights from the perspective of both Islamic and public international law.

The importance of the contribution of Islamic thought to the ethical and intellectual heritage of mankind is often underestimated. At earlier times of history, particularly in the Middle Ages, there seems to have been much more cross-fertilization between Islamic, Jewish and Christian thinking than in the modern era. Muslim philosophers like Avicenna (Ibn Sīna) and Averroes (Ibn Rushd) had a strong influence on European thinkers. The great Jewish philosopher Maimonides moved from Cordoba in Andalusia to Cairo at the age of thirty, and stayed there for the rest of his life, writing mostly in Arabic. Thomas Aquinas was very familiar with Arab philosophy and science. Unfortunately, at present there is more misunderstanding than mutual understanding between the Muslim and Western worlds. Hilmi M. Zawati's book helps to dispel some of the former while contributing to intellectual dialogue between the two civilizations.

As far as human rights are concerned, I have often said and written that it is wrong to believe that they suddenly walked onto the stage of history in the late 18th century, in Europe and North America. The aspiration to the recognition of human dignity can be traced in earlier periods of history, in different regions of the world and in different cultures and religions. Presenting Islam as the "natural" and perennial enemy of human rights is certainly a distortion of history. As Hilmi

M. Zawati shows, many rules and principles, which we now call human rights or humanitarian law were centuries ago already spelled out in Islamic law and tradition. The tendency of Western countries to appropriate and monopolize human rights and their historical development is not in the interest of the universal recognition of these rights.

The relationship between culture and religion, human rights and political power raises difficult issues. Far too often, culture and religion have been used and abused to reinforce the power of political rulers, regimes and states. Frequently they have been conscripted as tools of totalitarian ideologies and practices. All religions, Islam as well as others, must beware of the danger of being exploited and used by ruthless political power against the human being and his or her dignity and fundamental rights. I strongly believe that it is essential to be constantly aware of this danger and to fight it unremittingly.

Historical experience also teaches us that the interpretation, which men give to religion and the consequences they draw from it evolve over time. Who in the present Christian world would preach or justify a crusade against the "infidels"? The Catholic Church, which for a long time rejected human rights and, in particular, freedom of conscience and religion, now strongly advocates respect for these rights. The interpretation given to religions is not immutable and human rights may offer a means of helping it to evolve. It is obvious that some of the rules referred to by Hilmi M. Zawati as provisions of Islamic law, e.g. those concerning the punishment of apostates, are in conflict with modern international human rights law. Likewise, some of the forms of punishment mentioned in his work would clearly be regarded as inhuman by present day standards. The Qur'anic precept "Let there be no compulsion in religion" is an admirable expression of tolerance. However, does freedom of religion include the right to leave the Muslim religion?

As far as the concept of "*jihād*" is concerned, the author writes that it "might be one of the most misinterpreted terms in the history of Islamic legal discourse". I would add that it is certainly one of the most misinterpreted terms in a certain Western, anti-Islamic discourse. Hilmi M. Zawati shows that the concept

Foreword

The word *Jihād* may be one of the most misinterpreted terms in the history of Islamic legal discourse. In the last two decades or so, particularly in the aftermath of the Islamic revolution in Iran, the birth of various Islamic resistance movements, and the end of the Cold War era, misconceptions of *Jihād* and the consequent branding Islam as the "new enemy", have become a hotly debated issue in Western literature.

The idea of this book crystallized after careful examination and analysis of a considerable number of recent scholarly and journalistic works on the concept of war in Islamic legal theory. Most of these works, which are generally speaking descriptive and polemical, have distorted their representations by relying heavily on misleading stereotypes and, at best, a number of minor secondary sources. The result has been a distortion of the term *Jihād* to the point where it is virtually synonymous in the public mind with terrorism.

The fictive constructs of these works were built on general misconceptions, wrong assumptions, and political bias. Many of the earlier authors, who engaged in the study of Islamic legal theory, judged Islamic law according to their own Western values and failed to read or understand classical Arabic; the language of the primary sources of Islamic law. Moreover, they built their hypotheses on acts of so-called "fundamental" Muslim groups, and on particular practices in some Muslim societies. As well, authors failed utterly to distinguish between Islamic law and the contemporary legislation of Muslim nations, which is in general not Islamic.

As its title suggests, the purpose of this book is to investigate, analyze and critically examine the theory of war under Islamic and public international law. The chief aim of this work is to counter the distorted image of *Jihād* and to demonstrate that *Jihād* is a just, defensive and exceptional form of warfare, geared to the maintenance of peace and the protection of human rights for all people, regardless of their race, sex, language or religious belief.

Through an examination of the norms of Islamic and public international law on armed conflict, the present study argues that peace is the rule and war the exception in Islam, and that no obligatory state of war exists between Muslims and the rest of the world. Accordingly, the division of the world into *dār al-Islām* (territory of Islam) and *dār al-ḥarb* (territory of war), far from being predicated on a state of mutual hostility, was dictated by particular events, and is not imposed by scripture.

Furthermore, this analysis asserts that the chief aim of *Jihād* is not to force unbelievers to embrace Islam, nor to expand the boundaries of the Islamic state, but to sanction warfare by Muslims whenever their security is threatened. Accordingly, the Lewis-Huntington's theory of "Islam's bloody borders" is inadequate and groundless. In contrast, the present study points out that Islamic international law considers the right to life as the most basic and supreme right, and one which human beings are entitled to enjoy without distinction of any kind.

A closer look at the provisions of the Islamic law of nations, which governs the doctrine of *Jihād*, reveals that it is realistic and practical. It regulates conduct during a *Jihād* on the basis of certain human principles compatible with those upon which modern international conventions are based. Furthermore, Islamic law made a great contribution to international humanitarian law more than a millennium before the codification of the four Geneva Conventions of 1949, and eight centuries before the appearance of Hugo Grotius's treatise "*De jure belli ac pacis libri tres,*" which was published in 1625.

It is hoped that this intercultural dialogue on one of the most complicated and controversial issues facing mankind today will provide an authentic analysis and interpretation of the norms of both Islamic and international public law based on its primary sources. It is also hoped that it will offer a corrective perspective to the literature and academic notions that have heretofore been accepted as the conventional wisdom about *Jihād* and the Islamic law of nations, and foster a better understanding of Islam's position on peace, security and armed conflict. Finally, this analysis concludes that there is a unique relationship between *Jihād* and the notion of just war, a matter which qualifies it as the *bellum justum* of Islam.

Hilmi M. Zawati
Montreal, April 20, 2001

Acknowledgements

I would like to express my sincere gratitude and thanks to Professors Wael B. Hallaq and Uner Turgay of the Institute of Islamic Studies, McGill University, and to Professors Irwin Cotler, Peter Leuprecht, Steven J. Toope, and Elobaid A. Elobaid of the McGill Law School, for their interesting comments and valuable suggestions on the draft chapters of this study.

I would also take this opportunity to recognize a debt of gratitude to the staff of the Islamic Studies Library, Mr. Adam Gacek, Ms. Salwa Ferahian, Mr. Steve Millier and Mr. Wayne St. Thomas, and to sincerely thank the staff of the McGill Law School Library, especially Ms. Mary Lourenço, Mr. Carlos Rojas, and Mr. John Kirkpatrick for their assistance during the preparation of this work.

My grateful thanks go to Professor Ali H. Hajjaj, University of Petra, for translating *Ḥijjat al-Wadā'* (The Farewell-Pilgrimage Sermon) into English and for reading the final version of this book. I am also indebted to Ms. Reem Meshal for helping me edit this work and to Mrs. Alison Morin for her painstaking care in typing the manuscript. I would also like to thank Mrs. Ibtisam Mahmoud for preparing the index of this study.

My deepest appreciation and thanks go to the following individuals and organizations, for giving permission to reprint the documents found in the annex to this analysis: Mr. Ahmad B. Chami, ABC GRAPHIKART, for the Arabic calligraphy on the front cover; Mr. Ahmed Salim, Islamic Gateway, for reprinting "The Treaty of Medina" and " The Pact of Najran"; Professor Patrick Buckley, Royal Irish Academy, for reprinting "The Treaty of Jerusalem" and "The Treaty of

Egypt"; Dr. Salem Azzam, Islamic Council of Europe, for reprinting "The Universal Islamic Declaration of Human Rights"; and Ambassador Mohamed Saleh Zaimi, Organization of the Islamic Conference, and Ms. Anne Cunningham, UN Publication Board, for reprinting "The Cairo Declaration on Human Rights in Islam".

I should also mention here that citations from the Holy Qur'ān are drawn, with the author's revisions, from the English version done by Abdullah Yusuf Ali entitled *The Holy Qur'ān: Text Translation and Commentary*, 2nd ed. (Kuwait: That Es-Salasil, 1984).

Finally, I wish to thank my wife and children for their patience and endless support, since this book was written during time that rightly belonged to them.

Introduction

Relying on a number of minor secondary sources, some scholars have argued that Islam was spread by the sword, force and compulsion,[1] and that a state of war must necessarily exist between Muslims and the rest of the world until the latter accepts Islam or submits to the power of the Islamic state.[2] They undoubtedly believe that every Muslim bears a religious duty to kill any unbeliever when *jihād* breaks out.[3] W. Montgomery Watt treats this issue in the following statement:

> "For many centuries most Europeans believed that Islam was a religion of violence which spread by the sword.[4] This was part of the distorted image of Islam, which, as I have argued elsewhere,[5] was the negative identity of Western Europe or Western Christendom - a picture of what it considered itself not to be."[6]

---

[1]Sobhi Mahmassani, "The Principles of International Law in the Light of Islamic Doctrine," *Recueil des Cours* 117 (1966): 241.

[2]Bernard Lewis, *The Political Language of Islam* (Chicago: The University of Chicago Press, 1988), 73; Majid Khadduri, *The Islamic Law of Nations:* Shaybānī's Siyar (Baltimore, Maryland: The John Hopkins University Press, 1966), 13.

[3]Farooq Hassan, *The Concept of State and Law in Islam* (New York: University Press of America, 1981), 202; W. Gardner, "Jihād," *The Moslem World* 2: 1 (January 1912): 348.

[4]On the contrary, Sir Thomas Arnold conceives that the expansion of the Islamic religion has transpired through peaceful methods particularly preaching. See Thomas W. Arnold, *The Preaching of Islam: A History of the Propagation of the Muslim Faith* (Lahore, Pakistan: Muhammad Ashraf Publications, 1961), 115-119.

[5]W. Montgomery Watt, *The Influence of Islam on Medieval Europe* (Edinburgh: The University Press, 1972), 72-84.

[6]W. Montgomery Watt, "The Significance of the Theory of Jihād," in *Akten des VII. Kongresses für Arabistik und Islamwissenschaft*, eds. Herausgegeben Von and Albert Dietrich (Göttingen:

Among Western scholars who propagate this "distorted image" is Bernard Lewis, who views Islam "as a militant, indeed as a military religion, and its followers as fanatical warriors, engaged in spreading their faith and their law by armed might."[7] A similar approach was adopted by D. B. Macdonald in his article *"djihād"* in "The Encyclopaedia of Islam."[8] Macdonald claimed that *"djihād"* consists of military action with the object of the expansion of Islam."[9]

Moreover, since the breakdown of the former Soviet Union and the end of the Cold War, an oriental school of thought has flourished in the West. This school, which is represented by Bernard Lewis, Samuel Huntington and Daniel Pipes, deems that hostility is a deep-rooted feature of the Muslim psyche,[10] and that Islam

---

Vandenhoeck and Ruprecht, 1976), 390.

[7]Bernard Lewis, *supra note* 2, at 71. In this sense, Max Weber stated that "Islam was never really a religion of salvation. It is a warrior religion." See Bryan S. Turner, *Weber and Islam: A Critical Study* (London: Routledge & Kegan Paul, 1974), 34; Max Weber, *Economy and Society: An Outline of Interpretive Sociology*, 3 vols. (New York: Bedminster Press, 1968), 2:624-626; Ralph Schroeder, *Max Weber and the Sociology of Culture* (London: Sage Publications, 1992), 65-70.

[8]*The Encyclopaedia of Islam*, 2nd ed., s.v. "Djihād," by D.B. Macdonald.

[9]In his book entitled "*Promesses de L'Islam*," Roger Garaudy refutes Macdonald's notion. In the following statement, Garaudy points out that: "Il est de tradition, chez les Occidentaux, de traduire *djihād* par «guerre sainte», c'est-à-dire guerre entreprise pour la propagation de l'Islam. Le rédacteur de l'article «Djihad» dans l'*Encyclopédie de l'Islam*, l'orientaliste D.B. Macdonald, commence par affirmer: «L'expansion de l'Islam par les armes est un devoir religieux pour tous les musulmans.»

Ore, *djihad* ne signifie pas «guerre» (il existe un autre mot pour cela: *ḥarb*), mais «effort» sur le chemin de Dieu. Le Coran est parfaitement explicite: «Pas de contrainte en matière de religion» (II, 256).

Tous les textes que l'on a invoqués pour faire de l'Islam un épouvantail, une «religion de l'épée», ont été invariablement séparés de leur contexte. On a, par exemple, appelé «verset de l'épée» le verset 5 de la IXe sourate en détachant «tuez les polythéistes partout où vous les trouverez» du verset précédent (IX,4) qui précise qu'il s'agit de combattre ceux qui ayant conclu un pacte l'ont ensuite violé, ou ceux qui prétendent empêcher les musulmans de professer et de pratiquer leur foi.

En un mot, si la guerre n'est pas exclue, elle n'est acceptée que pour *la défense* de la foi lorsque celle-ci est menacée, et non pas pour *la propagation* de la foi par les armes.

La guerre ne se justifie, selon le Coran, que lorsqu'on est victime d'une agression ou d'une transgression, actes que les musulmans eux-mêmes s'interdisent formellement s'ils obéissent au Coran: «Combattez dans le chemin de Dieu *ceux qui luttent contre vous*. Ne soyez pas transgresseurs; Dieu n'aime pas les transgresseurs.» Le Corân, II: 190."

[10]For opposing viewpoints see Fred Halliday, *Islam and the Myth of Confrontation: Religion and Politics in the Middle East* (London: I.B. Tauris & Co. Ltd., 1996), 112; Michael Jansen, "Terrorism is a Response to Western Hypocrisy," in *Islam: Opposing Viewpoints*, ed. Paul A. Winters (San Diego: Greenhaven Press, Inc., 1995), 164-168.

has replaced communism as the new world threat.[11] Bernard Lewis argues that Islamists display an antagonism, which is tinged with humiliation, envy and fear. In his article entitled "the Roots of Muslim Rage", Lewis states that:

> "It should by now be clear that we are facing a mood and a [fundamental Muslim] movement for transcending the level of issues and policies and the governments that pursue them. This is no less than a clash of civilizations - the perhaps irrational but surely historic reaction of an ancient rival against our Judeo-Christian heritage, our secular present, and the world-wide expansion of both."[12]

Samuel Huntington seizes and expands upon this notion of a clash of civilizations.[13] In a widely read article published in *Foreign Affairs* in the summer of 1993, Huntington points out that:

> "In Eurasia the great historic fault lines between civilizations are once more aflame. This is particularly true along the boundaries of the crescent-shaped Islamic bloc of nations from the bulge of Africa to central Asia. Violence also occurs between Muslims, on the one hand, and Orthodox Serbs in the Balkans, Jews in Israel, Hindus in India, Buddhists in Burma and Catholics in the Philippines. Islam has bloody borders."[14]

---

[11]Shireen T. Hunter, "The Rise of Islamist Movements and the Western Response: Clash of Civilizations or Clash of Interests?" in *The Islamist Dilemma: The Political Role of Islamist Movements in the Contemporary Arab World*, ed. Laura Guazzone (Berkshire: Ithaca Press, 1995), 321. This theory has been reflected in the works of many Western Scholars, particularly: Daniel Pipes, "Political Islam is a Threat to the West," in *Islam: Opposing Viewpoints*, ed. Paul A. Winters (San Diego: Greenhaven Press, Inc., 1995), 190; Joseph Grinstein, "Jihād and the Constitution: The First Amendment Implications of Combating Religiously Motivated Terrorism," *The Yale Law Journal* 105:5 (March 1996): 1348; Steven Emerson, "Political Islam Promotes Terrorism," in *Islam: Opposing Viewpoints*, ed. Paul A. Winters (San Diego: Greenhaven Press, Inc., 1995), 160.

In his work "*Islam and Colonialism*," Rudolph Peters emphasizes that "The Islamic doctrine of *jihād* has always appealed to Western imagination. The image of the dreadful Turk, clad in a long robe and brandishing his scimitar, ready to slaughter any infidel that might come his way and would refuse to be converted to the religion of Mohamet, has been a stereotype in Western literature for a long time. Nowadays this image has been replaced by that of the Arab 'terrorist' in battledress, armed with a Kalashinkov gun and prepared to murder in cold blood innocent Jewish and Christian women and children." Rudolph Peters, *Islam and Colonialism: The Doctrine of jihād in Modern History* (The Hague, The Netherlands: Mouton Publishers, 1979), 4.

[12]Bernard Lewis, "The Roots of Muslim Rage," *The Atlantic Monthly* 266 (September 1990), 60.

[13]"Not Again: A Survey of Islam and the West," *The Economist* (August 6-12, 1994): 3.

[14]Samuel P. Huntington, "The Clash of Civilizations?" *Foreign Affairs* 72:3 (Summer 1993): 35. In his lecture on "Clash of Civilizations or Clash of Definition?" delivered in London, February 1995, and in Montreal, October 1996, Professor Edward Said, of Columbia University, has refuted

Taking into consideration the conscientious endeavours of other scholars to refute the above allegations,[15] a comparative analytical study, based on the primary sources of Islamic and public international law, reveals that Islam's so-called "bloody borders" and Lewis-Huntington's theory on *jihād* are fictive constructs. This study attempts a critical examination of the theory of war in Islamic and public international law in an effort to formulate an alternative view and demonstrate that *jihād* is a just, defensive, and exceptional form of warfare geared to achieve the ideal Islamic public order, and to secure justice and equality among all people.[16] To do so, the first chapter of this book will discuss in a comparative fashion the concept of war and belligerent occupation in Islamic and public international law. It will try mainly to establish clear and satisfactory answers to the following questions: what are the motives of *jihād* if its primary aim is not to convert unbelievers by force, or to expand the Islamic state? Is *jihād* a holy war? Is Majid Khadduri correct in surmising that *jihād* is equivalent to the Christian concept of the crusade?[17] Is there an obligatory state of war between Muslims and the rest of the world as argued by Bernard Lewis and Majid Khadduri?[18] What is the concept of war and belligerent occupation in Islamic international law? What are the characteristics of the duty of

---

Huntington's theory. Said implied that Huntington had lost his edge as one of the leading political theoreticians of the Cold War era, and has since branded Islam as the new enemy, knowing that the issue is a hot potato in the West.

In the same fashion, Judith Miller, the former Cairo Bureau chief of the New York Times, has alleged, in her 574-page book, that Islamic militants, since the days of the Prophet Muhammad, were bloody, fanatic, and intolerant. She attempts to confirm that only Westerners believe firmly in the inherent dignity of the individual and the value of human rights and legal equality for all. See Judith Miller, *God has Ninety-Nine Names Reporting from a Militant Middle East* (New York: Simon and Schuster, 1996), 88-94.

[15]See, for example, Gustave Le Bon, *La Civilisation des Arabes* (Paris: Librairie de Firmin-Didot et C[ie], 1884), 110-154; John Kelsay, *Islam and War* (Louisville, Kentucky: Westminster/John Knox Press, 1993), 29-36; Marcel A. Boisard, *jihād: A commitment to Universal Peace* (Indianapolis, Indiana: The American Trust Publications, 1988), 23; and Rudolph Peters, *jihād in Mediaeval and Modern Islam* (Leiden, The Netherlands: E.J. Brill, 1977), 3.

[16]Majid Khadduri, *supra note* 2, at 17.

[17]*Ibid.*, at 15.

[18]Bernard Lewis, "Politics and War," in *The Legacy of Islam*, eds. Joseph Schacht and C.E. Bosworth (Oxford: The Clarendon Press, 1974); 175; Majid Khadurri, *supra note* 2, at 13.

jihād? What are permissible and forbidden acts of hostility according to the doctrine of *jihād*? and when can *jihād* be terminated?

On the other hand, chapter two examines the Islamic State's relations with other nations in light of the doctrine of *jihād*. It investigates the legal status of protected minorities and enemy persons, their rights and obligations under Islamic Law, and demonstrates that the dividing of the world into *dār al-Islām* and *dār al-ḥarb*, by Muslim jurists, was dictated by particular events, and did not necessitate a permanent state of hostility between these territories. Furthermore, this chapter will show that Muslim jurists fourteen centuries ago developed an Islamic theory of international relations, in the modern sense of the term, to regulate inter-state relations between *dār al-Islām* and other territories in times of peace and armed conflict. Thus, Islamic laws on concluding treaties and mutual relations; namely, reciprocity, diplomatic intercourse, foreign trade, arbitration and neutrality will be the object of a comparative discussion.

Chapter three tries to address the crucial question, "to what extent did Islamic humanitarian law contribute to the protection of civilians' personal rights during wars and armed disputes?" To this end, a number of these rights will be examined in light of the norms of Islamic and international law of human rights, particularly the right to life, the prohibition of torture and inhuman treatment, and the right to respect of one's religious beliefs, customs and traditions. All this indicates that civilians' rights are not only recognized by Islamic law, but are also protected by practical, realistic legal and administrative rules, which were designed to ensure their application without distinction of any kind. Moreover, this chapter reveals that Islamic humanitarian law regards the right to life as a sacred right, and holds that any transgression against this right is considered a crime against the entire community.[19] On the other hand, it will be seen that the individual's right to freedom of belief, including the right to choose one's religion, is explicitly guaranteed by Islamic law, and treated as a component of the individual's

---

[19] *The Holy Qur'ān*, V: 32.

fundamental right to the freedom of opinion and expression.[20]

Chapter four is devoted to formulating a clear response to the main issue of this analysis, namely "is *jihād* a just war?" To begin with, this chapter attempts to work out exactly what is meant by "just war" by scrutinizing the chronological development of the term within its historical context. Through an examination of the relevant major primary juristic works of both Western and Muslim writers, this chapter concludes that *jihād* is a defensive war, based on certain humane principles, all of which argues for it being considered a "just war."

The sources of Islamic international law and the sources of public international law, as indicated in Article 38(1) of the statute of the International Court of Justice, bear similarities. The texts of international covenants may be compared to the texts of the *Holy Qur'ān* and the true Prophetic *ḥadīths*. In many respects, the international agreements are equivalent to the treaties made by the Prophet Muhammad, the rightly-guided Caliphs (*al-Khulafā' al-Rāshidūn*) and later Muslim rulers. Moreover, the opinions of Western scholars often parallel the legal opinions and works issued by Muslim jurists.

Methodologically, in examining the theory of *jihād*, this study relies heavily on the *Holy Qur'ān* and the Prophetic Traditions as law. The principles of *jihād* occupy twenty-eight chapters (*sūra*), which is one-fourth of the *Holy Qur'ān*. Furthermore, it should be made clear that the main features of the theory of *jihād* are explicitly outlined in the *Holy Qur'ān*, while juristic works,[21] from classical,

---

[20] *Ibid.*, II: 256; X: 99.

[21] See for example: Abū al-Ḥasan al-Māwardī, *al-Aḥkām al-Sulṭāniyya wal-Wilāyāt al-Dīniyya* (Cairo: Dār al-Fikr lil-Ṭibā'a wal-Nashr, 1983), 32-58 [hereinafter al-Māwardī] Abū Muḥammad 'Alī Ibn Ḥazm, *al-Iṣāl fī al-Muḥallā bil-Āthār*, 12 vols. (Beirut: Dār al-Kutub al-'Ilmiyya, 1988), 11:333-362 [hereinafter Ibn Ḥazm]; Abū al-Walīd Muḥammad Ibn Rushd, *Bidāyat al-Mujtahid wa Nihāyat al-Muqtaṣid*, 2 vols. (Beirut: Dār al-Ma'rifa, 1986), 380-407 [hereinafter Ibn Rushd]; Abū Ya'lā al-Farrā', *al-Aḥkām al-Sulṭāniyya* (Cairo: Maṭba'at Muṣṭafā al-Bābī al-Ḥalabī 1938), 23-44 [hereinafter al-Farrā']; 'Alā' al-Dīn al-Kāsānī, *Kitāb Badā'i' al-Ṣanā'i' fī Tartīb al-Sharā'i'*, 7 vols. (Cairo: al-Maṭba'a al-Jamāliyya, 1910), 7:97-142 [hereinafter al-Kāsānī]; Imām al-Ḥaramayn Abū al-Ma'ālī al- Juwaynī, Ghiyāth al-Umam fī *Iltiyāth al-Ẓulam* (Alexandria: Dār al-Da'wa lil-Ṭab' wal-Nashr, 1979), 260-264 [hereinafter al-Juwaynī];Muḥammad Ibn Idrīs al-Shāfi'ī, *Kitāb al-Umm*, 7 vols. (Cairo: al-Hay'a al-Miṣriyya al-'Āmma lil-Kitāb, 1987), 6:202-336 [hereinafter al-Shāfi'ī]; Muḥammad Ibn Ismā'īl al-Ṣan'ānī, *Subul al-Salām Sharḥ Bulūgh al-Marām min Jam' Adillat al-Aḥkām*, 4 vols. (Beirut: Dār Maktabat al-Ḥayāt, 1989), 4:53-100 [hereinafter al-

medieval and modern times, focus on the consequences of *jihād*, particularly the division of the world into the territory of Islam (*dār al-Islām*) and the territory of war (*dār al-ḥarb*); treaties; peaceful mutual relations; treatment of civilians in times of war, wounded combatants, and prisoners of war.

Before we proceed further with our examination, a clarification of the terms justice (*'adl*) and human rights (*ḥuqūq al-'ibād*), frequently employed in this study, is due. Although no consensus has ever been reached on the definition of these terms, one may argue that according to the *Holy Qur'ān* justice embodies equity and fairness between individuals and communities of mankind. Justice can thus take legal, ethical, social, political and theological forms. When we approach the concept of justice in the doctrine of *jihād*, our attention is necessarily drawn to the concept of justice among nations, which is essentially a legal and procedural concept. On the other hand, human rights in Islam, are linked to human interests sanctioned by Qur'anic injunction and protected by Islamic law. These basic rights include: respect of religious beliefs, customs and traditions; a right to life, and the prohibition of torture or inhumane treatment; children's rights to life, custody and education; the right to individual ownership and private property; and the right to freedom of thought, opinion and expression. In light of the theory of *jihād*, Islamic concepts of justice and human rights are integrated and overlapping, as the doctrine of *jihād* includes notions of human rights, the equality of all people, and the need for the rule of law.

Ṣan'ānī]; Muḥyī al-Dīn Yaḥyā Ibn Sharaf al- Dīn al-Nawawī, *Minhāj al-Ṭālibīn* (London: W. Thacker & Co., 1914), 457-471 [hereinafter al-Nawawī]; Muwaffaq al- Dīn Ibn Qudāma and Shams al- Dīn 'Abd al-Raḥmān Ibn Qudāma, *al-Mughnī wa Yalīhi al-Sharḥ al-Kabīr,* 12 vols. (Beirut: Dār al-Kitāb al-'Arabī, 1983), 10:48-635 [hereinafter al-Mughnī]; Shāh Waliy Allāh al-Dahlawī, *Ḥujjat Allāh al-Bāligha*, 2 vols. (Beirut: Dār al-Ma'rifa, n.d.), 2: 170-178 [hereinafter al-Dahlawī]; Shams al- Dīn Ibn Qayyim al-Jawziyya, *Zād al-Ma'ād fī Huda Khayr al-'Ibād*, 2 vols. (Cairo Maṭba'at Muṣṭafā al-Bābī al-Ḥalabī, 1950), 1:38-43 [hereinafter Ibn al-Qayyim]; Shams al-Dīn al-Sarakhsī, *Kitāb al-Mabsūṭ*, 30 vols. (Cairo: Maṭba'at al-Sa'āda, 1324 A.H.), 10:2-144 [hereinafter al-Sarakhsī]; Shams al-Islām Aḥmad Ibn Taymiyya, "Qā'ida fī Qitāl al-Kuffār," in *Majmū'at Rasā'il Ibn Taymiyya*, ed. Muḥammad Ḥāmid al-Faqī (Cairo: Maṭba'at al-Sunna al-Muḥammadiyya,1949), 116-146 [hereinafter Rasā'il Ibn Taymiyya]; Shaykh al-Islām Aḥmad Ibn Taymiyya; *al-Siyāsa al-Shar'iyya fī Iṣlāḥ al-Rā'i wal-Ra'iyya* (Beirut: Dār al-Kutub al-'Arabiyya, 1966), 102-144 [hereinafter Ibn Taymiyya]; Shaykh al-Islām Burhān al-Dīn al-Marghīnānī, *al-Hidāya Sharḥ Bidāyat al-Mubtadā*, 4 vols. (Beirut: Al-Maktaba al-Islāmiyya, n.d.), 2:135-156 [hereinafter al- al-Marghīnānī].

Finally, this work intends to counter the distorted image of *jihād*, as it is one of the most misunderstood terms in the history of Islamic legal discourse. This issue cannot be addressed without examining and elucidating some of the finer points of the doctrine of *jihād* according to the primary sources of Islamic international law, to which we now turn.

Chapter One

Theory of War in Islamic and Public International Law

Ibn Khaldūn, the pioneer Arab sociologist, observed that humanity has experienced wars and disasters of its own making, since the beginning of human society, which are rooted in a vengeful human imperative.[22] Since then, war has developed as a social phenomenon and accompanied humanity on its sojourn through history. Moreover, today, war remains a path to which modern nations resort in securing their various interests, in spite of so-called civilizational stride in the development of the human mind and thought.[23]

The rule of "might is right" was the mode of inter-state settlements. In the Grecian era, war was an absolute prerogative of nations, exercised without restraint. Nevertheless, ancient Rome drew a line between the so-called "just" war and "unjust" war, and upheld, what they termed, "the voice of God and Nature". The Romans, who believed in this doctrine, feared the wrath of God or nature, when

---

[22] ʻAbd al-Raḥmān Ibn Khaldūn, *Muqaddimat Ibn Khaldūn* (Beirut: Dār al-Qalam, 1984), 270.

[23] In a study on world wars in history, from 1496 B.C. to 1861 A.D., that is a period of 3,357 years, it was concluded that there was only a short period of 227 years of peace as opposed to 3,310 years of war: one year of peace per 13 years of war. In a more recent study, it was found, furthermore, that in 5,555 years, from the beginning of known human history until 1990, a total of 14,531 wars have been fought. Since the end of World War II, the world has witnessed 270 wars, some lasting for no more that a few months or even weeks, but some for much longer. This means that humanity faces a new war every four months or so. See Herbert K. Tillema, *International Armed Conflict Since 1945: A Bibliographic Handbook of Wars and Military Interventions* (London: Westview Press, 1991), 276-286.

waging an unjust war.[24] In turn, the attitudes adopted by the heavenly religions were different one from the other. Judaism permitted war and imposed no restrictions on its conduct.[25] Christianity, on the other hand, rejected the use of force, "for all those who take up the sword, shall perish by the sword."[26] Islam, however, viewed war as a necessary evil in exceptional cases sanctioned by *Allāh* in defence of Islam, its protection, and as a deterrent against aggression. Furthermore, such conduct is to be regulated by a fundamental respect for the freedom of belief of all communities.[27]

1. War and Belligerent Occupation in Islamic Legal Theory: Aims and Concepts

By examining the theory of war in Islamic international law, Sayyed Qutb concludes that peace is the rule, while war is the exception.[28] In the following statement, Qutb pinpoints the conditions, which should be met by Muslims prior to their engagement in war:

---

[24]William E. Hall, *International Law* (Oxford: The Clarendon Press, 1924), 446.

[25]*The Holy Scriptures*, Joshua VI: 21; I Samuel 15:2-3; and Deuteronomy 20:16-17. For more details see Gustave Le Bon, *Les premières civilisations* (Paris: C. Marpon et E. Flammarion, 1889), 81; Maurice Crouzet, *Histoire général des civilisation*, 7 vols. (Paris: Presses Universitaires de France, 1986), 1:270; Paul D. Hanson, "War and Peace in the Hebrew Bible," *Interpretation* 38:4 (October 1984): 341; Robert Carroll, "War in the Hebrew Bible," in *War and Society in the Greek World*, eds. John Rich and Graham Shipley (New York: Routledge, 1993), 36-40; Susan Niditch, *War in the Hebrew Bible; A Study in the Ethics of Violence* (New York: Oxford University Press, 1993), 128-137.

[26]*The New Testament*, Matthew XXVI: 52. For additional information, see Lisa Sowle Cahill, "Non-resistance, Defense, Violence, and the Kingdom in Christian Tradition," *Interpretation* 38:4 (October 1984): 380; Roland H. Bainton, *Christian Attitudes Toward War and Peace: A Historical Survey and Critical Re- evaluation* (New York: Abingdon Press, 1961), 38; Victor Paul Furnish, "War and Peace in the New Testament," *Interpretation* 38:4 (October 1984): 370.

[27]*The Holy Qur'ān*, II: 190. In this respect see al-Marghīnānī, *supra note* 21, at 135; Rasā'il Ibn Taymiyya, *supra note* 21, at 116-118; al-Ṣan'ānī, *supra note* 21, at 4:54; al-Sarakhsī, *supra note* 21, at 10:2.

[28]Sayyed Qutb, *Islam and Universal peace* (Indianapolis, Indiana: The American Trust Publications, 1977), 9. Influenced by Ibn Khaldūn's theory on war, Qutb discussed the unacceptable types of war according to Islamic law. These types are: "War based on racialism as contrary to the principles of the oneness of humanity, wars caused by ambition and exploitation, and wars of

> "In Islam, peace is the rule, and war is a necessity that should not be resorted to, but to achieve the following objectives: to uphold the rule of *Allāh* on earth, so that the complete submission of men would be exclusively to Him; to eliminate oppression, extortion and injustice by instituting the word of *Allāh*; to achieve the human ideas that are considered by *Allāh* as the aims of life; and to secure people against terror, coercion and injury."[29]

Similarly, John Kelsay perceives that the Islamic tradition presents evidence of both senses of peace: the desire to avoid conflict, and the interest in the achievement of an ideal social order. He proceeds to say:

> "In the Islamic tradition, one must strive for peace with justice. That is the obligation of believers; more than, it is the natural obligation of all of humanity. The surest guarantee of peace is the predominance of *al-Islām*, "the submission" to the will of God. One must therefore think in terms of an obligation to establish a social order in which the priority of Islam is recognized.... The Islamic tradition stresses, not the simple avoidance of strife, but the struggle for a just social order. In its broadest sense, the Islamic view of peace, like its Western counterpart, is in fact part of a theory of statecraft founded on notions of God, of humanity, and of the relations between the two."[30]

Accordingly, *jihād*, in Islamic legal theory, is a temporary legal device designed to achieve the ideal Islamic public order, and to secure justice and equality among all peoples.[31] As a matter of fact, there is not a single piece of evidence in Islamic legal discourse which instructs Muslims to wage perpetual war against those nations which fall outside of the sovereignty of the Islamic State, or to kill non-Muslims.[32]

The chief aim of *jihād* is not to force unbelievers to embrace Islam, nor to

---

ostentation which seek to magnify the pride and pomp of kings."

[29] *Ibid.*

[30] John Kelsay, *supra note* 15, at 30.

[31] Majid Khadduri, *supra note* 2, at 17.

[32] Abdulrahman Abdulkadir Kurdi, *The Islamic State: A Study Based on the Islamic Holy Constitution* (London: Mansell Publishing Limited, 1984), 97.

expand the boundaries of the Islamic state.[33] Ibn Taymiyya, for his part, notes that the *jihād* is a just war waged by Muslims whenever their security is threatened by the infidels.[34] Killing unbelievers who refuse to adopt Islam is worse than disbelief, and inconsistent with the spirit and the message of the *Holy Qur'ān*. This point is illustrated by Ibn Taymiyya, who argues that "if the unbeliever were to be killed unless he becomes a Muslim, such an action would constitute the greatest compulsion in religion,"[35] which contradicts the Qur'anic verse *Lā ikrāh fī al-Dīn* (Let there be no compulsion in religion).[36] Ibn Taymiyya deemed lawful warfare to be the essence of *jihād* and a means to securing peace, justice and equity. No one is to be killed for being a non-Muslim, for the *Holy Qur'ān* regards the subversion of faith and oppression as worse than manslaughter.[37] This point is emphasized in the Qur'anic verse "for tumult and oppression are worse than slaughter."[38] According to the basic Qur'anic rule of fighting, Muslims are instructed to "fight in the cause of *Allāh* those who fight you, but do not transgress limits, for *Allāh* loveth not transgressors."[39] Ibn Taymiyya marks out the following motives behind *jihād*: to defend Muslims against real or anticipated attacks; to guarantee and extend freedom of belief; and to defend the mission (*al-da'wah*) of Islam.[40] Based on the above argument, one concludes that peace is the rule and war is the exception in Islam, and that no obligatory state of war exists between Muslims and the rest of the world, nor

---

[33]Rudolph Peters, *supra note* 15, at 3.

[34]Rasā'il Ibn Taymiyya, *supra note* 21, at 123.

[35]*Ibid.* This point was emphasized by Maryam Jameelah, a contemporary American Muslim scholar, who deems that "*Jihād* is never used to compel anybody to embrace Islam against his will; its purpose is only to re-establish our freedom of operation." See Maryam Jameelah, *A Manifesto of the Islamic Movement* (Lahore, Pakistan: Mohammad Yusuf Khan Publications, 1979), 41.

[36]*The Holy Qur'ān*, II: 257.

[37]Ibn Taymiyya, *supra note* 21, at 107.

[38]*The Holy Qur'ān*, II: 192.

[39]*Ibid*, II: 191.

[40]Rasā'il Ibn Taymiyya, *supra note* 21, at 116-117.

is *jihād* to be waged until the world has either accepted the Islamic faith or submitted to the power of the Islamic state, as Bernard Lewis and Majid Khadduri suggest.[41] *Jihād* is a defensive war launched with the aim of establishing justice (*'adl*) and protecting basic human rights (*ḥuqūq al-'ibād*).[42]

Jihād cannot be understood out of its historical context, and can easily be misinterpreted if approached in terms of latter day occidental conceptions.[43] There is no exact equivalent in Islamic legal discourse to the concept of the "holy war" in Western Christendom.[44] Islamic law does not separate between state and religion and does not, as such, necessarily base the *Jihād* on religious motives.[45] Furthermore, there is no resemblance between the concept of the *Jihād*, as a religious collective duty, and the Christian concept of the crusade. Majid Khadduri's allegation that, "the *Jihād* was equivalent to the Christian concept of the crusade",[46] was refuted by Rudolph Peters, who argues: " 'Holy War' is thus, strictly speaking, a wrong translation of *Jihād*, and the reason why it is nevertheless used here is that the term has become current in Western literature."[47] In other words, the description of the *jihād* as a "holy war" is utterly misleading.[48]

Linguistically speaking, the term *jihād* is a verbal noun derived from the verb *jāhada*, the abstract noun *juhd*, which means to exert oneself, and to strive in doing

---

[41]Bernard Lewis, *supra note* 2, at 73; Majid Khadduri, *supra note* 2, at 13.

[42]Ahmed Zaki Yamani, "Humanitarian International Law in Islam: A General Outlook," *Michigan Yearbook of International Legal Studies* 7 (1985), 190.

[43]W. Montgomery Watt, *Islamic Political Thought: The Basic Concepts* (Edinburgh: Edinburgh University Press, 1968), 15.

[44]Bruce Lawrence, "Holy War (*Jihād*) in Islamic Religion and Nation-State Ideologies," in *Just War and Jihād Historical and Theoretical Perspectives on War and Peace in Western and Islamic Traditions*, eds. John Kelsay and James Turner Johnson (New York: Greenwood Press, 1991), 142.

[45]Rudolph Peters, *supra note* 15, at 4.

[46]Majid Khadduri, *supra note* 2, at 15.

[47]Rudolph Peters, *supra note* 15, at 4.

[48]W. Montgomery Watt, *supra note* 43, at 18; Patrick Bannerman, *Islam in Perspective: A Guide to Islamic Society, Politics and Law* (London: Routledge, 1988), 86.

things to one's best capabilities. Its meaning is, in fact, extended to comprise all that is in one's power or capacity.[49] Technically, however, *jihād* denotes the exertion of one's power in *Allāh's* path, encompassing the struggle against evil in whatever form or shape it arises.[50] This definition is forwarded in similar words in the different works of Muslim scholars. In his legal work *Badā'i' al-Ṣanā'i'*, al-kāsānī stipulates that, "according to Islamic law *(al-Shar' al-Islāmī), jihād* is used in expending ability and power in struggling in the path of *Allāh* by means of life, property, words and more."[51]

However, the exercise of *jihād* is the responsibility of the *Imām* or Caliph, who is the head of the Muslim State.[52] In other words, the *Imām* declares the call of *jihād*, not the public. This point was made by Abū Yūsuf, who states that "no army marches without the permission of the *Imām*." [53] Similarly, Abū al-Ḥasan al-Māwardī devotes a chapter in his work *al-Aḥkām al-Sulṭāniyya* to the duties of the *Imām*. The sixth of these basic duties, he argues, is the fight in the path of *Allāh*. Māwardī emphasizes the fact that a war cannot be waged without the permission of the *Imām*.[54]

---

[49]Abū al-Qāsim al-Zamakhsharī *Asās al-Balāgha* (Beirut: Dār al-Ma'rifa lil-Ṭibā'a wal-Nashr, n.d.), 67; Muḥammad Ibn Abī Bakr al-Rāzī, *Mukhtār al-Ṣiḥāḥ* (Beirut: Maktabat Lubnān, 1988), 48; Muḥammad Ibn Manẓūr, *Lisān al-'Arab al-Muḥīṭ*, 3 vol. (Beirut: Dār Lisān al-'Arab. n.d.), 2:190.

Similarly, Abū al-A'lā al-Mawdūdī advocates that "*jihād* means struggle to the utmost of one's capacity." See S. Abū al-A'lā al-Mawdudī, *Towards Understanding Islam* (Beirut: The Holy Qu'ān Publishing House, 1980), 140.

[50]Aḥmad al-Ṣāwī, *Bulghat al-Sālik li-Aqrab al-Masālik*, 2 vol. (Beirut: Dār al-Fikr lil-Ṭibā'a wal-Nashr wal-Tawzī', 1980), 1: 330 [hereinafter al-Ṣāwī]; Hasan Moinuddin, *The Charter of the Islamic Conference and Legal Framework of Economic Co-operation Among Its Member States* (Oxford: The Clarendon Press, 1987), 22; Majid Khadduri, *War and Peace in the Law of Islam* (Baltimore: The Johns Hopkins Press, 1955), 55; Moulavi Cheragh Ali, *A Critical Exposition of the Popular Jihād* (Delhi, India: Idarah-I Adabiyat-I Delli, 1884; Rudolph Peters, *Jihād in Classical and Modern Islam* (Princeton: N. J.: Markus Wiener Publishers, 1996), 1.

[51]al-Kāsānī, *supra note* 21, at 7:97.

[52]al-Mughnī, *supra note* 21, at 10:373; Noor Mohammad, "The Doctrine of *Jihād*: An Introduction," *Journal of Law and Religion* 3 (1985): 390.

[53]Abū Yūsuf Ya'qūb Ibn Ibrāhīm, *Kitāb al-Kharāj* (Beirut: Dār al-Ḥadātha, 1990), 349 [hereinafter Abū Yūsuf].

[54]al-Māwardī, *supra note* 21, at 33.

Unlike Shi'ite scholars, who hold that *jihād* can only be exercised under the leadership of the rightful *Imām*,[55] and contrary to the view held by the Kharijites who believe that *Jihād* is the sixth pillar of Islam,[56] Sunnite jurists conceive of *jihād*, in accordance with the nature of its obligation, as a collective duty (*farḍ Kifāya)* on the one hand,[57] and an individual duty (*farḍ 'ayn*) on the other.[58] When war is waged against infidels living in their own country, *jihād* is a collective duty; that is to say that *Jihād* is an obligation incumbent upon the Muslim community as a whole, which, if accomplished by a sufficient number of them, exempts the rest from being indicted for its neglect. If, however, no one performs this duty, all individual Muslims, qualified to take part in the *Jihād*, are sinning.[59] *Jihād* is considered an individual duty "*farḍ 'ayn*" when infidels invade Muslim territory. In this scenario, *Jihād* becomes a duty incumbent upon all the inhabitants of the occupied territory including the poor, women, minors, debtors and slaves without previous permissions.[60]

For his part, Bernard Lewis argues that "*Jihād*, in an offensive war, is an obligation, which is incumbent upon the Muslim community as a whole (*farḍ kifāya*); in a defensive war, it becomes a personal obligation of every adult male

---

[55]A. Querry, *Droit Musulman: Recueil de lois concernant les Musulman schyites*, 2 vols. (Paris: Imprimerie Nationale, 1871-1872), 1: 321-325; Abū Ja'far Muḥammad Ibn Jarīr al-Ṭabarī, *Kitāb Ikhtilāf al-Fuqahā'*, ed. Joseph Schacht (Leiden, The Netherlands: E.J. Brill, 1933), 12.

[56]'Abd al-Qāhir al-Baghdādī, *al-Farq Bayn al-Firaq* (Beirut: Dār al- Ma'rifa lil-Ṭibā'a wal-Nashr, n.d.), 84; Abū al-Fatḥ Muḥammad 'Abd al-Karīm al-Shahrastānī, *al-Milal wal-Niḥal* (Beirut: Dār al-Fikr lil-Ṭibā'a wal-Nashr, n.d.), 116-117; Majid Khadduri, *supra note* 50, at 67-69.

[57]"Nor should the believers all go forth together: if a contingent from every expedition remained behind, they could devote themselves to studies in religion, and admonish the people when they return to them." *The Holy Qur'ān*, IX: 123.

[58]"Go ye forth, (whether equipped) lightly or heavily, and strive, and struggle, with your goods and your persons in the cause of *Allāh*. That is best for you if ye knew." *The Holy Qur'ān*, IX: 42.

[59]Rudolph Peters, *supra note* 50, at 3.

[60]Abū 'Abd Allāh Muḥammad al-Qurṭubī, *al-Jāmi' li-Aḥkām al-Qur'ān*, 20 vols. (Beirut: Dār al-Kutub al-'Ilmiyya, 1988), 8: 186 [hereinafter al- al-Qurṭubī]; Ibn Rushd, *supra note* 21, at 1:381; al-Juwaynī, *supra note* 21, at 260-261; al-Kāsānī, *supra note* 21, at 98; al-Marghīnānī, *supra note* 21, at 2: 135; al-Mughnī, *supra note* 21, at 10: 364; al-Nawawī, *supra note* 21, at 457-458; al-Ṣāwī, *supra note* 50, at 330.

Muslim (*farḍ 'ayn*)."[61] Two things may be highlighted for criticism in that statement: the use of the term offensive war, and the misunderstanding of Muslim obligations where *Jihād* pertains to individual duty. In point of fact, only one kind of *Jihād* is acknowledged by Islamic law - the defensive one; whether it is waged against infidels living in their own country or when they attack Muslim territory.[62] With regards to the other claim in this statement, it should be made clear that *Jihād* is an obligation upon every Muslim, whether adult, minor, male, female, rich, poor, debtor or slave, only when it is *farḍ 'ayn*. In this case, *Jihād*, therefore, must be performed by the *levée en masse* of every competent Muslim person.[63]

However, as a collective duty, *Jihād* is incumbent upon every Muslim male, who is mature, sane, free, healthy and capable of adequate support.[64] Indeed, being a Muslim, adult and sane are the three necessary conditions for *bulūgh al-takālīf* (legal capacity.)[65] In this respect, females, according to the Prophet, are only to be engaged in non-combative *Jihād*; such as *ḥajj* and '*umra* (pilgrimage and the so-called minor pilgrimage to Mecca).[66] Thus, Islam exempts women from suffering wars' disasters and witnessing killing and bloodshed. In spite of this, however, women have taken part in the *Jihād*, side by side with men, from the outset of the Islamic mission, nursing the wounded;[67] transporting the injured;[68] cooking and

---

[61]Bernard Lewis, *supra note* 2, at 73.

[62]Needless to say, the adjectives added currently to the term *jihād*, like Islāmī and Muqaddas, are null and deceptive.

[63]Ahmed Rechid, "L'Islam et le droit des gens," *Recueil des cours* 60 (1937): 466-467.

[64]al-Mughnī, *supra note* 21, at 10: 366.

[65]*Ibid.*

[66]Abū 'Abd Allāh Muḥammad Ibn Ismā'īl al-Bukhārī, *Sahīḥ al-Bukhārī*, 8 vols. (Beirut: Dār al-Fikr lil-Ṭibā'a wal-Nashr, 1981), 3:220 [hereinafter al-Bukhārī]; Aḥmad Ibn 'Alī Ibn Ḥajar al-'Asqalānī, *Fatḥ al-Bārī bi-Sharḥ Ṣaḥīḥ al-Bukhārī* , 13 vols. (Beirut: Dār al-Ma'rifa, n.d.), 6:75 [hereinafter Fatḥ *al-Bārī*].

[67]Abū Muḥammad 'Abd al-Malik Ibn Hishām, *al-Sīra al-Nabawiyya*, 4 vols. (Beirut: Dār al-Jīl, 1987), 3:137 [hereinafter Ibn Hishām]; Khayr al-Dīn al-Ziriklī, *al-A'lām: Qāmūs Tarājim li-Ashhar al-Rijāl wal-Nisā' min al-'Arab wal-Musta'ribīn wal-Mustashriqīn*, 8 vols. (Beirut: Dār al-'Ilm lil-Malāyīn, 1980), 3:15; Muḥammad Ibn Aḥman al-Sarakhsī, *Sharḥ Kitāb al-Siyar al-Kabīr li-*

pouring water into the mouths of the soldiers;[69] scouting and intelligence;[70] fierce combat;[71] and army command.[72] The condition of freedom, mentioned earlier, is there because a slave is normally involved in taking care of his master's affairs.[73] In fact, the prophet used to take the pledge *(al-bay'a)* of free people for Islam and *jihād*, and that of slaves for Islam only.[74] The stipulation of good health means that the jihadist should be free of any permanent physical disability such as blindness, lameness or a chronic disease. The *Holy Qur'ān* explicitly excludes that: "no blame is there on the blind, nor is there blame on the lame, nor on the ill (if he does not join the war)."[75] In another verse, the *Holy Qur'ān* exempts the person who cannot earn his own household's daily living expenses, unless he is sponsored by the Muslim State, textually: "There is no blame on those who are infirm, or ill, or who find no resources to spend (on the cause), if they are sincere (in duty) to *Allāh* and His Apostle."[76] Finally, the *mujāhid* (Muslim fighter) should seek his parents'

Muḥammad Ibn al-Ḥasan al-Shaybānī, 5 vols. (Cairo: Maṭba'at Sharikat al-I'lānāt al-Sharqiyya, 1971-1972), 1: 184-186 [hereinafter al-Siyar al-Kabīr].

[68]al-Bukhārī, *supra note* 66, at 3:222; Khayr al-Dīn al-Ziriklī, *Ibid.*; al-Sarakhsī, *supra note* 21, at 10:70; al-Siyar al-Kabīr, *supra note* 67, at 1:185.

[69]Abū al-Ḥusayn Muslim Ibn al-Ḥajjāj al-Naysābūrī, Ṣaḥīḥ *Muslim*, 5 vols. (Beirut: Mu'ssasat 'Izz al- Dīn lil-Ṭibā'a wal-Nashr, 1987), 4:89 [hereinafter Muslim]; al-Bukhārī, *Ibid.*

[70]Ibn Hishām, *supra note* 67, at 2:95, and 1:295.

[71]Abū al 'Abbās Aḥmad Ibn Yaḥya al-Balādhurī, *Kitāb Futūḥ al-Buldān* (Beirut: Dār al-Nashr lil-Jami'iyyīn, 1957), 162 and 184 [hereinafter al-Baladhurī]; Abū Ja'far Muḥammad Ibn Jarīr al-Ṭabarī, *Tārīkh al-Ṭabarī: Tārīkh al-Umam wal-Mulūk*, 6 vols. (Beirut: Mu'assasat 'Izz al-Dīn lil-Ṭibā'a wal-Nashr, 1987), 2:201, 286, 291 and 298 [hereinafter al-Ṭabarī]; Ibn Hishām, *supra note* 67, at 3:136-137; Muslim, *supra note* 69, at 4:88-89; al-Siyar al-Kabīr, *supra note* 67, at 1:184.

[72]In the Battle of al-Jamal, 'A'isha, the wife of the Prophet, commanded the army to oppose 'Alī Ibn Abī Ṭālib. See Abū al-Fidā' al-Ḥāfiẓ Ibn Kathīr, *al-Bidāya wal-Nihāya*, 14 vols. (Beirut: Maktabat al-Ma'ārif, n.d.), 7:238 [hereinafter Ibn Kathīr]; al-Ṭabarī, *Ibid.*, 2:539.

[73]al-Juwaynī, *supra note* 21, at 262; al-Marghīnānī, *supra note* 21, at 135.

[74]Islamic law gives precedence to the service of the master over taking part in the *jihād*, because the first is a personal duty, while the second is a general obligation.

[75]*The Holy Qur'ān*, XLVIII: 17.

[76]*Ibid*, IX: 91.

permission before taking part in the *jihād*[77] and, if he is indebted to any person, including *dhimmīs*,[78] must ask for an excuse from his creditor.[79]

As long as Islam has sanctioned *jihād* for the very reasons quoted above, it is only natural that military actions will take place, culminating, as it were, in the Muslim army's entry into the territory of war (*dār al-ḥarb*) and ruling over. This is the so-called *al-fatḥ* (conquest or victory). According to *Lisān al-'Arab al-Muḥīṭ*, in linguistic usage, the word *al-fatḥ* means entering the house of war and conquering it.[80] *Allāh* promises the Prophet of the Conquest of Mecca, saying: "When comes the help of *Allāh* and victory."[81] In this sense, *al-fatḥ* in Islam is synonymous with belligerent occupation, in modern international law, regardless of the objectives underlying each. *Jihād* and *al-fatḥ*, which follows it, are therefore a response to a human request that righteousness and justice prevail, that wrongdoing be abolished, and that the message of *Allāh* be conveyed to all.

al-Fatḥ was regulated by Islamic international law. Muslim jurists treated issues related to *al-fatḥ* and the entry of the House of War in several works. Foremost among these works stands *Kitāb al-Siyar al-Kabīr* of Muḥammad Ibn al-Ḥasan al-Shaybānī, which included the principles and rules governing the conduct of the Islamic state during *al-fatḥ*. Where Hugo Grotius is considered as the legitimate father of the public international law, Muḥammad Ibn al-Ḥasan al-Shaybānī, for his part, is seen as the father of Islamic international law. Among other Islamic international law jurists is al-Awzā'ī (88-157 A.H.) who wrote

---

[77]al-Juwaynī, *supra note* 21, at 262; al-Mughnī, *supra note* 21, at 381.

[78]The free non-Muslim subjects living in Muslim countries, who enjoyed protection and safety in return for paying the capital tax. See Fakhr al-Dīn al-Ṭarīḥī, *Majma' al-Baḥrayn*, 6 vols. (Beirut: Dār wa Maktabat al-Hilāl, 1985), 6:66 [hereinafter al-Ṭarīḥī]; Ibn Rushd, *supra note* 21, at 1:322; Muḥammad Rawwās Qal'ajī and Ḥāmid Ṣādiq Qunaibī, *Mu'jam Lughat al-Fuqahā'* (Beirut: Dār al-Nafā'is, 1988), 95.

[79]al-Siyar al-Kabīr, *supra note* 67, at 4: 1448-1457.

[80]Muḥammad Ibn Manẓūr, *supra note* 49 at 2: 1044.

[81]*The Holy Qur'ān*, CX: 1.

extensively on Muslim conquests and expedition.[82] In *al-Siyar al-Kabīr,* al-Shaybānī establishes the rules which govern the conduct of the conquests, including specific rules for dealing with war spoils (*al-ghanā'im*), prisoners of war (*al-asrā*), the wounded and the dead. Furthermore, he establishes important international rules for settling disputes, treaties, peace and the rights and duties of the inhabitants of conquered territories.

However, Islamic international law did not make a terminological distinction between belligerent occupation without the use of force and belligerent occupation through the use of force. Either case is called *fatḥ* whether Muslim armed forces enter the *dār al-ḥarb* in the wake of fighting or peacefully in the light of agreements. For example, when Muslim armies entered Mecca without fighting, it was called a *fatḥ*,[83] and when these armies entered Iraq and *al-Sha'ām* (greater Syria), it was also called a *fatḥ*.[84] However, Islamic law draws a distinction between invasion and military occupation in their respective sense in modern international law. In Islamic international law, invasion is different from *fatḥ*; in the former, a group of Muslims invades enemy garrisons to achieve specific military objectives with no prior intention to stay in *dār al-ḥarb*, for example, the Tabūk expedition. In the latter, *fatḥ* involves the transfer of sovereignty over *dār al-ḥarb* to the Muslim army and annexation of that land to *dār al-Islām*.

In this respect, it is useful to mention that Gustave Le Bon concludes in his book "La civilisation des Arabes" that the Arabs did not use force as much as they used magnanimity in their attempt to spread Islam. The world's nations, he adds, have never known as merciful and tolerant a conqueror as the Arabs. Moreover, the

---

[82]'Abd al-Raḥmān Abū 'Amr al-Awzā'ī, "Kitāb Siyar al-Awzā'ī " in *Kitāb al-Umm*, 7 vols. ed. Abū 'Abd Allāh Muḥammad Ibn Idrīs al-Shāfi'ī (Cairo: al-Hay'a al-Miṣriyya al- 'Āmma lil-Kitāb, 1987), 6: 318 and 324 [hereinafter al-Awzā'ī].

[83]Mohammad Talaat Al Ghunaimi, *The Muslim Conception of International Law and the Western Approach* (The Hague, The Netherlands: Martinus Nijhoff, 1968), 21-22 [hereinafter Al Ghunaimi]; al-Ṭabarī, *supra note* 71, at 2:197.

[84]Alfred Morabia, *Le ǧihād dans l'Islam médiéval: Le «combat sacré» des origines au XIIᵉ siècle* (Paris: Albin Michel, 1993), 77-81; Muḥammad Ibn Isḥāq, *Sīrat Rasūl Allāh*, trans. A. Guillaume (Karachi, Pakistan: Oxford University Press, 1955), 549 [hereinafter Ibn Isḥāq].

Arabs were the only conquerors who conjoined *jihād* with tolerance towards the followers of other religions whom they conquered but left them free to pursue their own religious practices. Such mercy and tolerance were cornerstones in the expansion of the conquests and the conversion of many nations to the religion, regulations and language of the conqueror.[85] In this connection, al-Balādhurī and al-Ṭabarī reported that the people of Ṣughd, a small town close to Samarkand, complained to 'Umar Ibn 'Abd al-'Azīz, the Umayyad caliph, that Qutayba Ibn Muslim al-Bāhilī, a Muslim commander, has conquered their city without prior notice to the three options normally offered to conquered peoples by Muslim commanders.[86] They said: "*Allāh* has made known equity and justice, and Qutayba has oppressed and betrayed us, as well as usurped our town." 'Umar Ibn 'Abd al-'Azīz wrote the following message to Sulaymān Ibn Abī al-Surā, the Muslim governor of Samarkand:

> "The people of Samarkand have complained to me that Qutayba oppressed and maltreated them, and eventually expelled them from their territory. On account of that, if you receive this letter, let the case be heard by the judge, and if the judgement is in their favour force out the Arabs to their camps outside the town."

Finally, when the judge Jamī' Ibn Ḥāḍir adjudicated that the Arabs must withdraw to their camps in order to face the people of the town on an equal footing and offer them the three options, the people of the town willingly accepted the existing situation, chose peace, and embraced Islam in multitudes.[87]

2. The Concept of War and Belligerent Occupation in Public International Law

It can be inferred from the above that the concept of *jihād* in Islamic international law is based on the premise that an armed conflict arises between the

---

[85]Gustave Le Bon, *supra note* 15, at 110-154.

[86]al-Mughnī, *supra note* 21, at 8: 361; al-Sarakhsī, *supra note* 21, at 10:31; al-Shāfi'ī, *supra note* 21, at 4:172; al-Siyar al-Kabīr, *supra note* 67, at 1:78.

[87]Abū al-Ḥasan 'Alī Ibn al-Athīr, *al-Kāmil fī al-Tārīkh,* 12 vols. (Beirut: Dār al-Kutub al-'Ilmiyya, 1966), 5:22; al-Balādhurī, *supra note* 71, at 97; al-Ṭabarī, *supra note* 71 at 3:552.

Muslim State and non-Muslim State for the purpose of deterring aggression, protecting Islam, and defending the interests of the Muslim State.[88] Nevertheless, the concept of war in international law is, on the other hand, ambiguous. For example, we find that while international law jurists attempt to find a specific definition for the concept of war, the International Law Commission of the United Nations, for its part, decides not to include the concept of war in its agenda, on the grounds that the United Nations Charter considers war an illegal action.[89]

In an attempt to conclude a specific definition of war in international law, it is imperative therefore that we discuss various views posited by legists working on international law. Indeed, these views vary a great deal among themselves in this respect. To most legists, war is a real eventuality, which cannot be stemmed by law, but law comes at a later stage in the process of war, regulating its actions and attempting to safeguard its humane standards of conduct. To others, war is seen as a state between two or more disputing parties, which requires the law's intervention to regulate its action in relation to rights and commitments arising from the conduct of war.

In this respect, Fauchille defines war as:

> "La guerre est un état de fait contraire à l'état normal de la communauté internationale qui est la paix, état de fait dont la résolution, la fin, le but ultime est cette paix elle-meme."[90]

Oppenheim, for his part, defines it as:

> "War is a contention between two or more states through their armed forces, for the purpose of overpowering each other, and imposing such conditions of peace as the victor pleases. War is a fact recognized, and with regard to many points regulated, but not

---

[88]Sami A. Aldeeb Abu-Sahlieh, *Les Musulmans face aux droits de l'homme: religion & droit & politique* (Bochum, Germany: Winkler, 1994), 273-275.

[89]Hersch Lauterpacht, "The Problem of the Revision of the Law of War," *The British Year Book of International Law* 29 (1952): 361.

[90]Paul Fauchille, *Traité de droit international public*, Tome II, Guerre et neutralité (Paris: Rousseau, 1921), 5.

established, by international law."[91]

On the other hand, Hyde argues that war is "A condition of armed hostility between states."[92]

It is clear from these definitions that all law experts gravitate towards one definition despite ostensible differences. It is therefore plausible to define war as a condition of animosity arising between two or more parties, thereby terminating the peaceful state of co-existence between them through resorting to arms in settling disputes.

Moreover, international law is a recent phenomenon, dating back only to the writings of Hugo Grotius and the Treaty of Westphalia of 1648, which recognized states as units enjoying equal rights and responsibilities within the international community. It can be said that wars have raged ever since, as prevailing international practices do not impose any restrictions against countries resorting to power in their respective relations, regardless of the emergence of the so-called just wars, and Grotius' exclusion of preventive wars.[93] That is why Grotius's theory on the distinction between just and unjust wars did not last long, and was overshadowed, in the centuries after him, by the principle that states may resort to war as a legitimate right of sovereignty; a principle maintained until the conclusion of the Hague conventions of 1907.[94]

Reference to the Covenant of the League of Nations reveals that Articles 11 and 12 did indeed deal with the use of force among nations, whereas Article 12 also obliged member states to submit any dispute among them to an arbitration council, and not to resort to war until three months had lapsed since the arbitration ruling. Articles 13 and 15 provide that states should implement this ruling in good faith,

---

[91]L. Oppenheim, *International Law*, vol. 2, Disputes, war and Neutrality, 7th ed., revised by Hersch Lauterpacht (London: Longmans, Green and Co., Inc., 1952), 202.

[92]Charles Cheney Hyde, *International Law Chiefly as Interpreted and Applied by the United States*, 3 vols. (Boston: Little, Brown and Co., 1945), 3: 1686.

[93]Josef L. Kunz, "Bellum Justum and Bellum Legale," *AJIL* 45 (1951): 529.

[94]L. Oppenheim, *supra note* 91, at 180.

whereas Article 16, for its part, included the imposition of sanctions against a state that resorted to war contrary to its commitments not to do so according to Articles 12, 13 and 15.[95]

In 1924, the Geneva Protocol signaturies committed themselves not to resort to war except in certain cases specified by Article 2 of that Protocol. In 1925, member states signing the Locarno Treaty agreed among themselves not to resort to war against each other except in certain cases.[96] At the initiative of France and the United States, the General Treaty for the Renunciation of War (the Briand-Kellogg Pact, or Pact of Paris) was signed in Paris on August 27, 1928, by representatives of 15 governments; at a later stage, several other states also signed it. In its first article, the Treaty condemns the use of power in solving international disputes, and denounces it as a means of maintaining national sovereignty in international relations. Article 3 bans aggressive wars completely.[97]

The United Nations Charter does not use the word "war" except in its preamble in which member states pledge not to use armed force for other than common interest. Article 1 provides that among the purposes of the United Nations is the promulgation of effective measures for the prevention of threats to international peace and security, and for the suppression of acts of aggression.[98] Article 2 (4) proclaims that member states commit themselves to refrain from threatening or actually using force against the safety of the territory or political independence of any state.[99] The Charter, however, proclaims that members, individually or collectively, may use armed force in self-defence, if an armed

---

[95]Gerhard von Glahn, *Law Among Nations: An Introduction to Public International Law* (New York: The Macmillam Company, 1970), 518.

[96]*Ibid.*

[97]Leon Friedman, ed., *The Law of War: A Documentary History*, 2 vols. (New York: Random House, 1972), 1: 468; Quincy Wright, "The Meaning of the Pact of Paris," *AJIL* 27 (1933): 41.

[98]*United Nations Charter*, signed at San Francisco, 26 June 1945. Entered into force on 24 October 1945.

[99]*Ibid.*

aggression is perpetuated against them.[100] Nevertheless, the Geneva Conventions signed in the wake of World War II, in 1949, are seen as some of the most important agreements to establish international principles in the laws of war and armed disputes.

Ever since the signing of the UN Charter, the United Nations has failed to prevent wars, as a result of the fact that the Charter could not establish a workable alternative capable of preventing the use of force once disputes had erupted into armed conflicts. Another argument, is that the Great Powers have continued to bend the international laws to their own desires, and to retain the right to veto any and all the Security Council's resolutions.

International law experts do indeed draw a distinction between the cold war and the actual war, as well as between acts of revenge exercised by some states against other states, in order to achieve certain ends without terminating the state of peace between the war parties and replace it with belligerency. Furthermore, the articles related to war in international law have defined the principles by which war could be begun; the conduct of the warring states during the process of military operations; the type of weapons to be used; and the relations of the non-warring states with those engaged in the war through legal principles stated in the law of neutrality.[101]

In addition to international treaties and conventions governing the conduct of military actions among the warring parties, and seen as the primary sources of the laws of war, there are also other sources for this law, such as customary practices and international laws acceptable to the international community. Among such practices and laws, in addition to the Nuremberg judgements, 1945-1946; the Tokyo war crimes trial, 1948; the statute of the International Criminal Tribunal for the Former Yugoslavia, 1993; and the International Tribunal for crimes in Rwanda, 1994, are rulings and principles that have been concluded from court martial,

---

[100]Josef L. Kunz, "Individual and Collective Self-Defense in Article 51 of the Charter of the United Nations," *AJIL* 41 (1947): 873.

[101]L. Oppenheim, *supra note* 91, at 634-652.

particularly in the aftermath of World War I and World War II.[102]

Nevertheless, belligerent occupation, which is sometimes known as *occupatio bellica* in international humanitarian law, does not differ, from a procedural point of view, from that of *fatḥ* in Islamic international law. However, the first suggested definition of belligerent occupation is included in Articles 42-56 of the Hague Regulations,[103] Article 2 of the 1949 Geneva Conventions,[104] and Article 1 (3-4) of the 1977 Additional Protocol.[105] McNair, however, suggests three phases through which belligerent occupation goes: invasion, occupation and transfer of sovereignty as a consequence of concessions made in light of a treaty or by subjugation and annexation of a given territory. [106] Oppenheim argues that:

> "Belligerent occupation is invasion plus taking possession of enemy country for the purpose of holding it, at any rate temporarily. The difference between mere invasion and occupation becomes apparent from the fact that an occupant sets up some kind of administration, whereas the mere invader does not."[107]

Furthermore, Hyde, for his part, conceives that: "belligerent occupation is that stage of military operations which is instituted by an invading force in any part of an enemy's territory, when that force has overcome unsuccessful resistance and

---

[102]Among war crimes trials are the Trial of Captain Henry Wirz, 1865; Court-Martial of Major Edwin F. Glenn, 1902; Court-Martial of General Jacob H. Smith, 1902; Court-Martial of Lieutenant Preston Brown, 1902; Prosecution and Punishment of Major War Crimes of European Axis, 1945; Hirota, Dohihara, and Kido v. General MacArthur, 1948; The Eichmann Trial, 1961; and Court-Martial of William L. Calley, Jr., 1971.

[103]*The Hague Convention IV Respecting the Laws and Customs of War on Land*, signed on October 18, 1907, entered into force on January 26, 1910. J.B. Scott, ed., *The Hague Conventions and Declarations of 1899 and 1907*, 3rd. ed. (New York: Oxford University Press, 1918), 100-127 [hereinafter The Hague IV]; Hersch Lauterpacht, *supra note* 89, at 360.

[104]The four Geneva Conventions of August 12, 1949, common Article 2, 75 U.N.T.S. (1950) 31-417.

[105]Protocol I Additional to the Geneva Conventions of 12 August 1949, and Relating to the Protection of Victims of International Armed Conflicst, signed at Geneva on December 12, 1977, entered into force on December 7, 1978, UK Misc. 19 (1977), Cmnd. 6927 [hereinafter Protocol I].

[106]Lord McNair and A.D. Watts, *The Legal Effects of War*, 4th ed. (New York: Cambridge University Press, 1967), 319.

[107]L. Oppenheim, *supra note* 91, at 167.

established its own military authority therein."[108] From these definitions it is clear that belligerent occupation is the stage in war which immediately occurs after the belligerent state succeeds in entering the enemy territory and places it under its actual domination, culminating in the cessation of fighting and the end of military operations.

It must be emphasized that international humanitarian law draws a distinction between belligerent occupation and military occupation on the one hand, and that of invasion on the other. Belligerent occupation comes as a stage in the wake of fighting and armed military operations, as, for example, the occupation by the Axis forces of European territories during World War II. Military occupation, on the other hand, occurs as a result of the mutual surrender of antagonistic forces prior to the outbreak of war. In fact, a distinction is drawn between occupation and invasion, that the latter does not establish any new actual administration in the transgressed territory, but is, rather, a kind of attack and retreat without the imposition of a state of complete domination over a territory and the eradication of its entire resistance.[109]

In this respect, T.J. Lawrence has pointed out that belligerent occupation constitutes a three-phase process, namely: a state of war and armed dispute arising between two nations in which one succeeds in invading the other's territory and occupying it totally or in part; second, an interim actual state of war arising between two nations in which the armed forces of one occupies the territory of the other and places it under its own control. In this case, belligerent occupation is not seen as a legal condition but a *de facto* situation established by the conditions of war and the victory of the second party over the first; and third, occupation should be actual, and must not arise unless the armed forces of one nation imposes its authority over the occupied territory of the other, and subjecting it to its military authority.[110]

---

[108]Charles Cheney Hyde, *supra note* 92, at 2:361.

[109]*Ibid.*, at 362; Paul Reuter, *Droit international public* (Paris: Presses Universitaires de France, 1958), 344.

[110]T.J. Lawrence, *The Principles of International Law*, 7th ed. (London: Macmillan, 1927), 177.

Islamic international law, however, has not sanctioned belligerent occupation in its modern sense, for the *Holy Qur'ān* considers that a transgression against the rights of the others, "do not transgress limits, for *Allāh* loveth not transgressors,"[111] and "let there be no hostility except to those who practise oppression."[112] International humanitarian law considers belligerent occupation to be null and void, an act of illegal aggression unless it takes place as a form of legitimate self-defence, or sanctioned by the United Nations for the sake of maintaining world peace and security.[113] This is what the United Nations Charter states, and what has been emphasized by the UN Resolution 3734, in its 25th session by a majority of 140 votes, which states that nations commit themselves to refraining from threats to, or actual use of force, against the security of any territory, or the political independence of any other nation.

According to international humanitarian law, belligerent occupation does not abrogate the sovereignty of the victim state, nor does it transfer that sovereignty to the belligerent one, but rather maintains the sovereignty of the occupied nation over its own territory regardless of the fact that such sovereignty is suspended during the period of interim occupation. It was Vattle who became the first jurist to endorse this principle. Towards the end of the 19th century such views become more acceptable following their incorporation into the laws of land warfare.[114] In this respect, Fauchille states that belligerent occupation, in its capacity as an interim actual state, cannot replace the original authority over territory by that of the occupation.[115] In the same fashion, Liewellyn Johnes notes that sovereignty is not transferred to the belligerent nation, whether its occupation takes place peacefully or

---

[111]*The Holy Qur'ān*, II: 190.

[112]*Ibid.*, II: 193.

[113]Adam Roberts, "What is a Military Occupation?" *The British YearBook of International Law* 55 (1984): 293.

[114]Emmerich de Vattle, *Le droit des gens, ou principes de la loi naturelle, appliqués à la conduite et aux affaires de nations et des souverains*, 2 vols. (Paris: Chez Janet et Cotelle, 1820), 2:174.

[115]Paul Fauchille, *supra note* 90, at 215.

by military means.[116]

Thus, prior to the Hague's agreements of 1899 and 1907, belligerent occupation used to imply the annexation of occupied territories and their subjugation to the occupying army's authority. However, this implication becomes null and void and the annexation of occupied territory or the abrogation of nations' sovereignty is no longer seen as a necessary consequence of occupation. Accordingly, Kelsen, in his interpretation of the legal status of occupied Germany under the Allies, following World War II, argues for Germany's right to maintain complete sovereignty over its own territory despite the suspension of its jurisdiction.[117]

The modern principle of sovereignty originated in the sixteenth century with the emergence of the nation-state, and found its expression in the international arena after the establishment of the United Nations in 1945. Nonetheless, Islamic international law recognized this right as early as the seventh/eighth centuries. In *L'Arménie entre Byzance et l'Islam depuis la conquête arabe jusqu'en 886*, Joseph Laurent states that Mu'āwiya Ibn Abī Sufyān, the first Umayyad ruler, recognised the sovereignty of the Armenian peoples - i.e. the right to preserve an independent identity and to exercise control over their own territory - in 653 A.D. Another case in point is that of the peoples of *Samarkand v. Qutayba Ibn Muslim* in 702 A.D. The Muslim judge agreed with the claims of the peoples of Samarkand, and passed a judgement against Qutayba Ibn Muslim, the leader of the Muslim army. The judge ruled that the Muslim army must withdraw from the city, and take immediate steps to enable the peoples of Samarkand to exercise their right to territorial sovereignty and self-determination, peacefully and freely.[118]

---

[116]F. Liewellyn Johnes, *Military Occupation of Alien Territory in Time of Peace: Transactions of the Grotius Society* (London: Macmillan, 1923), 159.

[117]Hans Kelsen, "The Legal Status of Germany According to the Declaration of Berlin," *AJIL* 39 (1945): 518.

[118]Alen E. Buchanan, "The Right to Self-determination: Analytical and Moral Foundations," *Arizona Journal of International and Comparative Law* 8:2 (Fall 1991): 47; Ingrid Delupis, *International Law and the Independent State* (Glasgow: The University Press, 1974), 3-8; James Grawford, *The Creation of States in International Law* (Oxford, The Clarendon Press, 1979), 26-27; Joseph Laurent, *L'Arménie entre Byzance et l'Islam depuis la conquête arabe jusqu'en 886* (Paris: Fontemoing, 1919), 53; Nathaniel Berman, "Sovereignty in Abeyance: Self-determination and

3. Types of Jihād

In the course of discussing the theory of *jihād*, a considerable number of contemporary scholars have confused the types and modes of *jihād*. Nevertheless, while Ibn Qayyim al-Jawziyya distinguished four types of *jihād*: the struggle against the self; the struggle against evil; the struggle against non-believers; and the struggle against hypocrites,[119] al-Māwardī, for his part, divided *jihād* into two general categories: wars of public interest, and wars against polytheists and apostates.[120] In a similar vein, other Muslim jurists spelled out two types of *jihād*: the greater *jihād* and the lesser *jihād*.[121] The first type deals with the struggle against the self and evil, and may be performed by heart; and the second type deals with the strive against apostates and non-believers, which can be accomplished by tongue, wealth and self.[122] Based on the above categorization, and taking into consideration the current adaptation of the *Sharī'a* in a contemporary vein,[123] types of *jihād* can be subsumed under two categories: the moral struggle (greater *jihād*) and the armed struggle (lesser *jihād*). The first type is directed against the self and evil, while the second

---

International Law," *Wisconsin International Law Journal* 7:1 (Fall 1988): 52; Patrick Thornberry, "Self-determination, Minorities, Human Rights: A Review of International Instruments," *International and Comparative Law Quarterly* 38 (October 1989): 877; al-Ṭabarī, *supra note* 71, at 3:552.

[119]Ibn al-Qayyim, *supra note* 21, at 1:39-40; Sufyān Ibn 'Uyayna advocates that *Allāh* gave the Prophet Muḥammad four swords to strive against unbelievers: "The first against polytheists, which the prophet himself fought with; the second against apostates, which Abū Bakr fought with; the third against the people of the Book, which 'Umar fought with; and the fourth against dissenters, which 'Alī fought with." al-Sarakhsī *supra note* 21, at 10:3.

[120]al-Māwardī, *supra note* 21, at 50.

[121]Donna E. Arzt, "The Treatment of Religious Dissidents under Classical and Contemporary Islamic Law," in *Religious Human Rights in Global perspective: Religious Perspectives*, eds. John Witte, Jr. and Johan D. van der Vyver (The Hague, The Netherlands: Martinus Nijhoff Publishers, 1996), 388.

[122]al-Awzā'ī, *supra note* 82, at 330; al-Farrā', *supra note* 21, at 25, 35, 38 and 41; Ibn Ḥazm, *supra note* 21, at 333-361; al-Kāsānī, *supra note* 21, at 134-140; al-Sarakhsī, *supra note* 21, at 98-124.

[123]Shaykh 'Umar 'Abd al-Raḥmān, the leader of *al-Jihād* Movement, lecturing on *jihād* in Detroit in 1991. See *Jihād in America* (WNET television broadcast, Nov. 21, 1994), *available in* LEXIS, News Library, Curnws File.

type deals with Muslims (highway robbers, rebels, apostates and unjust rulers),[124] and with non-Muslims (polytheists and scripturaries).[125] Since this study is based on the rules of Islamic and public international law, it is best to concentrate on the armed *jihād*; which includes the struggle against Muslim dissidents and unjust rulers even if they claim to be Muslims; and the struggle against non-Muslims: polytheists and scripturaries. It is clear that the first type of fighting (against Muslims) falls within humanistic law, which deals with the rights of civilians and fighters in times of peace, while the other type (against non-Muslims) falls under humanitarian international law, which deals with the rights of civilians and combatants in times of international conflict.[126]

A. Jihād Against Muslim Dissidents and Unjust Rulers

However, *jihād* against dissidents, highway robbers, rebels, apostates and unjust rulers is in accord with the Muslim community's need to insure public security, social stability, and legal order.[127] Highway robbers (*al-Muḥaribūn*), are groups which raises weapons to take by force the property and life of travellers. This crime is defined as grand theft,[128] and explicitly discussed in the *Holy Qur'ān*:

> "The punishment of those who wage war against *Allāh* and His Prophet, and strive with might and main for mischief through the land is execution, or crucifixion, or have their hands and their feet cut off

---

[124]Contemporary Muslim scholars like al-Mawdūdī, al-Bannā, Quṭb and 'Abd al-Raḥmān call upon Muslims to wage *jihād* against unjust Muslim rulers. These teachings have been used by the militants of *al-Jihād* Movement to justify the assassination of Anwar al-Sādāt, the Egyptian president on October 6, 1981. See Michael Youssef, *Revolt Against Modernity: Muslim Zealots and the West* (Leiden, The Netherlands: E.J. Brill, 1985), 177; Tamara Sonn, "Irregular Warfare and Terrorism in Islam: Asking the Right Questions," in *Cross, Crescent, and Sword: The Justification and Limitation of War in Western and Islamic Tradition*, eds. James Turner Johnson and John Kelsay (Westport, Connecticut: Greenwood Press, 1990), 141.

[125]Relying on the works of Muslim jurists, Majid Khadduri called this type of *jihād* "*jihād* against unbelievers". Although he did not mention these works, one can argue that this naming is inaccurate since he treated scripturaries on the same footing as polytheists. In fact, the *Holy Qur'ān* is extremely strict in distinguishing between the two categories.

[126]Ahmed Zaki Yamani, *supra note* 42, at 192.

[127]Aly Aly Mansour, "Hudud Crimes," in *The Islamic Criminal Justice System*, ed. M. Cherif Bassiouni (New York: Oceana Publications, Inc., 1982), 196.

[128]*The Holy Qur'ān*, V: 37.

from opposite sides, or exile from the land. That is their disgrace in this world, and a great torment is theirs in the hereafter."

Although Muslim jurists disagree on the degree of punishment,[129] al-Farrā' argues that punishment should be devised according to the robbers' circumstances and not to their capacity:

> "For murder accompanied by plunder: beheading followed by crucifixion; for murder only: beheading; for plunder only without loss to life: the amputation of hand and foot on alternate sides; and for raising arms with the intent of plunder and murder only: deportation to another territory."[130]

Fighting against *al-Bughāt* (rebels), who secede from the Muslim community, or rebel against the *Imām* (Muslim ruler) is based on the following *Qur'anic* verse:

> "And if two parties among the Believers fall into a quarrel, make ye peace between them, but if one of them transgresses beyond bounds against the other, then fight ye [all] against the one that transgresses until it complies with the command of *Allāh*; but if it complies, then make peace between them with justice, and be fair; for *Allāh* loves those who are fair [and just]."[131]

From the verse above, one may deduce that rebels (*al-bughāt*) remain Muslims despite their rebellion, and are allowed to live in security in Muslim territory if they reconcile themselves to peace.[132] This is what was advocated by 'Alī Ibn Abī Ṭālib, the fourth rightly guided Caliph, who instructed his army before the battle of the Camel (*al-Jamal*), regarding the rebel forces:

"When you defeat them, do not kill their wounded, do not behead the

---

[129]Aly Aly Mansour, *supra note* 127, at 199.

[130]al-Farrā', *supra note* 21, at 41.

[131]*The Holy Qur'ān*, XLIX: 9.

[132]John Kelsay, *supra note* 15, at 86; Khalid Abou El Fadl, "Aḥkām al-Bughāt: Irregular War and the Law of Rebellion in Islam," in *Cross, Crescent and Sword: The Justification and Limitation of War in Western and Islamic Tradition*, eds. James Turner Johnson and John Kelsay (Westport, Connecticut: Greenwood press, 1990), 153; Al Ghunaimi, *supra note* 83, at 140.

> prisoners, do not pursue those who return and retreat, do not enslave their women, do not mutilate their dead, do not uncover what is to remain covered, do not approach their property except what you find in their camp of weapons, beasts, male or female slaves: all the rest is to be inherited by their heirs according to the *Qur'ān*."[133]

Unlike highway robbers or apostates, the punishment for a rebel, according to al-Māwardī, is not capital,[134] since the aim of fighting them is not to eliminate them, but to prevent them from disrupting peace and security.[135] This opinion cannot be taken for granted, as other jurists argue that rebels may be treated like apostates and polytheists if they have been forewarned of the battle.[136] A case in point is the *jihād* of 'Alī Ibn Abī Ṭālib against the *Khārijīs.* Before he crushed them in the battle of al-Nahruwān, he sent 'Abd Allāh Ibn 'Abbās to warn them and, thereby, to diminish the loss of Muslim life.[137] It is worth mentioning that rebels, according to al-Māwardī are entitled to what is so-called a *de facto* state in the modern sense of the term. They can collect revenue taxes and conclude treaties with foreign states.[138] However, the *jihād* against *al-bughāt* (rebels) may correspond to the fighting referred to in article 3 of the 1949 Geneva Convention I for the Amelioration of the Condition of Wounded and Sick in Armed Forces in the Field,[139] as well as to the 1977 Geneva Protocol II Additional to the Geneva Conventions of 12 August 1949, and Relating to the Protection of Victims of Non-

---

[133]Abū al-Ḥasan 'Alī Ibn al-Ḥusayn al-Mas'ūdī, *Murūj al-Dhahab wa Ma'ādin al-Jawhar*, 4 vols. (Beirut: Dār al-Fikr, 1973), 2:371 [hereinafter al- Mas'ūdī].

[134]al-Māwardī, *supra note* 21, at 54.

[135]al-Kāsānī, *supra note* 21, at 140.

[136]Ibn Ḥazm, *supra note* 21, at 333; al-Sarakhsī, *supra note* 21, at 128-129.

[137]al-Farrā', *supra note* 21, at 39; al-Marghīnānī, *supra note* 21, at 170; al-Mughnī, *supra note* 21, at 54.

[138]al-Māwardī, *supra note* 21, at 54; al-Sarakhsī, *supra note* 21, 130.

[139]*The Geneva Convention I for the Amelioration of the Condition of the Wounded and Sick in Armed Forces in the Field of August 12, 1949*, 75 U.N.T.S. (1950) 31-83 [hereinafter The Geneva I]. See Jean Pictet, *Humanitarian Law and the protection of War Victims* (Geneva: Henry Dunant Institute, 1975), 53.

International Armed Conflicts.[140] A comparison between the norms of Geneva Conventions, and its parallels in Islamic international law, reveals that the regulations of the Geneva Conventions relating to armed conflict of a non-international nature are weaker than those contained in the same conventions pertaining to international armed conflict. On the contrary, however, the regulations of Islamic international law pertaining to non-international armed conflict are stronger and more humane than those relating to international armed conflict of the same law.[141]

Waging war against apostates (*al-Murtaddūn*), who renounce Islam totally, or in part,[142] is justified by the Prophetic tradition:

> "A Muslim's blood shall not be lawfully shed except for three causes: atheism after belief; adultery after marriage; or killing a person otherwise than in retaliation for another person."[143]

Before taking any action against apostates, Muslim jurists emphasize that the *Imām* should negotiate with them for three days, trying to persuade them to return to Islam,[144] as *Allāh* says: "but if they repent, establish regular prayers, and give regular charity, then open the way for them."[145] The *Imām* should do the same with apostates who separate themselves and become a *de facto* state exercising

---

[140]*Protocol II Additional to the Geneva Conventions of August 12, 1949, and Relating to the Protection of Victims of Non-International Armed Conflicts*, 1125 U.N.T.S. 609 (opened for signature on December 12, 1977 and entered into force on December 7, 1978) [hereinafter Protocol II]. See Theodor Meron et al., "Application of Humanitarian Law in Non-International Armed Conflicts," *American Society of International Law Proceedings* 85 (1991): 84.

[141]Ahmed Zaki Yamani, *supra note* 42, at 195.

[142]Apostasy punishments would not apply to the insane, minors, the intoxicated, or those who became Muslims under coercion. Apostate women would not be killed, but imprisoned until returning to Islam. See al-Kāsānī, *supra note* 21, at 7:134; Majid Khadduri, *supra note* 2, at 205, 215 and 227; al-Marghīnānī, *supra note* 21, at 2:165 and 170; al-Sarakhsī, *supra note* 21, at 10:98 and 123.

[143]Muslim, *supra note* 69, at 3: 506-507.

[144]al-Farrā', *supra note* 21, at 35; al-Kāsānī, *supra note* 21, at 7: 135; Majid Khadduri, *supra note* 2, at 195.

[145]*The Holy Qur'ān*, IX: 5.

sovereignty over part of the territory of Islam (*dār al-Islām*), or who join the territory of war (*dār al-ḥarb*).[146] The apostates have to return to Islam or accept the challenge of *jihād*. In other words, they must choose between Islam or the sword;[147] they cannot be given *amān* (safeguard)[148] or allowed to become *dhimmīs*.[149] If apostates choose the sword after being notified and warned, *jihād* should be waged against them on the same terms that *jihād* is waged against *ḥarbīs* (the people of the territory of war).[150] Cases in point were the secession of the tribes of Arabia, except *Quraysh* and *Thaqīf*, after the death of the Prophet,[151] and the Karmathians (*al-Qarāmiṭa*) in the Abbasid era.[152] The Arab tribes who refused to return to Islam were severely fought by Abū Bakr, the first caliph, and the Karmathians were crushed by al-Muktafī bi-Allāh, the Abbasid caliph. Muslim jurists professed that apostates and their wives could not be enslaved,[153] nor could their property be confiscated.[154] If an apostate were killed, his property before renouncing Islam, would be distributed among his Muslim heirs,[155] while his property, after apostasy, would be taken over by the Islamic state as *fay*' (booty).[156] However, being treated like non-Muslim combatants, apostates, according to Islamic international law, are

---

[146]al-Kāsānī, *supra note* 21, at 7:136; al-Siyar al-Kabīr, *supra note* 67, at 5:1938.

[147]This issue has been expressed in the following verse: "Shall you fight, or they shall submit [to Islam]", *The Holy Qur'ān*, XLVIII: 16; al-Sarakhsī, *supra note* 21, at 10: 98-99.

[148]al-Farrā', *supra note* 21, at 37.

[149]*Ibid.*

[150]al-Sarakhsī, *supra note* 21, at 10:114; al-Siyar al-Kabīr, *supra note* 67, at 5:1941.

[151]al-Farrā', *Ibid.*; al-Ṭabarī, *supra note* 71, at 2: 157.

[152]Albert Hourani, *A History of the Arab Peoples* (Cambridge, Massachusetts: The Belknap Press of Harvard University Press, 1991), 40; Ibn Kathīr, *supra note* 72, at 11:82.

[153]al-Kāsānī, *supra note* 21, at 7:136; Majid Khadduri, *supra note* 2, at 216-217.

[154]al-Kāsānī, *Ibid.*; al-Marghīnānī, *supra note* 21, at 2:165.

[155]Majid Khadduri, *supra note* 2, at 196; al-Marghīnānī, *Ibid.*

[156]al-Farrā', *supra note* 21, at 36; al-Kāsānī, *supra note* 21, at 7:139; Majid Khadduri, *supra note* 2, at 201; al-Marghīnānī, *Ibid.*; al-Sarakhsī, *supra note* 21, at 10: 101.

not responsible for losses sustained as a result of war,[157] and their negotiators and ambassadors are entitled to diplomatic immunity in the modern sense of the term.[158]

The primary sources of Islamic law give final authority to the leaders of the Islamic State (*ulū al-amr*), and emphasize the need for their obedience and compliance by Muslims collectively and individually. The law concerning this issue is expounded in the *Holy Qur'ān* as follows:

> "O ye who believe! Obey *Allāh*, and obey the Prophet, and those charged with authority among you. If you differ in anything among yourselves, refer it to *Allāh* and His Prophet if you do believe in *Allāh* and the Last Day; that is best, and most suitable for final determination."[159]

However, Islamic law regulates the relationships between Muslims and their leaders. The subjects of the Islamic state owe a duty of obedience to the *Imām*, who in return has to defend their interests, enforce Islamic law, and establish public security.[160] Although many Muslim jurists argue that revolting against a corrupt *Imām* is worse than tyranny,[161] the Qur'anic verses and Prophetic traditions exhort Muslims to disobey the *Imām*, and even wage *jihād* (*sall al-sayf*) against him if he deviates from the right path, for "no obedience to any creature in disobedience to the Creator."[162] In other words, if the *Imām* commands something which violates the

---

[157]Majid Khadduri, *supra note* 2, at 202; al-Mughnī, *supra note* 21, at 10:73.

[158]The Prophet told the ambassadors of Musaylama *al-Kadhdhāb* "the liar" when they arrived at the Madīna: "By *Allāh* if you were not ambassadors, I would have ordered you to be beheaded." See Ibn Hishām, *supra note* 67, at 4: 183.

[159]*The Holy Qur'ān*, IV: 59.

[160]Abū al-Ḥasan 'Alī al-Māwardī, *Adab al-Dunyā wal-Dīn* (Mecca: Dār al-Bāz lil-Nashr, 1987), 138.

[161]al-Farrā', *supra note* 21, at 20; Qamaruddin Khan, *The Political Thought of Ibn Taymiyah* (Delhi, India: Adam Publishers & Distributors, 1988), 213; Shams al-Islām Ibn Qayyin al-Jawziyya, *I'lām al-Muwaqqi'īn 'an Rabb al-'Ālamīn*, 4 vols. (Cairo: al-Maktaba al-Tijāriyya al-Kubra, 1955), 3: 6-7 [hereinafter I'lām al- Muwaqqi'īn].

[162]Abū Muḥammad 'Ali Ibn Ḥazm, *al-Faṣl fī al-Milal wal-Ahwā' wal-Niḥal*, 5 vols. (Beirut: Dār al-Jīl 1985), 5:28 [hereinafter al-Milal wal-Niḥal]; Fakhr al-Dīn al-Rāzī, *al-Tafsīr al-Kabīr*, 32 vols. (Beirut: Dār Iḥyā' al-Turāth al-'Arabī, 1980), 4:42-43 [hereinafter al-Rāzī]; *The Holy Qur'ān*, II:124, V:47, 48, 50; al-Juwaynī, *supra note* 21, at 88; Qamaruddin Khan, *supra note* 161, at 205-210;

rules stated in the *Qur'ān* and the *Sunna*, the Muslims' duty of obedience, is null and void.[163] In his first speech, after his ascension to the position of the first guided Caliph, Abū Bakr addressed the believers: "Obey me as long as I remain loyal to *Allāh* and His Prophet, but if I disobey them none should accord obedience to me."[164] This point finds support in the *Qur'ān* and *ḥadīth* (prophetic tradition). *Allāh* puts the disbelievers and the rulers who do not enforce *Allāh's* laws, on an equal footing, "if any (rulers) do fail to judge by what *Allāh* has revealed, they are (no better than) unbelievers."[165] Through the glasses of this concept, the Prophet said: "The greatest *jihād* is a just word to a tyrant ruler."[166] In light of the above argument, it is obvious that the *bay'a* (homage) is a contract between the ruler and the ruled which, if breached by any of the two contracting parties, warrants a *jihād* against the violator until he follows the right path.[167]

B. Jihād against Non-Muslims

The other kind of lesser *jihād* is fighting against non-Muslims, polytheists and scripturaries (*Ahl al-Kitāb*). This external *jihād* may be called international *jihād*. As indicated earlier, it is important to emphasize that *jihād*, in any case, is a defensive war. In other words, according to the *Qur'ān* and the Prophetic traditions, Muslims are not allowed to wage *jihād* against polytheists and scripturaries before

---

Shihāb al-Dīn al-Sayyid Maḥmūd al-Alūsī al-Baghdādī, *Rūḥ al-Ma'ānī fī Tafsīr al-Qur'ān al-'Aẓīm wal-Sab' al-Mathānī*, 29 vols. (Beirut: Dār Iḥyā' al-Turāth al-'Arabī, 1980), 1: 376-378 [hereinafter al-Alūsī].

[163]al-Māwardī, *supra note* 21, at 15-16; Noel Coulson, "The State and the Individual in Islamic Law," *The International and Comparative Law Quarterly* 6 (1957): 57; Norman Anderson and Noel Coulson, "The Moslem Ruler and Contractual Obligations," *New York University Law Review* 33 (1958): 921.

[164]Ibn Kathīr, *supra note* 72, at 6:301; al-Ṭabarī, *supra note* 71, at 2:105.

[165]*The Holy Qur'ān*, V: 47.

[166]Abū 'Abd al-Raḥmān Aḥmad Ibn Shu'ayb al-Nasā'ī, *Sunan al-Nasā'ī*, 8 vols. (Cairo: Al-Maktaba al-Tijāriyya al-Kubrā, 1930), 7:161 [hereinafter al-Nasā'ī].

[167]al-Māwardī, *supra note* 21, at 40.

they attack Muslims or breach their conduct with them.[168]

In discussing this point, Majid Khadduri advocates that "no compromise is permitted with those who fail to believe in God, they have either to accept Islam or fight..."[169] "When *Allāh* sent the last of His Prophets to call them (scripturaries) to the truth, they accepted belief in *Allāh* but not in His Prophet or the *Qur'ān*. Hence, the scripturaries, like the polytheists must be punished."[170] In examining these statements, I recall this observation: "Rationality in drawing inferences means that the conclusion of an argument must follow from the premises and must not go beyond them; it must be true if the premises are true."[171] To disprove Khadduri's argument, and to show the invalidity of his inferences and his stereotyped conclusions, one must refer to the *Holy Qur'ān*, Prophetic traditions and precedents within the framework of Islamic legal theory.

It is obvious that Khadurri attempts to demonstrate the definitive hostility of Islam to all non-Muslims. In other words, he argues that polytheists and scripturaries are liable to punishment since they fail to believe in Islam; the polytheists should choose Islam or the sword, while the scripturaries can choose one of three: Islam, the poll tax (*jizya*), or the sword.[172] As has already been explained, waging *jihād* against non-Muslims on account of their denial of Muḥammad's mission is at variance with the *Qur'anic* teachings. This critical point has been expressed in the following verses:

> "Let there be no compulsion in religion."[173] "if it had been your Lord's will, all who are on earth would have believed (in Islam). Do

---

[168]*The Holy Qur'ān*, II: 190.

[169]Majid Khadduri, *supra note* 50, at 75.

[170]*Ibid.*, at 80.

[171]Wael B. Hallaq. "On Inductive Corroboration, Probability and Certainty in Sunni- Legal Thought," in *Islamic Law and Jurisprudence*, ed. N. Heer (Seattle: University of Washington Press, 1990), 3.

[172]Majid Khadduri, *supra note*, 50, at 80.

[173]*The Holy Qur'ān*, II: 256.

> you want to compel mankind, against their will, to believe."[174] "And say, the truth is from your Lord. Whosoever will, let him believe, and whosoever will, let him disbelieve."[175] "Those who believe (in the *Qur'ān*), those who follow the Jewish scriptures, and the Sabians, Christians, Magians, and Polytheists, *Allāh* will judge between them on the Day of Judgement, for *Allāh* is witness of all things."[176] "You have your religion and I have mine."[177]

Furthermore, one must make reference to the Islamic concept of religious liberty and tolerance, as well as to Islamic respect paid to the People of the Book (Jews and Christians) as outlined in the following Qur'anic verses:

> "Those who believe (in the *Qur'ān*), and those who follow the Jewish (scriptures), and the Christians and the Sabians, and who believe in *Allāh* and the Last Day, and work righteousness, shall have their reward with their Lord. On them shall be no fear, nor shall they grieve."[178]

> "And dispute ye not with the People of the Book, except with means better (than mere disputation), unless it be with those of them inflict wrong (and injury)."[179]

Accordingly, Muslims are not allowed to fight against the scripturaries and polytheists unless they commit an aggression. Even in the battlefield, Muslim soldiers were prohibited from starting the war. Although non-Muslims start killing Muslims, the latter are not allowed to do the same until they show them the killed person and say to them: Would it not be better for you to achieve peace and security by embracing Islam or by concluding a covenant safeguarding peace? If they accept Islam, or choose to remain scripturaries under safe conduct and quarter (*amān*), they

---

[174] *Ibid.*, X: 99.

[175] *The Holy Qur'ān*, XVIII: 29.

[176] *Ibid.*, XXII: 17

[177] *Ibid.*, CIX: 6.

[178] *Ibid.*, II: 62.

[179] *Ibid.*, XXIX: 46.

would be entitled to enjoy all the rights and obligations dictated by Islamic law.[180] If none of the choices above are accepted, Muslim soldiers are permitted to wage *jihād* in defence of their faith and land. This approach is illustrated by the following Prophetic traditions:

> "Narrated 'Abd Allāh Ibn Abī Awfā, the Prophet, during some of his battles, got up among the people and said: O people! Do not wish to face the enemy (in a battle) and ask *Allāh* to save you from calamities."[181]

> "The Prophet instructed Mu'ādh Ibn Jabal, when he sent him at the head of the Muslim army to conquer the Yemen. He said: Do not fight them before you call them [to be converted into Islam or to conclude a covenant]. And if they decline, do not fight them until they take the initiative, and when they do so, wait until they slay one of your men. Then show them the body of the slain and say to them: Is there no better way than this? If *Allāh* converts one single man through your example, it will be better for you than to own the whole world."[182]

4. The Development of the Doctrine of Jihād

A closer look at the verses of the *Holy Qur'ān* would reveal that *jihād* developed through four stages: the first was that of forbidding Muslims from fighting.[183] This is the earliest period in the life of the Muslims when they were still

---

[180]Majid Khadduri argues that if the People of the Book prefer to remain scripturaries at the sacrifice of paying the poll tax, they suffer certain disabilities, which reduce them to second-class citizens. Khadduri, however, does not mention any of these disabilities. See Majid Khadduri, *supra note* 50, at 80; Majid Khadduri, "The Islamic Theory of International Relations and Its Contemporary Relevance," in *Islam and International Relations*, ed. J. Harris Proctor (New York: Frederick A. Praeger Publishers, 1965), 26.

[181]al-Bukhārī, *supra note* 66, at 4:9.

[182]Muḥammad Abū Zahra, *Naẓariyyat al-Ḥarb fī al-Islām*, 4th ed. (Cairo: Wazārat al-Awqāf, 1961), 42; al-Sarakhsī, *supra note* 21, at 10:31; al-Siyar al-Kabīr, *supra note* 67, at 1:78; Wahba al-Zuḥaylī, *Āthār al-Ḥarb fī al-Fiqh al-Islāmī: Dirāsa Muqārana* (Damascus: Dār al-Fikr, 1992), 154.

[183]"Last thou not turned thy vision to those who were told to hold back their hands (from fighting) but established regular prayers and spend in regular charity, when (at length) the order for fighting was issued to them, behold! a section of them feared men as or even more that they should have

a weak community in Mecca prior to the *hijra* (emigration to Medina) and the establishment of the Islamic state. In this phase, the Prophet started the greater *jihād* (*al-jihād al-akbar*) by preaching non-violently, while Muslims were insulted, abused and persecuted for many years by the infidels of Mecca.[184] The second state is the one in which the Prophet stopped preaching inside Mecca and turned his attention to the neighbouring cities and countries. In this period, Muslims were given permission to fight, as the verse was revealed in the wake of the Muslims' forced departure from Mecca.[185] The third juncture is the one in which Muslims were given the order to fight. This significant development occurred following the establishment of the *post-Hijra* Muslim society in Medina, in a Qur'anic verse that was the first to explicitly orders Muslims to initiate a just war.[186] The fourth phase is the one in which Muslims received the order to fight against the polytheists (*al-Mushrikūn*) after they had dishonoured their pledges with Muslims.[187] This is the stage at which the Islamic state witnessed the peak of its strength in the days of the Prophet and when Muslims became established as a social and political force in Arabia.[188] In this period, the young Muslim State had become so vibrant as to extend its dominion over the entire Arabian Peninsula.

---

feared *Allāh*." *The Holy Qur'ān*, IV: 77.

[184]Aslam Siddiqi, "*Jihād*: An Instrument of Islamic Revolution," *Islamic Studies* 2 (1963): 383-384; Ibn Hishām, *supra note* 67, at 1: 258-259; Ibn Isḥāq, *supra note* 84, at 131.

[185] "To those against whom war is made, permission is given (to fight), because they are wronged; and verily, *Allāh* is Most Powerful for their aid. (They are) those who have been expelled from their homes in defiance of right (for no cause) except that they say: Our Lord is *Allāh*." *The Holy Qur'ān*, XXII: 39-40.

[186]"Fight in the cause of *Allāh* those who fight you, but do not transgress limits, for *Allāh* loveth not transgressors." *The Holy Qur'ān*, II: 190.

[187]"Fight those who believe not in *Allāh* nor the Last Day, nor hold that forbidden which hath been forbidden by *Allāh* and His Prophet, nor acknowledge the religion of truth, (even if they are) of the People of the Book; until they pay the *jizya* with willing submission and feel themselves subdued." *The Holy Qur'ān*, IX: 29.

[188]Jamilah Kolocotronis, *Islamic Jihād: A Historical Perspective*, (Indianapolis, Indiana: American Trust Publications, 1990), 74.

5. Forbidden Acts of Hostility According to the Doctrine of Jihād

Nevertheless, Islamic international law recognizes that war, by its nature, implies violence and suffering.[189] Therefore, as a highly practical and realistic law, it does not require Muslim jihadists to love their enemies nor to receive them with damask roses,[190] but, strictly, lays down humane rules governing the conduct of war, and the treatment of enemy persons and property.[191] Limiting violence to the necessities of war, Islamic international law differentiates between combatants and civilians, as well as between military and civilian objects in time of war.[192] Furthermore, it provides a set of forbidden acts that relate directly to the above categories; combatants, civilians, and civilian objects.

With respect to the first category, Islamic international law deters Muslim fighters from the following acts: (a) starting warfare before inviting their enemy to adopt Islam or to conclude a covenant.[193] Even if the enemy declines, Muslim fighters are still bound not to start the fighting until the enemy attacks;[194] (b) summary executions, decapitation and torturing of prisoners of war (*al-asrā*);[195] (c) delivering a *coup de grâce* to the wounded;[196] (d) burning captives to death;[197] (e)

---

[189]Sobhi Mahmassani, *supra note* 1, at 300.

[190]Marcel A. Boisard, "The Conduct of Hostilities and the Protection of the Victims of Armed Conflicts in Islam," *Hamdard Islamicus* 1:2 (Autumn 1978): 10.

[191]al-Kāsānī, *supra note* 21 at 7:101-102; al-Marghīnānī, *supra note* 21, at 2:136-137; al-Māwardī, *supra note* 21, at 38; al-Mughnī, *supra note* 21, at 10:542-544; al-Siyar al-Kabīr, *supra note* 67, at 1:39-55.

[192]Muḥammad Ibn ʻAlī al-Shawkānī, *Nayl al-Awṭār Sharḥ Muntaqā al-Akhbār min Aḥādīth Sayyid al-Akhyār*, 8 vols. (Cairo: Maṭbaʻat Muṣṭafā al-Bābī al-Ḥalabī, 1952), 7:258-263 [hereinafter al-Shawkānī]; al-Ṣanʻānī, *supra note* 21, at 4:62-64 and 85; al-Sarakhsī, *supra note* 21, at 10:30-77; al-Siyar al-Kabīr, *supra note* 67, at 4:1458-1467.

[193]Fatḥ al-Bārī, *supra note* 66 at 6:111; al-Kāsānī, *supra note* 21, at 107; Muslim, *supra note* 69, at 4:8; al-Siyar al-Kabīr, *supra note* 67, at 1:38-59.

[194]al-Sarakhsī, *supra note* 21, at 10:31.

[195]*Ibid.*, at 10:32; al-Siyar al-Kabīr, *supra note* 67, at 1:110-111, 3:1024-1041; 4:1148-1158.

[196]ʻIzz al-Dīn Abū Ḥāmid Ibn Abī al-Ḥadīd, *Kitāb Nahj al-Balāgha*, 4 vols. (Beirut: Dār al-Maʻrifa, n.d.), 3: 425 [hereinafter Nahj al-Balāgha].

mutilating dead bodies;[198] (f) treachery and perfidy;[199] (g) using poisoned weapons;[200] and (h) killing of an enemy *hors de combat*.[201] However, some of these prohibited acts are reflected in several conventions and protocols of international humanitarian law. Despite the inclusion of a general clause for participation which provides that their regulations are binding only to the High Contracting Parties,[202] the four Geneva Conventions of 1949 and its Additional Protocols of 1977, as well as the Hague Conventions of 1899 and 1907 are mainly devoted to the protection of war victims.[203] The Hague Regulations, annexed to the 1907 Hague Convention IV Respecting the Laws and Customs of War on Land, provide in Article 22 that, "the right of belligerents to adopt means of injuring the enemy is not unlimited."[204] More specifically, Article 23 of the same regulations prohibits the employment of poison or poisoned weapons, the killing or wounding of an enemy who has laid down his arms, and the employment of arms or material calculated to cause unnecessary suffering.[205] Similarly, these norms are affirmed by Article 3 of the

---

[197]Abū Dāwūd Sulaymān Ibn al-Ash'ath, *Sunan Abī Dāwūd*, 2 vols. (Beirut: Dār al-Janān, 1988), 2:61 [hereinafter Abū Dāwūd]; Al-Siyar al-Kabīr, *supra note* 67, at 4:1467.

[198] Abū Dāwūd, *supra note* 197, at 2:59; al-Shawkanī, *supra note* 192, at 7:262.

[199]*The Holy Qur'ān* explicitly discusses this point: "If thou fearest treachery from any group, throw back (their covenant) to them, (so as to be) on equal terms, for *Allāh* loveth not the treacherous." *The Holy Qur'ān*, VIII: 58. See Muslim, *supra note* 69, at 4:8; Said El-Dakkak, "International Humanitarian Law Lies Between the Islamic Concept and Positive International Law," *International Review of Red Cross* 275 (March-April 1990): 106.

[200]Muslim jurists clearly rule that using poisoned weapons against an enemy in warfare is unlawful. See Abū 'Abd Allāh Muḥammad al-Maghribī, *Kitāb Mawāhib al-Jalīl li Sharḥ Mukhtaṣar Khalīl*, 6 vols. (Beirut: Dār al-Fikr, 1992), 6:291 [hereinafter Mawāhib al-Jalīl].

[201]Nahj al-Balāgha, *supra note* 196, at 425.

[202]Waldemar A. Solf, "Protection of Civilians against the Effects of Hostilities under Customary International Law and under Protocol I," *The American University Journal of International Law and Policy* 1 (Summer 1986): 123.

[203]Su Wei, "The Application of Rules Protecting Combatants and Civilians against the Effects of the Employment of Certain Means and Methods of Warfare," in *Implementation of International Humanitarian law*, eds. Frits Kalshoven and Yves Sandoz (Dordrecht, The Netherlands: Martinus Nijhoff Publishers, 1989), 377.

[204]The Hague IV, *supra note* 103.

1949 Geneva Convention I for the Amelioration of the Condition of the Wounded and Sick in Armed Forces in the Fields,[206] as well as, by Article 35 of the 1977 Geneva Protocol I Additional to the Geneva Conventions of 12 August 1949, and Relating to the Protection of Victims of International Armed Conflicts.[207] Moreover, Article 37 of the same Protocol prohibits killing, injuring or capturing an adversary by resorting to perfidy.[208] Article 41 also includes provisions concerning the prohibition of extermination of the enemy and the killing of an enemy *hors de combat.*[209]

Islamic international law is rather cautious in dealing with civilians in times of war. It forbids (a) attacking, killing and molesting of non-combatant persons. This category includes children under 15 years of age, women, old men, monks, sick and disabled persons;[210] (b) rape in war and sexual molestation. Any Muslim fighter who may commit fornication, rape and other forms of gender-based sexual violence is subject to stoning to death or, to lashing, according to his status as single or married;[211] (c) ethnic cleansing, brutal massacres and collective blood baths;[212]

---

[205]*Ibid.*

[206]The Geneva I, *supra note* 139.

[207]Protocol I, *supra note* 105.

[208]*Ibid.*

[209]*Ibid.*

[210]Abū Dāwūd, *supra note* 197, 2:60-61; Abū Yūsuf, *supra note* 53, at 344; al-Bukhārī, *supra note* 66, at 4:21; al-Farrā', *supra note* 21, at 27; Ḥasan al-Bannā, *al-Jihād fī Sabīl Allāh* (Cairo: Maktabat al-Turāth al-Islāmī, n.d.), 89; Ibn Rushd, *supra note* 21, at 1:382; al-Kāsānī, *supra note* 21, at 7:101; al-Mughnī, *supra note* 21, at 10:541; al-Nawawī, *supra note* 21, at 459; al-Sarakhsī, *supra note* 21, at 10:32; al-Siyar al-Kabīr, *supra note* 67, at 4:1415-1419.

[211]Majid Khadduri, *supra note* 2, at 126; David Aaron Schwartz, "International Terrorism and Islamic Law," *Columbia Journal of Transnational Law* 29 (1991): 650. It is important to mention that Islamic international law has prosecuted and considered rape in war as a war crime, as early as fourteen centuries before the Geneva Conventions of 1949, and the statute of the International Criminal Tribunal for the Former Yugoslavia, 1993. In the case of *Khālid Ibn al-Walīd v. Ḍirār Ibn al-Azwar*, the former complained to 'Umar Ibn al-Khaṭṭāb, the second Muslim Caliph, that the latter, a Muslim army commander, had had sexual intercourse with a captive woman during the Muslim war against Banū Asad. In response, 'Umar wrote to Khālid ordering him to stone Ibn al-Azwar to death. Before Khālid had received 'Umar's judgment, however, Ibn al-Azwar had passed away. See Abū Bakr Aḥmad Ibn al-Ḥusayn al-Bayhaqī, *al-Sunan al-Kubrā*, 10 vols. (Ḥaydar Abād: Maṭba'at Majlis

and (d) killing of peasants, merchants, and diplomats.[213]

A closer look at the provisions of the international humanitarian law reveals that prior to the establishment of the International Criminal Tribunal for the former Yugoslavia, rape was viewed as a secondary human rights abuse during war.[214] Rape was neither mentioned in the Nuremberg Charter nor prosecuted in Nuremberg as a war crime under customary international law,[215] but it was prosecuted to a limited degree as a war crime in the Tokyo Tribunal.[216] However, Article 46 of the Hague Regulations of 1899 and 1907 can be broadly considered to cover rape, but has, in the past, been interpreted more narrowly.[217] Article 147 of the 1949 Geneva Convention IV, and Article 76 (1) of the 1977 Geneva Protocol I Additional to the Geneva Conventions of 12 August 1949 provide that, "women

---

Dā'irat al-Ma'ārif al-'Uthmāniyya, 1925), 9:104 [hereinafter al-Bayhaqī]; Abū Yūsuf, *supra note* 53, at 336; al-Mughnī, *supra note* 21, at 10:561; al-Shāfi'ī, *supra note* 21, at 7:322.

[212]In spite of the brutal and cruel treatment of the Meccans, the Prophet instructed the Muslim army, before marching to Mecca in A.D. 630, to avoid fighting or shedding of blood. The Prophet emphasized that after he heard Sa'd Ibn 'Ubāda, one of the four commanders to enter Mecca saying: "Today is a day of war, sanctuary is no more," the Prophet replied: "Today is a day of mercy," and he replaced Ibn 'Ubāda by 'Alī Ibn Abī Tālib. When he conquered Mecca, the Prophet asked the Meccans: "What do you think that I am about to do with you?" They replied: "Good. You are a noble brother, son of a noble brother." He said: "Go your way for you are the freed ones." Similarly, 'Umar Ibn al-Khaṭṭāb, the second well-guided Caliph, did when he conquered Jerusalem in A.D. 638. 'Umar gave a formal pledge (*al-'uhda al-'Umariyya*) to respect the Christian churches, crosses, and the extended security to the people of the city. See Appendix IV: The Treaty of Jerusalem "Mu'āhadat Ahl Īliyā'". As a matter of fact, it was the first time in history that Jerusalem was conquered without bloodshed. See Ibn Hishām, *supra note* 67, at 4:36; Ibn Isḥāq, *supra note* 84 at 553; Ibn Kathīr, *supra note* 72, at 4:292 and 7:55; al-Ṭabarī, *supra note* 71, at 2:21 and 304.

[213]al-Siyar al-Kabīr, *supra note* 67, at 1:296 and 2:515.

[214]M. Cherif Bassiouni, "The Commission of Experts Established Pursuant to Security Council Resolution 780: Investigating Violations of International Humanitarian Law in the Former Yugoslavia," *Criminal Law Forum* 5: 2-3 (1994): 280; Christine Clinkin, "Rape and Sexual Abuse of Women in International Law," *European Journal of International Law* 5 (1994): 326.

[215]*Agreement for the Prosecution and Punishment of the Major War Criminals of the European Axis Powers and Charter of the International Military Tribunal*, August 8, 1945, 82 U.N.T.S. 279, 59 Stat. 1544, E.A.S. No. 472.

[216]*Charter of International Military Tribunal for the Far East*, January 19, 1946, April 26, 1946, T.I.A.S. No. 1589, 4 Bevans 20.

[217]This Article provides that "Family honour and rights, the lives of persons, and private property, as well as religious convictions and practice, must be respected." Hague IV, *supra note* 103.

shall be especially protected against any attack on their honour, in particular against rape, enforced prostitution, or any form of indecent assault."[218] Accordingly, Islamic international law could be considered as the first international law to consider rape during armed conflict, a war crime.

Islamic international law prohibits unnecessary destruction of an enemy's real or personal property;[219] devastation of harvest and cutting fruitful trees; and demolition of religious, medical and cultural institutions.[220] Citing *Kitāb al-I'tibār* of Usāma Ibn Munqidh, Marcel A. Boisard states that starting with the 3rd/9th century Islamic international law gave amnesty to hospitals, medical and paramedical personnel. Furthermore, he argues that Muslims knew military field hospitals as early as the 9th century, while it was found in Spain only in the 16th century.[221]

Articles 13 to 26, of the 1977 Additional Protocol I, specify the immunity of civilian hospitals and medical personnel, and Article 53 refers directly to the protection of cultural objects and places of worship during armed conflicts.[222]

6. When Can Jihād be Terminated?

Being an exceptional, and purely defensive war designed to stem rebellion, repel aggression, or avert any danger to *dār al-Islām*, *jihād* could be terminated by

---

[218]*The Geneva Convention IV Relative to the Protection of Civilian Persons in Time of War of August 12, 1949*, 75 U.N.T.S. (1950) 287-417 [hereinafter The Geneva IV]. For more details concerning the protection of civilians, particularly women and children, in armed conflict, see Charles A. Allen, "Civilian Starvation and Relief during Armed Conflict: The Modern Humanitarian Law," *Georgia Journal of International and Comparative Law* 19:1 (Spring 1989): 23; Colleen C. Maher, "The Protection of Children in Armed Conflict: A Human Rights Analysis of the Protection Afforded to Children in Warfare," *Boston College Third World Law Journal* 9:297 (Summer 1989), 301; Geraldine Van Bueren, "The International Legal Protection of Children in Armed Conflicts," *International and Comparative Law Quarterly* 43:4 (October 1994): 810.

[219]David Aaron Schwartz, *supra note* 211, at 650.

[220]al-Bukhārī, *supra note* 66, at 4:22; al-Shawkānī, *supra note* 192, at 7:262-263.

[221]Marcel A. Boisard, *supra note* 190, at 10.

[222]Protocol I, *supra note* 105. See J.G. Starke, "the Concept of Open Cities in International Humanitarian Law," *Australian Law Journal* 56:11 (November 1982): 596.

causes which closely parallel the causes of terminating war in public international law.[223] According to *Kitāb al-Aḥkām al-Sulṭāniyya* of al-Māwardī,[224] and *al-Mughnī* of Ibn Qudāma,[225] *jihād* may be ended by one of the following ways: (a) surrender of the non-Muslim enemy by embracing Islam. According to the following Prophetic *ḥadīth* (tradition), enemy persons are entitled to acquire Muslims' rights and obligations on the same equal footing.

> "I am commanded to fight with men till they testify that there is no God but *Allāh*; when they do that, they will keep their life and their property safe from me, except what is due to them, and their reckoning will be at *Allāh's* hands."[226]

In this case, Muslim jurists hold that only the convert's young children become Muslims according to the Qur'anic verse "and those who believe and their families follow them in faith, to them shall we join their families,"[227] but this rule does not apply to their wives and dependent children, for *Allāh* says: "each individual is in pledge for his deeds";[228] (b) defeat of the enemy. In this case, lives and properties of enemy polytheists will be subject to the rules of spoils of war;[229] (c) concluding a treaty of peace (*muwāda'a*) or an armistice treaty (*muhādana*). This treaty is usually granted by the *Imām* for a short period of time, in consideration of the payment of an

---

[223]A war may end in one of several ways: by a simple cessation of hostilities; by subjugation; and by a treaty of peace. See Gerhard von Glahn, *supra note* 95, at 572.

[224]al-Māwardī, *supra note* 21, at 45.

[225]al-Mughnī, *supra note* 21, at 544-547.

[226]Abū Dāwūd, *supra note* 197, at 2:50.

[227]*The Holy Qur'ān*, LII: 21. See al-Kāsānī, *supra note* 21, at 7:104; al-Mughnī, *supra note* 21, at 8:143; Muḥammad Amīn Ibn 'Ābdīn, *Radd al-Muḥtār ʿalā al-Durr al-Mukhtār*, 5 vols. (Cairo: al-Maṭba'a al-Amīriyya, 1326 A.H.), 3:316 [hereinafter Ibn 'Ābdīn].

[228]*The Holy Qur'ān*, LII: 21. See Abū 'Abd Allāh Muḥammad al-Khirshī, *Fatḥ al-Jalīl 'alā Mukhtaṣar al-'Allāma Khalīl*, 8 vols. (Cairo: Maṭba'at Būlāq, 1299 A.H.), 3:166 [hereinafter al-Khirshī]; Ibn Ḥazm, *supra note* 21, at 7:309; Muḥammad Ibn Aḥmad Ibn 'Arafa al-Dusūqī, *Ḥāshiya 'alā al-Sharḥ al-Kabīr lil-Dardīr*, 4 vols. (Cairo: Maṭba'at Muṣṭafa Muḥammad, 1373 A.H.), 2:185 [hereinafter al-Dusūqī].

[229]al-Sarakhsī, *supra note* 21, at 10:7-8.

annual tribute to the Muslim State. The *Imām* may renew the treaty for a similar period if he feels that Muslims are not powerful enough to launch a *jihād*;[230] and (d) a cessation of hostilities by one or both parties, which does not necessitate victory of one of them over the other. A clear example of this, is the battle of Mu'ta, where both armies parted from each other, without concluding an agreement.[231] However, Muslim jurists excluded the possibility of a Muslim defeat as a reason for the termination of fighting.

[230]al-Shāfi'ī, *supra note* 21, at 4:110; al-Siyar al-Kabīr, *supra note* 67, at 5:1689.

[231]Ibn Hishām, *supra note* 67, at 4:7; al-Ṭabarī, *supra note* 71, at 2:18.

Chapter Two
Jihād and International Relations

During the first century and a half of the Islamic era, Islamic international humanitarian law developed and crystallized; when Muslim armies pounded on the gates of Europe, Africa, and the Far East,[232] to emancipate peoples, defend freedoms, establish human equality and spread justice.[233] Consequently, established regimes, particularly, the Byzantine and the Persian Empires, opposed Islam and plotted against its revolutionary rhetoric.[234] Although Muslim wars were merely exceptional and defensive;[235] and war, in general, is strictly prohibited in Islamic law unless in response to aggression,[236] Majid Khadduri alleges that the normal state between Muslims and non-Muslim communities is one of hostility.[237] Khadduri bases this statement on the works of a number of prominent scholars. By examining

---

[232]Bernard Lewis, *supra note* 18, at 176.

[233]Muḥammad Abū Zahra, *supra note* 182, at 33.

[234]*Ibid.*

[235]"Fight in the cause of *Allāh* those who fight you, but do not transgress limits, for *Allāh* loveth not transgressors." *The Holy Qur'ān*, II: 190.

[236]"There is the law of equality. If then anyone transgresses the prohibition against you, transgress ye likewise against him." *The Holy Qur'ān*, II: 194.

[237]Majid Khadduri, *supra note* 50, at 202.

the works cited by him, however, I found opposing viewpoints.[238]

In discussing the *jihād* theory, Muslim jurists divided the world into three parts: the territory of Islam (*dār al-Islām or dār al-salām or dār al-'adl*); the territory of covenant (*dār al-'ahd or dār al-muwāda'a or dār al-Ṣulḥ*); and the territory of war (*dār al-ḥarb or dār al-jawr*).[239] This division, which is not predicated on a state of hostility between the territory of Islam and other territories, was dictated by events and was not derived from Islamic legislation. Moreover, Marcel A. Boisard holds that "this division is not based upon geographical or juridical criteria but represents a state to be described rather than a situation which could be subjectively judged."[240]

Nevertheless, *dār al-Islām* includes all territories, which are ruled by Islamic law and are subject to the sovereignty of the Islamic State.[241] In other words, a territory can be deemed Islamic if the rules applied are Islamic, and if Muslims and all protected monotheistic minorities reside safely and enjoy liberty to practice their religion individually or collectively.[242] In this respect, al-Shawkānī argues that a territory can be considered *dār al-Islām* even if it is not under Muslim rule as long as a Muslim can reside there in safety and freely fulfil his religious obligations.[243]

Conversely, *dār al-ḥarb*, which stands in opposition to *dār al-Islām*, can be defined as a territory which does not apply Islamic rules, and where a Muslim

---

[238]For example, Hans Kruse advocates that, "In the theory of classical Muslim jurists, the external conduct of the one Islamic state, the *Ummah*, is governed by a special set of rules exposed in *fiqh* works, under the heading '*siyar*'. It is a wellknown fact that these rules demand the peaceful or even friendly relations between the *Ummah* and independent communities of the non-Muslim outer world." See Hans Kruse, "Al-Shaybānī on International Instruments," *Journal of the Pakistan Historical Society* 1 (1953): 90.

[239]al-Kāsānī, *supra note* 21, at 7:130-134; al-Māwardī, *supra note* 21, at 136; al-Mughnī, *supra note* 21, at 10:609; al-Sarakhsī, *supra note* 21, at 10: 19; al-Shāfi'ī, *supra note* 21, at 4:103.

[240]Marcel A. Boisard, *supra note* 15, at 53; Muḥammad Abū Zahra, *supra note* 182, at 32.

[241]*The Encyclopaedia of Islam*, 2nd ed., s.v. "Dār al-Islām," by A. Abel; Al Ghunaimi, *supra note* 83, at 156; Marcel A. Boisard, *supra note* 15, at 6; Rudolph Peters, *supra note* 11, at 11; Sobhi Mahmassani, *supra note* 1, at 250.

[242]Al Ghunaimi, *supra note* 83, at 156-157.

[243]al-Shawkānī, *supra note* 192, at 8:29.

cannot publicly adhere to the ritual practices of his faith.[244] Marcel Boisard maintains that a state which authorizes oppression; violence; tyranny; religious coercion; usury; gambling; and any other form of activity prohibited by Islamic law should be deemed *dār al-ḥarb* even if its leaders claim to be Muslim. On the other hand, Boisard continues, a non-Muslim State which does not threaten the community of believers, respects justice, and guarantees freedom of worship, should not be considered *dār al-ḥarb*.[245] Boisard's definition is complimented by Abū Ḥanīfa who cites three pre-conditions to the designation of any territory as *dār al-ḥarb*: (1) the prevalence of non-Islamic rules; (2) the country in question is directly adjacent to the *dār al-ḥarb*; and (3) Muslims, and those under their protection, no longer enjoy security except by obtaining a given pledge.[246] For his part, al-Kāsānī, has expressly discussed Abū Ḥanīfa's argument which would not define a country as *dār al-Islām* or *dār al-ḥarb* by virtue of its being Muslim or non-Muslim. He discerns that Abū Ḥanīfa's argument is based on the premise of security and fear (*al-amn wal-khawf*).[247] In other words, *dār al-ḥarb* is the country where Muslims lack security, except by a given pledge, and *dār al-Islām* is the country where Muslims and *dhimmīs* enjoy protection and security. Although the majority of jurists classify a country as *dār al-Islām* or *dār al-ḥarb* according to the prevalence or absence of Islamic law, Abū Ḥanīfa's conception may be considered the nearest to the concept of *jihād* defended here, namely, establishing peace and resisting aggression.[248]

While Hanafites hold the opinion that a territory must be either *dār al-Islām* or *dār al-ḥarb*,[249] the Shafi'ites observe *dār al-'Ahd* as a temporary and often

---

[244] *The Encyclopaedia of Islam*, 2nd ed., s.v. "Dār al-Ḥarb," by A. Abel; Rudolph Peters, *supra note* 11, at 12.

[245] Marcel A. Boisard, *supra note* 15, at 8-9.

[246] al-Kāsānī, *supra note* 21, at 7:130.

[247] *Ibid.*

[248] Muḥammad Abū Zahra, *supra note* 182, at 36-37.

[249] *The Encyclopaedia of Islam*, 2nd ed., s.v. "Dār al-'Ahd," by Halil Inalcik; Al Ghunaimi, *supra*

intermediate territory between *dār al-Islām* and *dār al-ḥarb*.[250] However, this tributary land is recognized as an independent nation by the Islamic state on the condition that the latter pays to the former an annual tribute, *al-kharāj*. Moreover, a development occurred within the Hanafite school when Muḥammad Ibn al-Ḥasan al-Shaybānī coined *dār al-Muwāda'a*, as yet another type of territory.[251] It is worthwhile to mention here that *dār al-'ahd* is protected by the Islamic state, as far as the former pays the *kharāj* and respects the provisions of the treaty. According to the Shafi'ite school, *dār al-'ahd* becomes *dār al-ḥarb* if people of the former land breach the agreement, while the Hanafites hold them as rebels, since, in their view, *dār al-'ahd* is not sovereign from the Muslim State.[252]

The foregone historical scenarios were met in the case of Najrān and Nubia. In the former case, the Prophet Muḥammad concluded a treaty with the Christians of Najrān, giving them rights and imposing certain obligations on them.[253] Another case in point is that of Nubia, where 'Abd Allāh Ibn Abī al-Sarḥ concluded a treaty ('ahd) with the Nubians in the reign of 'Uthmān Ibn 'Affān, the third Muslim Caliph, imposing on them an annual tribute of 360 slaves.[254] More recent examples

---

note 83, at 156-157.

[250]al-Māwardī, *supra note* 21, at 128; Rudolph Peters, *supra note* 11, at 11; al-Shāfi'ī, *supra note* 21, at 4:103-104; Yaḥyā Ibn Ādam al-Qurashī, *Kitāb al-Kharāj* (Beirut: Dār al-Ḥadātha, 1990), 398 [hereinafter al-Kharāj].

[251]al-Kāsānī, *supra note* 21, at 7:109; al-Siyar al-Kabīr, *supra note* 67, at 5:1689-1724.

[252]The Encyclopaedia of Islam, *supra note* 249.

[253]Abū 'Ubayd al-Qāsim Ibn Sallām, *Kitāb al-Amwāl* (Beirut: Dār al-Ḥadātha, 1988), 198-199 [hereinafter Ibn Sallām]; Abū Yūsuf, *supra note* 53, at 185-187; al-Balādhurī, *supra note* 71, at 65; Ibn al-Qayyim, *supra note* 21, at 2:40; Majid Khadduri, *super note* 2, at 278; Muḥammad Ḥamī dullāh, *Majmū'at al-Wathā'iq al-Siyāsiyya lil-'Ahd al-Nabawī wal-Khilāfa al-Rāshida* (Beirut: Dār al-Irshād, 1969), 140-142; Muḥammad Ibn Sa'd Ibn Manī' al-Zuhrī, *Kitāb al-Ṭabaqāt al-Kabīr*, 14 vols. (Cairo: Dār al-Taḥrīr, 1388 A.H.), 1:35-36 [hereinfater Ibn Sa'd]; Taqī al-Dīn Aḥmad Ibn 'Alī al-Maqrīzī, *Imtā' al-Asmā'* (Cairo: Maṭba'at Lajnat al-Ta'līf wal-Tarjama wal-Nashr, 1941), 1:502 [hereinafter al-Maqrīzī]. See also Appendix II: The Pact of Najrān "'Ahd Najrān".

[254]Abū al-Qāsim 'Abd al-Raḥmān Ibn 'Abd al-Ḥakam, *Futūḥ Miṣr wa Akhbāruhā* (Cairo: Maktabat Madbūlī, 1991), 188-189 [hereinafter Ibn 'Abd al-Ḥakam]; al-Balādhurī, *supra note* 71, at 236; J. Spencer Trimingham, *Islam in the Sudan* (London: F. Cass, 1949), 61-62; Taqī al-Dīn Aḥmad Ibn 'Alī al-Maqrīzī, *Kitāb al-Khiṭaṭ al-Maqrīziyya*, 4 vols. (Cairo: Maṭba'at al- Nīl, 1325 A.H.),

include the *ahdnames* (peace treaties) granted by the Ottoman sultans to the tributary Christian princes. In his *ahdname*, the Sultan ensures the prince's peace, security and respect of religious beliefs upon the payment of an annual *Kharāj*. If the prince failed to fulfil any of his obligations, the Sultan, according to the Ḥanafī doctrine, could consider him a rebel and designate his land *dār al-ḥarb*.[255]

Furthermore, al-Māwardī classifies *dār al-Islām* into a variety of divisions and subdivisions. According to him, *dār al-Islām* consists of three main divisions: the ḥaram, Ḥijāz and the rest of the Muslim territory.[256] The ḥaram, place of security,[257] includes Mecca and the sanctified territory surrounding it. Other scholars, however, argue that the ḥaram includes *al-ḥaramayn al-sharīfayn*, Mecca and Medina.[258] According to the Shāfi'ī doctrine, this territory is exclusively reserved for Muslims, but Abū Ḥanīfa argues that non-Muslims (*dhimmīs* and the people of *dār al-'ahd*) are permitted to pass through this territory not to reside there.[259] Moreover, the Prophet Muḥammad prohibited bloodshed in the vicinity of al-haram, and declared its residents immune from war, even if they rebel against the *Imām*.[260] The Ḥijāz represents the second division of *dār al-Islām*. According to a Prophetic *ḥadīth*, non-Muslims are permitted to travel through this territory, but not allowed to live there permanently.[261] The remaining part of the Muslim territory is

---

3:290 [hereinafter al-Khiṭaṭ].

[255]The Encyclopaedia of Islam, *supra note* 249; Halil Inalcik, "Ottoman Methods of Conquest," *Studia Islamica* 2 (1953): 107.

[256]al-Māwardī, *supra note* 21, at 136.

[257]*The Holy Qur'ān*, III: 97.

[258]Ibn 'Abd al-Ḥakam, *supra note* 254, at 1; al-Farrā', *supra note* 21, at 181.

[259]al-Farrā', *supra note* 21, at 179; al-Māwardī, *supra note* 21, at 144.

[260]On the contrary, the Saudi security armed forces, assisted by American and French commando units, massacred hundreds of the members of the Saudi political opposition, after they resorted to the Holy Mosque (*al-Masjid al-ḥarām*) in Mecca in 1979. Another time, the Saudi forces killed and injured hundreds of the Iranian pilgrims in a peaceful protest marched in Mecca in 1988.

[261]al-Māwardī, *supra note* 21, at 145; al-Mughnī, *supra note* 21, at 8:613-615.

the largest geographical division. This territory is open to the protected people, (*dhimmīs*) where they may live, and open to the people of *dār al-'ahd* where they may travel with a permit.[262] Nevertheless, al-Māwardī divides this territory into four categories, three of them are called *'Ushūr* (tithe) lands: the land of the people who embraced Islam; the uncultivated land reclaimed by Muslims; and the land taken by force of arms. The fourth category is the land acquired by peace treaties, and falls into two categories: *waqf* land, which becomes the common property of the Muslim community. The original owners remain on their land and become *dhimmīs* paying a *kharāj* while their territory becomes *dār al-Islām*. The second type remains with its original people, and is called *dār al-'ahd*. The original owners of this land are allowed to keep their estates through contract, and through the payment of *kharāj* as a *jizya* (poll tax).[263]

Needless to say, Islamic law is not simply a collection of religious precepts and rules, but a comprehensive legal system styled to preserve the interests of Muslims and to regulate their relations with the rest of the world in times of peace and war. In the light of Qur'anic injunctions,[264] Prophetic tradition,[265] and the doctrine of *jihād*, Muslim jurists unanimously agree on the permissibility of concluding peace treaties with the enemy. They also consent to diplomatic, commercial, and political ties with non-Muslim States,[266] in order to protect the public interest of Muslims,[267] whether they live in *dār al-Islām*, under Islamic

---

[262] Marcel A. Boisard, *supra note* 15, at 7.

[263] *The Encyclopaedia of Islam*, 2nd ed., s.v. "Dār al-Ṣulḥ," by D.B. Macdonald and A. Abel; al-Māwardī, *supra note* 21, at 149.

[264] "But if the enemy incline towards peace, do thou (also) incline towards peace, and trust in *Allāh*." *The Holy Qur'ān*, VIII: 61; "Those who fulfill the covenant of *Allāh* and fail not in their plighted word." *The Holy Qur'ān*, XIII: 20.

[265] "When one has covenant with people, he must not strengthen or loosen it till its term comes to an end or he brings it to an end in agreement with them." Abū Dāwūd, *supra note* 197, at 92.

[266] Aḥmad Ibn 'Alī al-Qalqashandī, *Ṣubḥ al-A'shā fī Ṣinā'at al-Inshā*, 14 vols. (Beirut: Dār al-Kutub al-'Ilmiyya, 1987), 14:5 [hereinafter al-Qalqashandī]; Ibn Sallām, *supra note* 253, at 156; al-Siyar al-Kabīr, *supra note* 67, at 5:1689; al-Shawkānī, *supra note* 192, at 8:30.

[267] al-Dasūqī, *supra note* 228, at 2:205.

dominion, or in other territories.[268] The afore-mentioned relations could be classified under so-called Islamic theory of international relations, in the modern sense of the term, namely: (a) *al-mu'āhadāt* (treaties), which include *al-amān* (safe-conduct); *al-hudna* (armistice); and *al-dhimma* (pact, security); (b) *al-mu'āmala bil-mithl* (reciprocity); (c) *al-taḥkīm* (arbitration); (d) *al-ḥiyād* (neutrality); (e) *tabādul al-wufūd wal-safārāt* (diplomatic exchange); and (f) *al-tijāra al-Khārijiyya* (foreign trade). The implication of this theory will be the object of discussion in the following pages.

1. Treaties (al-Mu'āhadāt)

Many years before Islam, *al-mu'āhadāt* (treaties) were known in Arabia under the terms *muḥālafa, muṣālaḥa* or *muwālāh.*[269] Islamic law imposes the respect of treaties even above the respect of religious solidarity.[270] In other words, if the *Imām* concludes a treaty with the enemy, this treaty is binding upon all Muslims.[271] Moreover, Islamic law prohibited Muslims from assisting their fellow believers if the former were in violation of a treaty of peace concluded with the enemy.[272]

---

[268] In fact, Islam, as a religion, has prevailed behind the borders of the Islamic State, and demanded all Muslims to comply with its rules. See al-Shāfi'ī, *supra note* 21, at 4:165; 7:322.

[269] Arabian tribes concluded various alliances and treaties before Islam to regulate their social, economic and public life. Among those alliances were *Ḥilf al-Muṭayyibīn* and *Ḥilf al-Fuḍūl.* See Abū al-Qāsim 'Abd al-Raḥmān Ibn Aḥmad al-Khath'amī al-Suhaylī, *al-Rawḍ al-Anaf fī Sharḥ al-Sīra al-Nabawiyya li-Ibn Hishām*, 7 vols. (Cairo: al-Maṭba'a al-Jamāliyya, 1914), 1:91 [hereinafter al-Suhaylī]; Ibn Hishām, *supra note* 67, at 1:120-122.

[270] Sobhi Mahmassani, *supra note* 1, at 268.

[271] "O ye who believes! fulfill (all) obligations." *The Holy Qur'ān*, V:1; "Fulfill the covenant of *Allāh* when ye have entered into it, and break not your oaths after ye have confirmed them." *The Holy Qur'ān*, XVI: 91.

[272] "But if they seek your aid on account of religion, it is your duty to help them, except against a people with whom you have a treaty of mutual alliance." *The Holy Qur'ān*, VIII: 72.

This point has been emphasized in the following Prophetic *ḥadīth.* "Fulfill the trust towards the one who trusted you, and do not betray the one who betrayed you." See Muḥammad 'Abd al-Ra'ūf al-Mināwī, *Mukhtaṣar Sharḥ al-Jāmi' al-Ṣaghīr*, 2 vols. (Cairo: Dār Iḥyā al-Kutub al- 'Arabiyya, 1954), 1:21.

As early as the migration (*hijra*) of the Prophet Muḥammad from Mecca to Medina, Muslims knew various types of treaties, which varied according to their nature and aim. Treaties concluded with *dhimmīs* were permanent in nature, while those made with *ḥarbīs* were temporary and did not exceed ten years.[273] Wahba al-Zuhayli, an eminent scholar of Islamic international humanitarian law, argues that the first treaty concluded between Muslims and non-Muslims was *Ṣaḥīfat al-Madīnah*,[274] while other scholars argue that the *Ṣaḥīfa* was the first constitution of the Islamic state.[275] Reading the *Ṣaḥīfa* carefully, one may conclude that it is neither a treaty nor a constitution. It is not a treaty because it was dictated by the Prophet Muḥammad without the interference of other parties. On the other hand, treaties are usually concluded after negotiations and require an offer (*ījāb*) from one party and acceptance (*qabūl*) by the other, attributes which the *Ṣaḥīfa* lacks.[276] However, the *Ṣaḥīfa* could also be considered a constitutional charter as it organized relations between the Muslim and Jewish tribes of Medina. This charter emphasized the unity of the nation and underscored the freedom of religion and other fundamental rights.[277]

The Ḥudaybiya treaty might be considered as the first real *mu'āhada* between Muslims and non-Muslims.[278] In 6 A.H., the Prophet Muḥammad with a number of

---

[273]Ibn Rushd, *supra note* 21, at 388; Ibn Sallām, *supra note* 253, at 170; al-Kāsānī, *supra note* 21, at 7:108; al-Mughnī, *supra note* 21, at 10:518; al-Qalqashandī, *supra note* 266, at 14:9; al-Shāfi'ī *supra note* 21, at 4:109; al-Sarakhsī, *supra note* 21, at 10:88.

[274]Wahba al-Zuḥaylī, *supra note* 182, at 352. See also Appendix III:The Farewell-Pilgrimage Sermon " Khuṭbat Ḥijjat al-Wadā'"; Ismā'īl Ibrāhīm Abū Sharī'a, *Naẓariyyat al-Ḥarb fī al-Sharī'a al-Islāmiyya* (Kuwait: Maktabat al-Falāḥ, 1981), 439; Majid Khadduri, *supra note* 50, at 205; Najīb al-Armanāzī, *al-Shar' al-Dawlī fī al-Islām* (London: Riad El-Rayyes Books, 1990), 187.

[275]Muḥammad 'Amāra, *al-Islām wa Ḥuqūq al-Insān:Ḍarūrāt lā Ḥuqūq*, 'Ālam al-Ma'rifa, no. 89 (Kuwait: al-Majlis al-Waṭanī lil-Thaqāfa wal-Funūn wal-Ādāb, 1985), 152.

[276]'Abd al-Razzāq al-Sanhūrī, *Maṣādir al-Ḥaqq fī al-Fiqh al-Islamī,* 6 vols. (Beirut: al-Majma' al-'Ilmī al-'Arabī al-Islāmī, n. d.), 6:30.

[277]Ibn Hishām, *supra note* 67, at 2:106-107; Muḥammad Ḥamīdullah, *supra note* 253, at 41-47.

[278]al-Maqrīzī, *supra note* 253, at 1:297-298; Muḥammad Ḥamīdullah, *supra note* 253, at 58-59; al-Sarakhsī, *supra note* 21, at 30:169.

his followers, marched to Mecca with the intention of making a pilgrimage. The Meccans blocked the Prophet entry, and denied his right to visit Mecca. The Prophet proffered a token of peace to Quraysh, which the latter accepted. The treaty concluded is known as *Ṣulḥ al-Ḥudaybiya*. It was broken by the Meccans two years later, a matter which motivated Muslims to march to Mecca and conquer it peacefully in 8 A.H.[279] In the year 17 A.H., ʻUmar Ibn al-Khaṭṭāb signed a *dhimma* pact with the Patriarch of Jerusalem. This treaty might be construed as a basic charter for *dhimmī* subjects in the Islamic legal discourse.[280]

Another type of treaty was developed during Muslim civil wars. During the conflict over power with ʻAlī Ibn Abī Ṭālib, the fourth well-guided Caliph, Muʻāwiya Ibn Abī Sufyān signed a treaty with the Byzantine emperor to deter him from attack on the boundaries of the Muslim State. Accordingly, Muʻāwiya paid an annual tribute to the emperor.[281] However, this type of treaty was subject of controversy among Muslim jurists. Muḥammad Ibn al-Ḥasan al-Shaybānī argued against it and accepted it only when it was a matter of effectual necessity, while al-Shāfiʻī advised against its validity. On the other hand, al-Awzāʻī and al-Thawrī approved it under certain conditions.[282]

In addition to the afore-mentioned treaties, another type was concluded during the Abbasid period called *al-mufādāh* (ransoming). Through these treaties, Muslims were able to set free prisoners of war, whether by interchange or by paying a certain amount of money.[283] Later on, Ṣalāḥ al-Dīn al-Ayyūbī concluded several

---

[279]Ibn Kathīr, *supra note* 72, at 4:293; al-Ṭabarī, *supra note* 71 at, 2:21.

[280]Aḥmad Ibn Abī Yaʻqūb Ibn Jaʻfar al-Yaʻqūbī, *Tarīkh al-Yaʻqūbī,* 3 vols. (al-Najaf, Iraq: al-Maktaba al-Murtaḍawiyya, 1964), 2:167 [hereinafter al-Yaʻqūbī];al-Balādhurī, *supra note* 71, at 138; Muḥammad Ḥamīdullah, *supra note* 253, at 379-380; al-Ṭabarī, *supra note* 71, at 304-305. See also Appendix IV: The Treaty of Jerusalem "Muʻāhadat Ahl Īliyā'".

[281]Abū al-Ḥasan ʻAlī Ibn al-Ḥusayn al-Masʻūdī, *Kitāb al-Tanbīh wal-Ishrāf,* 8 vols. (Leiden, The Netherlands: E.J. Brill, 1967), 2:91 [hereinafter al-Tanbīh wal-Ishrāf]; al-Balādhurī, *supra note* 71, at 216; al- Ṭabarī, *supra note* 71, at 3:169.

[282]Ikhtilāf al-Fuqahā', *supra note* 55, at 17-20; al-Shāfiʻī, *supra note* 21, at 4:110; al-Siyar al-Kabīr, *supra note* 67, at 5:1692.

[283]Ibn Rushd, *supra note* 21, at 1:309; al-Kāsānī, *supra note* 21, at 7:120; Majid Khadduri, *supra*

treaties with the crusaders. Based on these treaties, he released a great number of poor crusaders for no charge, and imposed *fidya* on the wealthy; twenty *dīnars* for a man, ten *dīnars* for a woman, and one *dīnar* for a child.[284] However, the Islamic states of North Africa treated the European Christians on the same premise.[285] Below are three types of treaties, which mirror this approach.

First, the *amān* (safe-conduct), in Islamic humanitarian law, is a pledge of security, granted to an enemy person for a limited period, under which his life, freedom, and property are protected by the sanctions of law.[286] This pledge is binding upon all Muslims, and substantiated by the Qur'anic verse, "If one amongst the Pagans ask thee for asylum, grant it to him, so that he may hear the Word of *Allāh*; and then escort him to where he can be secure."[287] However, Muslim jurists identified two types of *amān*,[288] the first of which is collective, granted only by the *Imām* or his representative to a *ḥarbī* town or territory; and individual, bestowed upon an enemy person or persons, by any Muslim male or female, of full age, free,

---

note 50, at 217; al-Siyar al-Kabīr, *supra note* 67, at 4:1650.

[284]'Abd al-Raḥmān Ibn Ismā'īl Abū Shāma, *Kitāb al-Rawḍatayn fī Akhbār al-Dawlatayn*, 2 vols. (Cairo: Maṭba'at Lajnat al-Ta'līf wal-Tarjama wal-Nashr, 1956), 2:79-81 [hereinafter Abū Shāma]; Bahā' al-Dīn Yūsuf Ibn Shaddād, *al-Nawādir al-Sulṭāniyya wal-Maḥāsin al-Yūsufiyya* (Cairo: al-Dār al-Miṣriyya lil-Ta'līf wal-Tarjama, 1962), 64 [hereinafter Ibn Shaddād]; Ibn al-Athīr, *supra note* 87, at 11:538; Jamāl al-Dīn Muḥammad Ibn Wāṣil, *Mufarrij al-Kurūb fī Akhbār Banī Ayyūb*, 5 vols. (Cairo: Maṭba'at Jāmi'at Fu'ād al-Awwal, 1953-1972), 2:195-196 [hereinafter Ibn Wāṣil]; Jamāl al-Dīn Yūsuf Ibn Taghrībirdī, *al-Nujūm al-Zāhira fī Mulūk Miṣr wal-Qāhira*, 12 vols. (Cairo: Maṭba'at Dār al-Kitāb, 1930), 6:35 [hereinafter Ibn Taghrībirdī]; Taqī al-Dīn Aḥmad Ibn 'Ali al-Maqrīzī, *al-Sulūk li-Ma'rifat Duwal al-Mulūk*, 4 vols. (Cairo: Maṭba'at Lajnat al-Ta'līf wal-Tarjama wal-Nashr, 1957), 1:94 [hereinafter al-Sulūk].

[285]Louis de Mas-Latrie, *Relations et commerce de l'Afrique septentrionale ou Magreb avec les nations Chrétiennes ou moyen-âge* (Paris: Firmin-Didot, 1886), 79-94.

[286]*The Encyclopaedia of Islam*, 2nd ed., s.v. "Amān," by Joseph Schacht; Rudolph Peters, *supra note* 11, at 29; al-Siyar al-Kabīr, *supra note* 67, at 1:283.

[287]*The Holy Qur'ān*, IX:6.

[288]Aḥmad Ibn Idrīs Ibn 'Abd al-Raḥmān al-Qarāfī, *al-Furūq*, 4 vols. (Cairo: Maṭba'at Muṣṭafā al-Bābī al-Ḥalabī, 1344 A.H.), 3:24 [hereinafter al-Qarāfī]; al-Kāsānī, *supra note* 21, at 7:106; Muḥammad al-Sharbīnī,al-Khaṭīb, *Mughnī al- Muḥāj ilā Sharḥ al-Minhāj*, 4 vols. Cairo: Maṭba'at Muṣṭafā al-Bābī al-Ḥalabī, 1933), 4:236 [hereinafter al-Khatīb].

and sensible.[289] The Prophet Muḥammad approved the *amān* granted by Muslim women, when he expressly authorized Umm Hāni' Bint Abī Ṭālib to accord *amān* in the year of the conquest to a man from the polytheists, by saying, "We have given security to those to whom you have given it."[290] Another case in point is the Prophet's validation of the *amān* granted by his daughter, Zaynab, to Abū al-'Āṣ, her husband.[291]

Moreover, Muslim jurists permitted the *amān* given by a slave, except Abū Ḥanīfa and Abū Yūsuf, who argued against its sanction, unless the slave is permitted to fight by his master.[292] In this connection, jurists also rejected the *amān* given by a minor or insane.[293] The *amān* accorded by a discerning minor is approved by Mālik Ibn Anas, Aḥmad Ibn Ḥanbal, and Muḥammad Ibn al-Ḥasan,[294] but repudiated by Abū Ḥanīfa, Abū Yūsuf and al-Shāfi'ī.[295] Saḥnūn, for his part,

---

[289]Ikhtilāf al-Fuqahā', *supra note* 55, at 30; al-Kāsānī, *supra note* 21, at 7:106; al-Khatīb, *supra note* 288, at 4: 237; al-Khirshī, *supra note* 228, at 3:124; al-Marghīnānī, *supra note* 21 at 2:139; al-Mughnī, *supra note* 21, at 8:396; al-Shāfi'ī, *supra note* 21, at 4: 196; al-Siyar al-Kabīr, *supra note* 67, at 1:252-257; al-Shawkānī, *supra note* 192, at 8:30-31.

[290]Abū Dāwūd, *supra note* 197, at 2:93.

[291]al-Kāsānī, *supra note* 21, at 7:106.

[292]al-Awzā'ī, *supra note* 82, at 319; al-Kāsānī, *supra note* 21, at 7:106; al-Marghīnānī, *supra note* 21, at 2:139; al-Siyar al-Kabīr, *supra note* 67, at 1:255; Zayn al-Dīn Ibn Ibrāhīm Ibn Nujaym, *al-Baḥr al-Rā'q Sharḥ Kanz al-Daqā'iq*, 8 vols. (Cairo: Maṭba'at Muṣṭafā al-Bābī al-Ḥalabī, 1334 A.H.), 5:81 [hereinafter Ibn Nujaym].

[293]Abū Bakr Muḥammad Ibn Aḥmad al-Qaffāl al-Shāshī, *Ḥilyat al-'Ulamā' fī Ma'rifat Madhāhib al-Fuqahā'*, 8 vols. (Amman: Maktabat al-Risāla al-Ḥadītha, 1988), 3:449 [hereinafter al-Shāshī]; Muḥammad Ibn 'Abd al-Wāhid Ibn al-Humām, *Fatḥ al-Qadīr Sharḥ al-Hidāya lil-Marghīnānī*, 10 vols. (Beirut: Dār al-Fikr, 1990), 4:302 [hereinafter Ibn al-Humām]; Mālik Ibn Anas, al-Mudawwana al-Kubrā, 5 vols. (Cairo: Maṭba'at al-Sa'āda, 1323 A.H.), 3:41 [hereinafter al-Mudawwana]; al-Mughnī, *supra note* 21, at 8:398; al-Shāfi'ī, *supra note* 21, at 4:196; Ṣiddīq Ibn Ḥasan al-Qannujī, *al-Rawḍa al-Nadiyya Sharḥ al-Durar al-Bahiyya lil-Shawkānī*, 6 vols. (Cairo: al-Maṭba'a al-Munīriyya, 1941), 2:253 [hereinafter al-Rawḍa al-Nadiyya].

[294]al-Mudawwana, *supra note* 293, at 3:41; al-Mughnī, *supra note* 21, at 8:397; Muḥammad Ibn Aḥmad al-Kalbī, *al-Qawānīn al-Fiqhiyya* (Tunus: Maṭba'at al-Nahḍa, 1344 A.H.), 157 [hereinafter al- Qawānīn]; al-Siyar al-Kabīr, *supra note* 67, at 1:257.

[295]Abū Ḥāmid al-Ghazālī, *al-Wajīz fī Fiqh Madhhab al-Imām al-Shāfi'ī*, 2 vols. (Cairo: Maṭba'at al-Ādāb wal-Mu'ayyad, 1899), 2:194 [hereinafter al-Ghazālī]; Aḥmad Ibn Yaḥyā Ibn al-Murtaḍā, *al-Baḥr al-Zakhkhār al-Jāmi' li-Madhāhib 'Ulamā' al-Amṣār*, 5 vols. (Beirut: Mu'assasat al-Risāla, 1975), 5:452 [hereinafter al-Baḥr al-Zakhkhār]; al-Khatīb, *supra note* 288, at 4:237; al-

upheld this *amān*, so long as it is explicitly approved by the *Imām.*[296] On the other hand, Muslim jurists denied the *amān* granted by *dhimmīs*,[297] except al-Awzā 'ī, who endorsed it under two conditions: if *dhimmīs* were fighting to defend *dār al-Islām*, and if the *amān* were confirmed by the *Imām.*[298]

The *amān* is granted for a limited time. On the strength of the Qur'anic verse, "Go ye, then, for four months, backwards and forwards throughout the land, but know that you cannot frustrate *Allāh*, and *Allāh* will cover with shame the polytheists,"[299] Shafi'ites and Malikites argue that the period of *amān* should not exceed four months.[300] The Hanafites, however, state that the period should not exceed one lunar year, and that if the *Musta'min* (the person who has received the *amān*), prolongs his stay beyond this period, he becomes subject to the *jizya.*[301] On the other hand, the Hanbalites hold that no *jizya* is to be imposed on the *Musta'min* regardless of the *amān's* length of time[302] However, the *amān* may be terminated if

---

Siyar al-Kabīr, *supra note* 67, at 1:257.

[296]Abū al-Walīd Sulaymān Ibn Khalaf al-Bājī, *al-Muntagā Sharḥ Muwatta' Imām Dār al-Hijra*, 7 vols. (Cairo: Maṭba'at al-Sa'āda, 1332 A.H.), 3:173 [hereinafter al-Muntaqā]; 'Alī al-Ṣa'īdī al-'Adawī, *Ḥāshiya 'alā Kifāyat al-Ṭālib al-Rabbānī li-Risālat Ibn Abī Zayd al-Qayrawānī fī Madhhab Mālik*, 2 vols. (Cairo: al-Maṭba'a al-Azhariyya al-Miṣriyya, 1309 A.H.), 2:7 [hereinafter al-'Adawī]; Muḥammad Ibn 'Abd Allāh al-Qafṣī, *Lubāb al-Lubāb* (Tunus: Al-Maṭba'a al-Tūnusiyya, 1346 A.H.), 72 [hereinafter al-Lubāb].

[297]al-Mudawwana, *supra note* 293, at 3:42; Muḥammad Ibn Shihāb Ibn al-Bazzāz, "al-Fatāwī al-Bazzāziyya aw al-Jāmi' al-Wajīz," in *al-Fatāwī al-'Ālimkīriyya*, 6 vols. (Cairo: al-Maṭba'a al-Amī riyya bi-Būlāq, 1310 A.H.), 6:608 [hereinafter Ibn al-Bazzāz]; al-Sarakhsī, *supra note* 21, at 10:70; al-Shāfi'ī, *supra note* 21, at 4:196-197.

[298]Badr al-Dīn Mahmūd Ibn Aḥmad al-'Aynī, *'Umdat al-Qārī Sharḥ Ṣaḥīḥ al-Bukhārī*, 25 vols. (Cairo: al-Maṭba'a al-Munīriyya, 1348 A.H.); 15:93 [hereinafter al-'Aynī]; Fatḥ al-Bārī, *supra note* 66, at 7:319; Ikhtilāf al-Fuqahā', *supra note* 55, at 25; al-Mughnī, *supra note* 21, at 10:432; al-Shāfi'ī, *supra note* 21, at 7:319; al-Shawkānī, *supra note* 192, at 8:25.

[299]*The Holy Qur'ān*, IX: 2.

[300]Aḥmad Ibn Ḥijr al-Haytamī, *Tuḥfat al-Muḥtāj ilā Sharḥ al-Minhāj*, 8 vols. (Cairo: Maṭba'at Muṣṭafā al-Bābī al-Ḥalabī,1933), 8:61 [hereinafter Tuḥfat al-Muḥtāj]; al-Qawānīn, *supra note* 294, at 154; al-Shāfi'ī, *supra note* 21, at 4:111.

[301]Abū al-Muẓaffar Muhyī al-Dīn Ūrānk 'Ālimkīr, *al-Fatāwī al-Hindiyya wa Tu'raf bil-Fatāwī al-'Ālimkīriyya*, 6 vols. (Cairo: al-Maṭba'a al-Amīriyya bi-Būlāq, 1310 A.H.), 2:234 [hereinafter al-Fatāwī al-Hindiyya].

[302]al-Mughnī, *supra note* 21, at 10:436.

the *Musta'min* violates it, or it expires, or the *Musta'min* returns to his territory.

The second type of treaty is the *hudna* (armistice). The term derives linguistically from the past verb *hādana* (to make peace)[303] and is also known in Islamic international law as *muʿāhada*, *muhādana*, *muwāda'a*, *musālama*, and *ṣulḥ*. Technically, *muhādana* denotes the process of entering into a peace agreement (*hudna*) with the enemy.[304] Concluding a *hudna* with the enemy is permitted on the basis of the divine injunction, "Fulfil the covenant of *Allāh* when you have entered into it, and break not your oaths after you have confirmed them."[305] As mentioned, the Prophet Muḥammad concluded the Ḥudaybiya treaty with the unbelievers of Mecca in 6 A.H., setting a precedent for subsequent treaties by his successors. Predicated on the most authoritative sources, *hudna* was established in Islamic international law, and validated by practice.

The Shafi'ites, Hanbalites, and Malikites concur that *hudna*-making power rests in the hands of the *Imām*, and that any *hudna* concluded by individuals or even by Muslim commanders is considered null and void. Malikites, on the other hand, deem that the *Imām* has the right to repudiate or accept the treaty based on its conformity with the interests of the Muslim community.[306] In general, Muslim jurists stipulate the fulfilment of an immediate interest when the *Imām* concludes a *hudna*, but the Hanafites argue that the interest should be one, which persists as long as the treaty is valid. In the absence of interest, the *Imām* has the right to terminate a *hudna* by denunciation (*nabdh*).[307] Pursuant to the Qur'anic verse, "so lose not heart, nor fall into despair for you must gain mastery if you are true in faith,"[308] the Hanafites pronounce that an *Imām* can only conclude a *hudna* with the enemy when

---

[303]Muḥammad Ibn Manẓūr, *supra note* 49, at 3:786.

[304]*The Encyclopaedia of Islam*, 2nd ed., s.v. "Hudna" by Majid Khadduri.

[305]*The Holy Qur'ān*, XVI: 91.

[306]al-'Aynī, *supra note* 298, at 15:97; Fatḥ al-Bārī, *supra note* 66, at 6: 196; Ibn Rushd, *supra note* 21, at 1:309; al-Khatīb, *supra note* 288, at 4:260; al-Mughnī, *supra note* 21, at 8:459.

[307]al-Dasūqī, *supra note* 228, at 2:205.

[308]*The Holy Qur'ān*, III: 139.

the Muslim State has declined in force or power.[309] This opinion is based on the Qur'anic verse, "But if the enemy inclines towards peace, do thou (also) incline towards peace, and trust in *Allāh*."[310] For his part, however, Ibn Ḥazm, denied the validity of *hudna*,[311] arguing that the Prophet's example of *Ṣulḥ al-Ḥudaybiya* was abrogated by divine legislation.[312]

In general, Muslim jurists hold that *hudna* must be concluded for a certain period of time; not exceeding four months except in cases of absolute necessity.[313] Once the *hudna* is accepted by the *Imām*, its observation becomes an obligation upon all Muslims.[314] In this case, it is the *Imām's* responsibility to protect the *mu'āhidūn* (the enemy individuals) as long as they travel in *dār al-Islām*.[315] In this connection, al-Qalqashandī adds four stipulations to be considered before the conclusion of a *hudna*: it should be concluded by the *Imām* or his representative; it should serve the interests of the Muslim community; it must not include invalid provisions, such as returning the women of the enemy who have converted to Islam; and finally, the treaty must be concluded for a definite period of time.[316] However, the *hudna* will be terminated: if the treaty comes to its end; if the enemy terminates it by an explicit declaration; if the enemy takes up arms or propagates military information; and if the enemy kills a Muslim.[317]

---

[309]al-Kāsānī, *supra note* 21, at 7:108; al-Sarakhsī, *supra note* 21, at 10:86; al-Siyar al-Kabīr, *supra note* 67, at 5:1689.

[310]*The Holy Qur'ān*, VIII: 61.

[311]Ibn Ḥazm, *supra note* 21, at 7:307.

[312]"Renunciation by *Allāh* and his Apostle of the Pagans with whom you have made treaties." *The Holy Qur'ān*, IX:1.

[313]al-Mughnī, *supra note* 8, at 10:518.

[314]"So fulfill your treaties with them to the end of their term." *The Holy Qur'ān*: IX: 4. On the other hand, the Prophet Muhammad said: "And the Muslims abide by their conditions." See Abū Dāwūd, *supra note* 197, at 2:328; al-Bukhārī, *supra note* 66, at 3:52.

[315]"As long as these (the Pagans) stand true to you, stand ye true to them." *The Holy Qur'ān*, IX:7.

[316]al-Qalqashandī, *supra note* 266, at 14: 8-9.

[317]al-Nawawī, *supra note* 21, at 470.

Third, the Qur'anic basis for the status of *dhimma* is found in the verse which refers to the *jihād* against those who have failed to recognize the new faith of Islam.[318] According to this treaty, usually concluded by the *Imām* or his representative,[319] *dhimmīs* (Christians, Jews, Sabians, Samaritans and Magians) may acquire the rights to permanent residence in *dār al-Islām*, as well as the protection of Islamic law, in view of the payment of the *jizya* (poll tax), and the performance of certain duties.[320] Historically, the *jizya* was known as early as in the pre-Christian period of the Roman Empire. The Jewish Bible points to the *jizya* paid by Hoshe'a, the King of Judah, to Shalmane'ser, the King of Assyria.[321] Furthermore, Jews and Zoroastrians had also paid a fixed due (one *dīnār* per annum by every person) to the imperial treasury of the Roman Empire.[322]

Under Islamic law, *jizya* has different connotations. According to the Qur'anic text, "Until they pay the *jizya* readily and submissively,"[323] *dhimmīs* have

---

[318]"Fight those who believe not in *Allāh* nor in the Last Day, and do not forbid what *Allāh* and His Apostle have forbidden, and do not acknowledge the religion of truth, (even if they are) of the People of the Book, until they pay the *jizya* readily and submissively." *The Holy Qur'ān*, IX: 29.

This issue has also been illustrated in the following *ḥadīth:* "Fight in the name of *Allāh* and in His path. Combat (only) those who disbelieve in *Allāh*. Do not cheat or commit treachery, nor should you mutilate anyone or kill children. Whenever you meet the Polytheists who are your enemy, summon them to one of three things, and accept whichever of them they are willing to agree to, and refrain from them. Invite them to Islam, and if they agree, accept it from them, and refrain from them. Then summon them to leave their territory to the territory of the Emigrants (*dār al-Muhājirīn*), and tell them if they do so, they will have the same rights and responsibilities as the Emigrants; but if they refuse and choose their own abode, tell them that they will be like the desert Arabs who are Muslims, subject to *Allāh's* jurisdiction which applies to the believers, but will have no spoil or booty unless they strive with the Muslims. If they refuse (Islam), demand *jizya* from them, and if they agree, accept it from them, and let them alone; but if they refuse, seek *Allāh's* help and combat them." Abū Dāwūd, *supra note* 197, at 2:43.

[319]A clear wording of the *dhimma* treaty is mentioned in al-Shāfi'ī's legal work "*Kitāb al-Umm*," vol. 4, p. 118.

[320]*The Encyclopaedia of Islam*, 2nd ed., s.v. "Dhimma," by C. Cahen; al-Kāsānī, *supra note* 21, at 7:110; al-Mughnī, *supra note* 21, at 10:584; Sobhi Mahmassani, *supra note* 1, at 257.

[321]*The Holy Scriptures*, 2 Kings XVII: 1-5.

[322]Abū al-Qāsim 'Abd Allāh Ibn Khurradādhbih, *al-Masālik wal-Mamālik*, ed. Michel Jan de Goeje (Leiden, The Netherlands: E.J. Brill, 1889), 111.

[323]*The Holy Qur'ān*, IX: 29.

to pay an annual tribute in lieu of military service and protection. Hence, *jizya* is only due from every male adult, sane, free and able. On the other hand, women, minors, monks, the blind, the insane, slaves, crippled and other disabled persons are exempt.[324] Two precedents were advanced for this criteria by 'Umar Ibn al-Khaṭṭāb. When ʿUmar saw an old Jew begging to collect money for the payment of the *jizya*, he exempted him from the tribute and ordered him a pension from the public funds (*bayt al-māl*).[325] It is also reported that ʿUmar had directed his general Abū 'Ubayda neither to oppress the *dhimmīs* nor to harm them. When the Muslim army failed to protect the people of Ḥimṣ in Syria, ᶜUmar ordered Abū 'Ubayda to refund any *jizya* paid by the *dhimmīs* to the Muslim leader. Furthermore, depending on variant sources, Laurent mentions that Mu'āwiya Ibn Abī Sufyān instructed his commanders to treat the Armenians kindly.[326]

Muslim jurists differed as to the amount of the *jizya*; 'Umar Ibn al-Khaṭṭāb asked 'Uthmān Ibn Ḥanīf, the regent of Kūfa, to impose *jizya* on *dhimmīs* as follows: forty-eight dirhams from the rich, twenty-four from the middle class, and twelve from low-income persons.[327] While the Hanafites followed 'Umar's example, Mālik, for his part, classified *jizya* into three categories: one *dīnār* from the poor; two *dīnārs* from the middle class and four *dīnārs* from the wealthy. al-Shāfi'ī held the same view, leaving to the *Imām* the authority to scale up or down the *jizya* to a minimum of one *dīnār* per person.[328] It is worth mentioning here that

---

[324]Abū Isḥāq Ibrāhīm Ibn 'Alī al-Shīrāzī, *al-Muhadhdhab*, 2 vols. (Cairo: Maṭba'at Muṣṭafā al-Bābī al-Ḥalabī, 1343 A.H.), 2:269 [hereinafter al-Shīrāzī] ; Kāsānī, *supra note* 21, at 7:111; al-Marghīnānī, *supra note* 21, at 2:166; Shams al-Dīn Ibn Qayyim al-Jawjiyya, *Aḥkām Ahl al-Dhimma*, 2 vols. (Damascus: Maṭba'at Jāmi'at Dimashq, 1961), 1:47-51 [hereinafter Aḥkām Ahl al-Dhimma].

[325]Abū Yūsuf, *supra note* 53, at 255; Aḥkām Ahl al-Dhimma, *supra note* 324, at 1:38; Ibn Sallām, *supra note* 253, at 55.

[326]Abū Yūsuf, *supra note* 53, at 271; al-Balādhurī, *supra note* 71, at 187; Joseph Laurent, *supra note* 118, at 53.

[327]Ibn Sallām, *supra note* 253, at 68-69.

[328]Abū Yūsuf, *supra note* 53, at 253; Aḥkām Ahl al-Dhimma, *supra note* 324, at 1:28; Ibn al-Humām, *supra note* 293, at 4:368; al-Kāsānī, *supra note* 21, at 7:112; al-Khirshī, *supra note* 228, at 2:443; al-Māwardī, *supra note* 21, at 126; al-Shīrāzī, *supra note* 324, at 2:267.

except for the Shafi'ites, Muslim jurists agreed that the failure to pay the *jizya* for legitimate reasons does not constitute a breach of the *dhimma* treaty,[329] for the Prophet Muḥammad said: "I will be the opponent of whoever oppresses a *dhimmī* or over burdens him beyond his ability."[330]

Besides paying the *jizya*, there are certain duties to be performed by *dhimmīs*. What the Christians of Syria accepted as part of their request for *amān*, submitted to 'Abd al-Raḥmān Ibn Ghunm and 'Umar Ibn al-Khaṭṭāb, became the basis for concluding subsequent treaties with the *dhimmīs*.[331] The Christians of Syria took upon themselves not to build any new churches, or repair those falling into ruin; to hospitalize Muslim travellers for up to three days; not to shelter spies or harm the Muslims in any way; not to teach the *Qur'ān* to their children; not to celebrate their religious services publicly; not to prevent any of their people from freely embracing Islam; to respect Muslims and not imitate them in matters of dress or hairstyle; not to use riding-beasts with saddles, or to bear any arms; not to sell alcoholic drinks; to shave the front of the head and to wear *al-zunnār* (girdle); not to parade the emblem of the cross publicly in Muslim markets, or to ring the *nāqūs* (bell) or to chant loudly.[332]

On the other hand, al-Māwardī has classified these duties into two main categories. The first is the deserved (*mustaḥaq*) obligations, which include showing respect for the *Holy Qur'ān*, the Prophet, and the religion of Islam; not marrying or

---

[329]Abū Yūsuf, *supra note* 53, at 161; Aḥkām Ahl al-Dhimma, *supra note* 324, at 1:35; al-Kāsānī, *supra note* 21, at 7:113; al-Marghīnānī, *supra note* 21, at 2:161; al-Shīrāzī, *supra note* 324, at 2:273.

[330]Abū Dāwūd, *supra note* 197, at 1:72; Abū Yūsuf, *supra note* 53, at 254. In this connection, Ann Elizabeth Mayer concludes that "it is fair to say that the Muslim World, when judged by the standards of the day, generally showed far greater tolerance and humanity in its treatment of religious minorities than did the Christian West. In particular, the treatment of the Jewish minority in Muslim societies stands out as fair and enlightened when compared to the dismal record of Christian European persecution of Jews over the centuries." See Ann Elizabeth Mayer, *Islam and Human Rights: Tradition and Politics*, 2nd ed. (Boulder, Colorado: Westview press, Inc., 1995); 148.

[331]Aḥkām Ahl al-Dhimma, *supra note* 324, at 2:891.

[332]Abū Yūsuf, *supra note* 53, at 256-257; C.E. Bosworth, "The Concept of *Dhimma* in Early Islam," in *Christians and Jews in the Ottoman Empire: The Functions of a Plural Society*, 2 vols., eds. Benjamin Braude and Bernard Lewis (New York: Holmes & Merier Publishers, Inc., 1982), 1:46; al-Kāsānī, *supra note* 21, at 7:113-114; al-Mughnī, *supra note* 21, 10:606-607.

committing adultery with a Muslim woman; not persuading Muslims to abandon their faith;[333] and not supporting the enemy (*ahl al-ḥarb*). The commendable (*mustaḥab*) obligations are: wearing *al-zunnār*; not building houses higher than those of Muslims; not ringing their bells; not drinking wine in public or bringing crosses or pigs into view; burying the dead privately; and not riding horses, but mules or donkeys.[334]

By paying the *jizya*, an essential duty, and observing the above obligations, which are in most cases not imposed by scripture, *dhimmīs* are entitled to the same rights as Muslims: right to life and prohibition of torture and inhuman treatment;[335] respect of their dignity and their family rights;[336] respect of religious beliefs, customs and traditions;[337] and right to individual ownership and respect for private property rights. These rights are protected by Islamic law and the *dhimma* treaty, which is binding on all Muslims (*pacta sunt servanda).* Moreover, breaching the dhimma treaty, for a Muslim, is an offence and a renouncement of an obligation towards *Allāh,* Who considers Himself a third party in any treaty concluded by Muslims.[338] The *Holy Qur'ān* explicitly discusses the principle of equality between the citizens of *dār al-Islām*, notwithstanding their different faiths: "Those who believe (in the *Qur'ān*), those who follow the Jewish (scriptures), and the Sabians and the Christians, and any who believe in *Allāh* and the Last Day, and work

---

[333]In 383 A.D. the Council of Byzantine bishops had forbidden apostasy from Christianity, and death penalty was prescribed to any Jew who persuaded Christians to abandon their faith. See C.E. Bosworth, *supra note* 332, at 38; *Encyclopaedia Judaica,* 2nd ed., s.v. "Byzantine Empire."

[334]al-Māwardī, *supra note* 21, at 126-127.

[335]The Caliph 'Alī Ibn Abī Tālib declared that the *dhimmīs'* property and blood are as sacred as that of the Muslims. See al-Kāsānī, *supra note* 21, at 7:111.

[336]'Umar Ibn al-Khaṭṭāb exhorted an Egyptian Copt to whip the son of 'Amr Ibn al-'Āṣ, who was then the governor of Egypt, in retaliation for an offence of this type.

[337]In 638 A.D., 'Umar Ibn al-Khaṭṭāb signed a *dhimma* treaty with the people of Jerusalem, in which he guaranteed their lives, property, churches, and crosses. See Appendix IV: The Treaty of Jerusalem "Mu'āhadat Ahl Īliyā'".

[338]*The Holy Qur'ān,* V: 1; VI: 152; XVI: 91; XVII: 34.

righteousness; on them shall be no fear, nor shall they grieve."[339]

In spite of being oppressed during the reigns of al-Mutawakkil and al-Ḥākim,[340] the *dhimmīs* were appointed to various governmental posts at certain periods. In the Umayyad, Abbasid, Fatimid and Ottoman caliphates, Christians and Jews occupied the posts of secretaries, prison warders, and *wazīrs* (ministers).[341] However, it must be emphasized, as has been indicated earlier, that the *dhimma* treaty is binding on all Muslims, and cannot be abjured by the *Imām* in any case. In contrast, the *dhimmīs* may terminate the treaty, according to al-Kāsānī, by embracing Islam, joining *dār al-ḥarb*, or taking up arms and revolting against Muslims.[342]

2. Reciprocity (al-Mu'āmala bil-Mithl)

The law concerning this issue is provided in the *Qur'ān* as follows: "if then any one transgresses the prohibition against you, transgress ye likewise against him, and fear *Allāh*, and know that *Allāh* is with those who restrain themselves."[343] "And if you punish them, punish them no worse than they punish you, but if you show patience, that is indeed the best (course) for those who are patient."[344] Accordingly, Muslim soldiers are ordered to deal on a reciprocal basis with their enemy in the battlefield. In other words, Muslim jihadists are bound in their actions by the conduct of the enemy; if the enemy enslaves Muslim captives or use a certain weapon, Muslim soldiers should do the same.[345]

---

[339]*The Holy Qur'ān*, V: 72.

[340]I. Lichter Stadter, "The Distinctive Dress of Non-Muslims in Islamic Countries," *Historia Judaica* 5 (1943): 37; *The Encyclopaedia of Islam*, 2nd ed., s.v. "Ghiyār," by M. Perlman.

[341]Aḥkām Ahl al-Dhimma, *supra note* 324, 1:210-225; al-Māwardī, *supra note* 21, at 24.

[342]al-Kāsānī, *supra note* 21, at 7:112-113.

[343]*The Holy Qur'ān*, II: 194.

[344]*Ibid.*, XVI: 126.

[345]Muḥammad Abū Zahra, *supra note* 182, at 55.

A careful examination of the above verses shows, however, that Muslim troops are commanded to exercise self-restraint as much as possible, and fear *Allāh* by showing adherence to virtue and ethical considerations. Consequently, if the enemy declares killing Muslim captives lawful, or mutilates the bodies of the dead Muslims, Muslims are not allowed to imitate the enemy or indulge in similar brutality. In this connection, two cases are in point. The first one is that Ṣalāh al-Dī n al-Ayyūbī released a large number of enemy captives when he could not find enough food for them. In contrast, the Crusader leader, Richard the Lion Heart, executed three thousand Muslim captives who had surrendered to him after having obtained his pledge to spare their lives.[346] The second case was an act of Byzantine treachery toward Muslims. In the Umayyad era, the Byzantines concluded peace treaties with the first Umayyad ruler, Mu'āwiya Ibn Abī Sufyān, who accordingly held a number of Byzantine hostages in Baalbek. When the Byzantine breached their treaties with Mu'āwiya, the latter spared the hostages' blood and released them all, saying: "loyalty against treachery is better than treachery against treachery."[347]

Nevertheless, reciprocity has been substantiated in the instruments of both customary and modern international humanitarian law. Article 62 of the Instructions for the Government of the Armies of the United States in the Field, of 1863, proclaims that troops giving no quarter were entitled to receive none.[348] Furthermore, the Convention on Treatment of Prisoners of War, of 1929, the 1949 Geneva Conventions, and the 1977 Geneva Protocol I Additional to the Geneva Conventions prohibit reprisals against prisoners of war.[349] Despite the limitation of

[346]Gustave Le Bon, *supra note* 15, at 340-341.

[347]Ibn Sallām, *supra note* 253, at 174-175.

[348]The manual Instructions for the Government of the Armies of the United States in the Field was drafted by Professor Francis Lieber and issued to the Union Army, after minor revisions, on April 24, 1863. See Gerhard von Glahn, *The Occupation of Enemy Territory: A Commentary on the Law and Practice of Belligerent Occupation* (Minneapolis: University of Minnesota Press, 1957), 8-16.

[349]D.W. Greig, "Reciprocity, Proportionality, and the Law of Treaties," *Virginia Journal of International Law* 34 (Winter 1994): 333; *Geneva Convention III Relative to the Treatment of Prisoners of War of August 12, 1949*, 75 U.N.T.S. (1950) 135-285 [hereinafter Geneva III]; René Provost, "Reciprocity in Human Rights and Humanitarian Law," *The British Year Book of International Law* 65 (1994): 405.

reciprocity by the minimum standards given in these conventions, parties to the conflict should take the necessary measures to ensure the application of equal treatment for all prisoners of war. However, a comparison between concepts of reciprocity under Islamic and international humanitarian law reveals that the reciprocal basis, according to Islamic humanitarian law, must not exceed the bounds of human decency. On the contrary, it is limited and can be turned into reprisals under customary international law.[350]

3. Arbitration (al-Taḥkīm)

Arbitration is as old as disputes and nations themselves. Ralston argues that the Greek city-states had developed institutions of arbitration by which they settled disagreements and concluded peaceful treaties. To resolve their disputes, the Greek litigant parties used to submit their disputes in a comprehensive procedural detail for arbitration.[351] However, in pre-Islamic Arabia, arbitration was resorted to as a legal institution to settle inter-tribal disputes. The *Naqīb* (tribal chief) of another tribe usually led this judicial machinery.[352] It was reported that Haram Ibn Sinān and al-Ḥirth Ibn 'Awf had settled the fierce war of *Dāḥis* and *al-Ghabrā'* between the *'Abs* and *Fazāra* tribes.[353] A short time before the emergence of Islam, the Prophet Muḥammad was elected, by the tribal chiefs of Mecca as an arbitrator (*ḥakam*) to settle disputes which arose between them concerning the lifting of the Black Stone of the *Ka'ba*. At a later time, the Prophet acted as an arbitrator to settle a historical dispute between the *Aws* and the *Khazraj* tribes of *al-Madīnah*.

The word *taḥkīm* is derived from the root *ḥakama*, which means to decide,

---

[350]William Hall, *A Treatise on International Law* (Oxford: The Clarendon Press, 1924), 495.

[351]Jackson H. Ralston, *International Arbitration from Athens to Locarno* (Stanford, California: Stanford University Press, 1929), 11-15.

[352]Muhammad Hamidullah, "Administration of Justice in Early Islam," *Islamic Culture* 9 (1937): 165.

[353]Abū ᶜAbd Allāh al-Ḥusayn Ibn Aḥmad al-Zawzanī, *Sharh al-Mu'allaqāt al-Sab'* (Beirut: Dār al-Qāmūs al-Ḥadīth, n.d.), 98.

judge, or rule.[354] Both words, *ḥakam* (judge) and *ḥakīm* (wise), are among the ninety-nine attributes of *Allāh*. Moreover, the word *hakama* and its derivatives are cited in more than one hundred and forty verses in the *Holy Qur'ān*. Apart from the linguistic meanings, *al-taḥkīm*, as a preventive measure and a preliminary peaceful step before resorting to war, has played a prominent role in settling disputes and promoting international justice.[355]

After the emergence of Islam, *al-taḥkīm* was recognized as a peaceful means of settling disputes both in civil and public international law.[356] During the first century of the Islamic era there were two cases in point: the first case was *al-taḥkīm* between the Prophet Muḥammad and Banū Qurayẓa; and the second was between 'Alī Ibn Abī Ṭālib, the fourth Caliph, and Mu'āwiya Ibn Abī Sufyān, the governor of Syria. In the first case, both parties agreed to submit their dispute to Sa'd Ibn Mu'ādh, as an arbitrator,[357] and in the second precedent, each of the parties agreed to submit his dispute to an appointed *ḥakam* (arbitrator). 'Alī appointed Abū Mūsa al-Ash'arī, and Mu'āwiya appointed 'Amr Ibn al-'Āṣ.[358]

However, according to Islamic law, *al-taḥkīm* procedure can be characterized as follows: first, the free selection of arbitrators; second, arbitrators must respect the rules of Islamic law; third, parties who agree to submit their dispute to arbitration must respect its ruling, and comply with its provisions; fourth, no arbitration in *al-ḥudūd* and *al-Qiṣāṣ* (punishments stipulated in the *Qur'ān*); fifth, the award is considered null and void in two cases: if the arbitrator is not chosen freely by the parties, and if he is a close relative to one of the litigants; and finally, the arbitrator

---

[354]Abū al-Qāsim al-Zamakhsharī, *supra note* 49, at 91; Aḥmad Riḍā, *Mu'jam Matn al-Lugha*, 5 vols. (Beirut: Dār Maktabat al-Ḥayā, 1958), 2: 139; Muḥammad Ibn Abī Bakr al-Rāzī, *supra note* 49, at 62; Muḥammad Ibn Manẓūr, *supra note* 49, at 1: 688.

[355]Sobhi Mahmassani, *supra note* 1, at 273.

[356]Majid Khadduri, *supra note* 50, at 233; Sobhi Mahmassani, *supra note* 1, at 272.

[357]For more details see Ibn Hishām, *supra note* 67, at 3: 145-146; al-Siyar al-Kabīr, *supra note* 67, at 2: 587-593.

[358]al-Ṭabarī, *supra note* 71, at 3: 31-38.

must be a wise and just believer.[359]

4. Neutrality (al-Ḥiyād)

The term neutrality is derived from the Latin *neuter*. According to Oppenheim, neutrality, which may be defined as the attitude of impartiality adopted by third states towards belligerents, was not recognized as an institution of international law before the writings of Grotius.[360] It is perceived that the concept of neutrality has been connected with the development of the idea of the international community.[361] Even Grotius did not know or use the term neutrality in its modern sense. He dealt briefly with this concept under the title *De his, qui in bello medii funt* to support his theory of the just war.[362] In Vattel's time, as a result of the growing importance of international trade, belligerent states agreed to respect the neutrality of those states who decided to remain outside war.[363]

Although neutrality was accepted as a legal status by the end of the nineteenth century, the definitions of both neutral rights and duties remained unclear until the convening of the Hague Peace Conference in 1907, when two conventions on neutrality were adopted.[364] However, the failure of the Hague Conventions, to

---

[359]*The Encyclopaedia of Islam*, 2nd ed., s.v. "Ḥakam," by E. Tyan; al-Marghīnānī, *supra note* 21, at 3:108-109.

[360]L. Oppenheim, *supra note* 91, at 514.

[361]Gerhard von Glahn, *supra note* 95, at 625.

[362]Hugo Grotius, *De jure belli ac pacis libri tres* (Amstelodami: Apud Viduam Abrahami Asomeren, 1701), 828-833. However, Emmerich de Vattel (1714-1767), whose writings appeared in 1758, one hundred and thirty-three years after Grotius treatise, has used the term neutrality, and defined it as: "Les peuples neutres, dans une guerre, sont ceux qui n'y prennent aucune part, demeurant amis communs des deux partis, et ne favorisant point les armes de l'un au préjudice de l'autre." See Emmerich de Vattel, *supra note* 114, at 2:565.

[363]Gerhard von Glahn, *supra note* 95, at 626; L. Oppenheim, *supra note* 91, at 490.

[364]*The Hague Convention V Respecting the Rights and Duties of Neutral Powers and Persons in Case of War on Land, of 1907*, 3 Martens NRG, 3ème sér. (1862-1910) 504-532 (opened for signature on October 18, 1907, and entered into force on January 26, 1910) [hereinafter Hague V]; The Hague Convention VIII Relative to the Laying of Automatic Submarine Contact Mines, of 1907, 3 Martens NRG, 3ème sér. (1862-1910) 580-603 (opened for signature on October 18, 1907, and entered into force on January 26, 1910) [hereinafter Hague VIII].

lay down precise rules on neutrality, led to different amendments being adopted in the Declaration of London of 1909; the Covenant of the League of Nations, (Article 16); the Pact of Paris of 1928; the United Nations Charter of 1945, (Article 2, paragraph 5 and 6); and the four Geneva Conventions of 1949.[365]

Examining the concept of neutrality in Islamic international law, Majid Khadduri maintained that such an institution did not exist in Islamic legal theory, since Islamic humanitarian law never recognized an attitude of impartiality on the part of other states.[366] He proceeded to say:

> "If neutrality is taken to mean the attitude of a state which voluntarily desires to keep out of war by not taking sides, no such a status is recognized in Muslim legal theory. For Islam must *ipso jure* be at war with any state which refuses to come to terms with it either by submitting to Muslim rule or by accepting a temporary peace arrangement."[367]

A careful examination of the main sources of Islamic law, however, shows the contrary. It is obvious that Khadduri's viewpoint is based on his earlier claim that, "the normal relationship between Islam and non-Muslim communities is a state of hostility."[368] This notion is drawn from three irrelative cases,[369] of which Khadduri himself acknowledges, "such states were not neutral, in the sense of the modern law

---

[365]Based on Article 2 (paragraph 5), and Article 41 of the United Nations Charter, Member States of the United Nations have no absolute right of neutrality. They may be called upon to apply enforcement measures against a state or states engaged in war pursuant to a decision passed by the Security Council. For example, the Security Council's Resolution 661, of August 6, 1990, calling upon all States, including non-member States of the United Nations, to take measures against Iraq after Iraq's invasion of Kuwait. Furthermore, rules of neutrality proved quite out of date, and could not be applied in many instances during World War I (1914-1918) and World War II (1939-1945). See J.G. Starke, *An Introduction to International Law* (London: Butterworths, 1977), 613.

[366]Moreover, in discussing the Islamic conception of justice, Khadduri claimed that Islamic law leaves no room for neutrality. He alleged that, "justice under neutrality had no place in accordance with the Islamic public order, if neutrality were taken to mean the attitude of a political community which voluntarily decided to refrain from hostile relations with belligerent parties." See Majid Khadduri, *The Islamic Conception of Justice* (Baltimore: The Johns Hopkins University Press, 1984), 168.

[367]Majid Khadduri, *supra note* 50, at 251.

[368]*Ibid.*, at 202.

[369]The cases of Ethiopia, Nubia and Cyprus.

of nations."[370] Moreover, Khadduri ignores the Qur'anic verse, which the theory of neutrality, in Islamic legal discourse, is based on. This verse reads: "therefore if they withdraw from you (*I'tazalūkum*), and wage not war against you and offer you peace, then *Allāh* hath opened no way for you (to war against them)."[371] Both the context and the wording of the verse testify to the main components of the theory of neutrality: a war has broken out between two subjects of the law; a third political community voluntarily desires not to take sides with or against belligerent parties; and the warring parties fully recognize the rights of the neutral state. The verse, strictly speaking, indicates that the Islamic state must be committed to recognizing and respecting the neutrality of the states who have declared their impartiality toward the belligerent powers.[372] This shows clearly that the Islamic concept of neutrality is compatible with the same concept as it appears under international law in the modern sense of the term.

Although the classical juridical works do not leave much room for neutrality, a historical case in point is the treaty concluded in the second year of the *hijra*, between the Islamic city-state in *Medina* and the quasi-state of the tribe of *Banū Ḍamra.* The treaty, which was signed by the Prophet Muḥammad and Makhshī Ibn 'Amr al-Ḍamrī, runs as follows: "the Prophet will not attack *Banū Ḍamra* nor will they attack him or swell the troops of his enemies nor help his enemies in any way."[373]

Furthermore, the Gulf crisis, that followed Iraq's invasion of Kuwait in August 1990, gave rise to the most recent examples of neutrality in the Muslim

---

[370]Majid Khadduri, *supra note* 50, at 252.

[371]*The Holy Qur'ān*, IV: 90.

[372]David Aaron Schwartz, *supra note* 211, at 645; Marcel A. Boisard, *supra note* 15, at 10; Al Ghunaimi, *supra note* 83, at 217; Mustansir Mir, "Jihād in Islam," in *The Jihād and Its Times*, ed. Hadia Dajani-Shakeel (Michigan: The University of Michigan, 1991), 121.

[373]Aḥmad Ibn Yaḥyā al-Balādhurī, *Ansāb al-Ashrāf*, 5 vols. (Jerusalem: Hosta'at Sefarim, 1938), 1:287 [hereinafter al-Ansāb]; Ibn Hishām, *supra note* 67, at 2:170-171; Ibn Sa'd, *supra note* 253, at 2:27; al-Maqrīzī-, *supra note* 253, at 1:53; Muhammad Hamidullah, *Muslim Conduct of State* (Lahore, Pakistan: Muhammad Ashraf, 1961), 296; al-Suhaylī, *supra note* 229, at 2:58-59; al-Ṭabarī, *supra note* 71, at 1:519-520.

World. In spite of the popular support of their citizens for Iraq against the Western Coalition, Jordan, the Sudan and Yemen maintained a formal state of neutrality throughout the crisis.[374]

By contrast, the cases of Ethiopia, Nubia and Cyprus, which were cited by Khadduri, could not constitute a formal state of neutrality. In contrast, true neutrality requires sovereignty and independence, for a neutral state is one whose independence and integrity, both political and territorial, allow her to possess sovereignty over her subjects and affairs.[375] Although Ethiopia was an independent state, it did not in fact announce its neutral status. Muslims themselves voluntarily abstained from attacking Ethiopia and declared its immunity from war.[376] Moreover, Ethiopia may be considered *dār al-Islām* rather than a neutral territory, for its King had accepted the Prophet's invitation of Islam;[377] protected those Muslims who escaped persecution in Mecca and sought asylum in Ethiopia; and allowed Muslims to reside safely and to outwardly practice their religion individually and collectively.[378]

Soon after they failed to annex Nubia, Muslims were successful in concluding a treaty of interdependence with the Nubians on a reciprocal basis. This treaty, which was signed in 31 A.H., ensured security and peace between both parties. According to the norms of the treaty, Nubians shall pay an annual tribute of three hundred and sixty slaves to the chief of the Muslims. In return, the Muslims are bound by the treaty to supply the Nubians with wheat, horses and clothing.[379] It

---

[374]David Aaron Schwartz, *supra note* 211, at 645.

[375]J.G. Starke, *supra note* 365, at 113 and 140.

[376]Abū Dāwūd, *supra note* 197, at 2:101; al-Bayhaqī, *supra note* 211, at 9:176; Ibn Rushd, *supra note* 21, at 1:369; Nūr al-Dīn 'Alī Ibn Abī bakr al-Haythamī, *Majma' al-Zawā'id wa Manba' al-Fawā'id*, 10 vols. (Cairo: Maktabat al-Qudsī, 1353 A.H.), 5:304 [hereinafter al-Haythamī].

[377]Ibn Kathīr, *supra note* 72, at 3:84; al-Qalqashandī, *supra note* 266, at 6:466-467; Ibn al-Qayyim, *supra note* 21, at 3:60-61; al-Ṭabarī, *supra note* 71, at 1:643-644.

[378]Al Ghunaimi, *supra note* 83, at 156-157; al-Shawkānī, *supra note* 192, at 8:29.

[379]al-Balādhurī, *supra note* 71, at 236; Ibn 'Abd al-Ḥakam, *supra note* 254, at 188-189; al-Khiṭaṭ, *supra note* 254, at 1:323-324.

is clear that the Muslims and the Nubians signed a reciprocal trade agreement, not a treaty of neutrality. Therefore, it may be argued that Nubia was *dār al-'ahd*, not *dār al-ḥiyād.*

Finally, from the legal point of view, Cyprus was not a sovereign state when it was attacked by the Muslim army. It was a Byzantine tributary island. Due to the fact that the annexation of Cyprus to *dār al-Islām* might lead the Muslims into a real confrontation with the Byzantine Empire, the Muslims and Cypriots concluded a peace treaty, which provided that the latter pay an annual tribute of seven thousand, two hundred *dīnārs.* According to this treaty, the Muslims would refrain from waging war against the Cypriots.[380] However, in spite of its neutral attitude and acting as a buffer state between Muslims and Byzantines, Cyprus' neutral status was *ipso facto*, the thing which categorized it as being within *dār al- 'ahd.*

5. Diplomatic Exchange (Tabādul al-Wufūd wal-Safārāt)

Generally speaking, no exclusive definition of diplomacy has been yet made.[381] The Oxford English Dictionary calls it "the management of international relations by negotiation," or "the method by which these relations are adjusted and managed."[382] However, based on the doctrine of *jihād*, in which "peace is the rule, war is the exception," diplomacy has played a distinct role in the peaceful missionary work of Islam.[383] Conversely, Majid Khadduri claims that the adoption of diplomacy by Islam was not essentially for peaceful purposes "as long as the state of war was regarded as the normal relation between Islam and other nations."[384]

---

[380]al-Balādhurī, *supra note* 71, at 152-153 and 155-156; *The Encyclopaedia of Islam*, 2nd ed., s.v. "Cyprus," by R. Hartmann; Ibn al-Athīr, *supra note* 284, at 3:37; Ibn Sallām, *supra note* 253, at 174.

[381]Norman D. Palmer and Howard C. Perkins, *International Relations: The World Community in Transition* (New York: Houghton Mifflin Company, 1953), 84.

[382]Lesley Brown, ed., *The Oxford English Dictionary on Historical Principles*, 2 vols. (Oxford: The Clarendon Press, 1993), 1:678.

[383]"Invite (all) to the way of *Allāh* with wisdom and beautiful preaching; and argue with them in ways that are best and most gracious." *The Holy Qur'ān*, XVI: 125.

[384]Majid Khadduri, *supra note* 50, at 239.

Despite the apparent differences, Islamic historical and juristic works show that diplomacy, as an organized profession, arose very early in the Islamic era. Thus, the following study will discuss the historical background of diplomacy and the functions, privileges and immunities of diplomats.

Until the late seventeenth century the word diplomacy meant verifying ancient documents. It is derived from the Greek verb *diploun* meaning to fold. The Romans used the word *diploma* for official documents, particularly those relating to foreign communities or tribes.[385] Diplomacy, meaning the management of international relations, was used for the first time in England in 1796, and was recognized as a distinct profession by the Congress of Vienna in 1875.[386]

In Arabic, the term *rasūl* (messenger) or *safīr* (ambassador) refers to a diplomatic agent. The word *rasūl*, which is derived from the verb *arsala* (to dispatch), has a religious connotation. The term *safīr* is derived from the verb *safara*, which means mediation and conciliation.[387] It must be pointed out that according to Muslim chronicles and jurists, diplomatic agents should display the following qualities: elegance, intelligence, dignity, eloquence, politeness, loyalty and education.[388] However, diplomatic relations were known to Arab tribes before Islam. In Mecca, foreign affairs were entrusted to Banū 'Uday, and 'Umar Ibn al-Khaṭṭāb was the last Qurashite ambassador to other Arab tribes before Islam.[389]

---

[385]Harold Nicolson, *Diplomacy* (London: Oxford University Press, 1969), 4.

[386]*Ibid.*

[387]Abū 'Alī al-Ḥusayn Ibn Muḥammad Ibn al-Farrā', *Kitāb Rusul al-Mulūk wa-man Yaṣluḥ lil-Risāla wal-Safāra*, ed. Ṣalāḥ al-Dīn al-Munajjid (Cairo: Lajnat al-Ta'līf wal-Tarjama wal-Nashr, 1947), 3 [hereinafter Rusul al-Mulūk]; Abū al-Qāsim al-Zamakhsharī, *supra note* 49, at 162 and 212; Muḥammad Ibn Abī Bakr al-Rāzī, *supra note* 49, at 102 and 127; Muḥammad Ibn Manẓūr, *supra note* 49, at 1: 1165 and 2:154.

[388]Muḥammad Ibn 'Alī Ibn Ṭabātaba Ibn al-Ṭaqtaqī, *al-Fakhrī fī al-Ādāb al-Sulṭaniyya wal-Duwal al-Islāmiyya* (Cairo: Maṭba'at Muḥammad 'Alī Ṣubayḥ, n.d.), 57[hereinafter Ibn al-Ṭaqtaqī]; Rusul al-Mulūk, *supra note* 387, at 20-29; al-Siyar al-Kabīr, *supra note* 67, at 2:471; Sobhi Mahmassani, *supra note* 1, at 266.

[389]Aḥmad Shalabī, *Mawsū'at al-Tārīkh al-Islāmī*. 10 vols. (Cairo:Maktabat al-Nahḍa al-Miṣriyya, 1984), 1:570; al-Sayyid al-Jamīlī, *Manāqib Amīr al-Mu'minīn 'Umar Ibn al-Khaṭṭāb* (Beirut: Dār al-Kitāb al-'Arabī, 1985), 21.

Following the emergence of Islam, diplomatic intercourse was developed to a considerable extent. In the sixth year of the *Hijra,* after he concluded the *Ḥudaybiya* Treaty with the pagans of Mecca, the Prophet Muḥammad dispatched envoys to various Arab and non-Arab kingdoms, inviting them to Islam. He sent Ḥāṭib Ibn Abī Balta'a to Muqawqas, the governor of Alexandria; 'Abdullāh Ibn Ḥudhāfa al-Sahmī to the King of Persia; Daḥiyya Ibn Khalīfa al-Kalbī to Heraclius, the Byzantine emperor, 'Amr Ibn Umayya al-Ḍamrī to the Negus, the Emperor of Abyssinia; 'Amr Ibn al-'Āṣ to the Kings of Oman; Salīṭ Ibn 'Amr to the Kings of Yamama; al-'Alā' Ibn al-Ḥaḍramī to the King of Al-Bahrain; Shujā' Ibn Wahb al-Asadī to the Ghassanid King; al-Muhājir Ibn Abī Umayya al-Makhzūmī to the Himyarite King; and Mu'ādh Ibn Jabal to the Kings of Yemen.[390] Through a close look at the letters carried by the above ambassadors, one may observe a refined etiquette on the part of the Prophet.

On the other hand, the Prophet Muḥammad received delegations and embassies at *usṭuwānat al-wufūd* (the pillar of embassies) in his mosque. He received deputations from Ṭā'if; Najrān; Banū Sa'd; Banū Ṭay'; Banū Tamīm; Banū Ḥanīfa; the Kings of Ḥimyar; and the Kings of Kinda.[391] At the time of the ceremonial reception of emissaries, the Prophet and his companions usually put on fine dress.[392] Before ceremonials took place, usually, envoys were instructed by a person who was later called the master of ceremonials.[393] In many cases the Prophet and his successors exchanged gifts with envoys as part of the diplomatic ceremonies. The gifts received by the prophet and the Muslim Caliphs went to the general exchequer.[394] In the time of the Prophet, there were a number of large

[390]Ibn Hishām, *supra note* 67, at 3: 232; Ibn Sa'd, *supra note* 253, at 2:15-38; al-Qalqashandī, *supra note* 266, at 6: 376-377; al-Suhaylī, *supra note* 229, at 2:352-358; al-Ya'qūbī, *supra note* 280, at 2:83.

[391]Ibn Hishām, *supra note* 67, at 4:152-181; Ibn Kathīr, *supra note* 72, at 5: 40-98; al-Maqrīzī, *supra note* 253, at 1:509; Ibn Sa'd, *supra note* 253, at 1:153; al-Ṭabarī, *supra note* 71, at 2:48.

[392]al-Maqrīzī, *supra note* 253, at 1:509; Ibn Sa'd, *supra note* 253, at 1:153.

[393] al-Ṭabarī, *supra note* 71, at 2:49.

[394]*Ibid.* When the wife of 'Umar Ibn al-Khaṭṭāb received a gift from the wife of the Emperor of

houses (*dār al-ḍīfān*) in Medina to accommodate envoys according to their personal status and the rank of whom they represented.[395] In this connection, it might be important to mention here that diplomatic intercourse flourished and achieved great success in the late Islamic periods. In the times of the rightly-guided caliphs, as well as in the Umayyad and Abbasid periods, the Islamic state came into more sophisticated diplomatic relations when they negotiated and concluded truce and peace treaties with neighbouring kingdoms.[396] Moreover, the Fatimid, Mamluk, Ayyubid, and Ottoman regimes exchanged diplomatic representatives with European and Asian countries.[397]

Nevertheless, based on customary and conventional international law, diplomatic agents enjoy a considerable range of privileges and immunities to ensure their efficient performance and function.[398] According to the Vienna Convention on Diplomatic Relations, concluded on April 18, 1961, diplomatic envoys have the right to inviolability. In other words, the person of the diplomatic agent is inviolable. Article 29 of the above Convention proclaims that diplomatic agents are protected from molestation of any kind, as well as from arrest or detention by the local authorities. The second privilege is extraterritoriality. This concept involves a number of exemptions from local jurisdiction. Accordingly, diplomatic envoys are exempt from the jurisdictions of the receiving state, including local civil and criminal jurisdiction. Moreover, they cannot be asked to appear as a witness in a tribunal. Exemption from taxes and customs duties is provided in Articles 34 and 36 of the Vienna Convention. In addition, there are a number of minor immunities

---

Constantinople, ʻUmar confiscated it for the Muslim state treasury. See Ibn al-Athīr, *supra note* 284, at 3:74.

[395]Ibn Saʻd, *supra note* 253, at 1:153; al-Maqrīzī, *supra note* 253, at 1:509; Muhammad Hamidullah, *supra note* 373, at 147.

[396]al-Qalqashandī, *supra note* 266, at 421-463.

[397]B. Sen, *A Diplomat's Handbook of International Law and Practice* (The Hague, The Netherlands: Martinus Nijhoff Publishers, 1965), 5.

[398]J.G. Starke, *supra note* 365, at 444. These privileges and immunities are minutely discussed in Articles 20 to 41 of the Vienna Convention on Diplomatic Relations, of April 18, 1961.

embodied in the articles of the convention, namely: the right to move and travel freely in the territory of the receiving state, except in prohibited security zones; the freedom of communication for official purposes; exemption from social security provisions; and exemption from services and military obligations.[399]

Thus, diplomatic envoys enjoy specific immunities and privileges corresponding to those provided by public international law. In this sense, Bernard Lewis concludes that "the rights and immunities of envoys, including those from hostile rulers, were recognized from the start, and enshrined in the *Sharī'a*."[400]

To enable them to exercise their duties and functions, diplomatic agents enjoy full personal immunity under Islamic international law. They are not to be killed, maltreated or arrested even if they are convicted or have a criminal record.[401] The Prophet Muḥammad granted these privileges and immunities to diplomatic envoys in his lifetime. Two incidents are on record: first, the Prophet granted immunity to Ibn al-Nawwāḥa and Ibn Āthāl, the emissaries of Musaylama – the liar - , in spite of their extremely rude behaviour towards him. The Prophet said: "I swear by *Allāh* that if emissaries were not immune from killing, I would have ordered you to be beheaded."[402] Second, the Prophet treated kindly Waḥshī, the ambassador of the people of al-Ṭā'if, who had murdered Ḥamza, the Prophet's uncle, at the battle of Uḥud. The Prophet's generous treatment convinced him to embrace Islam.[403] Moreover, Islamic law accorded *droit de chapelle* to diplomatic

---

[399] *Vienna Convention on Diplomatic Relations*, Articles 26, 27, 33 and 35. See Gerhard von Glahn, *supra note* 95, at 42, 199, and 386-394; J.G. Starke, *supra note* 365 at 440-445; L. Oppenheim, *supra note* 91, at 1: 629-636; Norman D. Palmer and Howard C. Perkins, *supra note* 381 at 90-91.

[400] Bernard Lewis, *supra note* 2, at 76.

[401] Afzal Iqbal, *The Prophet's Diplomacy: The Art of Negotiation as Conceived and Developed by the Prophet of Islam* (Cape Cod, Massachusetts: Claude Stark & Co., 1975), 54-55; al-Mas'ūdī, *supra note* 133, at 2:309; Muhammad Hamidullah, *supra note* 373, at 147.

[402] Abū Dāwūd, *supra note* 197, at 2:92-93; Aḥmad Ibn Ḥanbal al-Shaybānī, *al-Musnad*, 6 vols. (Beirut: al-Maktab al-Islāmī, 1969), 1:390 [hereinafter Ibn Ḥanbal]; al-Bayhaqī, *supra note* 211, at 9:211; Ibn Hishām, *supra note* 67, at 4:165; Ibn al-Qayyim, *supra note* 21, at 2:75; al-Sarakhsī, *supra note* 21, at 10:92; al-Shawkānī, *supra note* 192, at 8:34; al-Ṭabarī, *supra note* 71, at 2:69.

[403] Ibn Hishām, *supra note* 67, at 3:21-23; Ibn Kathīr, *supra note* 72, at 4:17-19; al-Ṭabarī, *supra note* 71, at 1:576.

agents. The Prophet allowed a delegation from the Christians of Najrān to hold their service in his mosque.[404]

In addition to the above privileges, the property of diplomatic agents is exempt from customs duties and other taxes during their stay in *dār al-Islām.*[405] This privilege could be provided on a reciprocal basis.[406] In this sense, Muslim jurists deem that diplomatic agents of foreign states enjoy the same privileges granted to Muslim envoys in such states.[407] To enjoy these privileges and immunities, foreign envoys must commit themselves to good breeding and fidelity. In committing any prohibited acts, which might disturb the peace and security of *dār al-Islām*, like engaging in espionage or exporting weapons from *dār al-Isālam* to *dār al-ḥarb*, an envoy will be declared *persona non grata* and expatriated safely to his state of origin.[408] In this case, however, the emissary will not be killed or in any way molested or badly treated, for the rule is "loyalty against treachery is better than treachery against treachery."[409] In light of the above discussion, one may ask: On what grounds is Majid Khadduri standing when he concludes, "if hostilities began when the emissaries were still on Muslim soil, they were either insulted or

---

[404]Afzal Iqbal, *supra note* 401, at 55; Ibn Hishām, *supra note* 67, at 2:160; Ibn Kathīr, *supra note* 72, at 5:52-56; Mohammad Ali Homoud, *Diplomacy in Islam: Diplomacy During the Period of Prophet Muḥammed* (Jaipur, India: Printwell, 1994), 232.

[405]Abū Yūsuf, *supra note* 53, at 334-335; al-Khaṭīb, *supra note* 288, at 4:247; al-Shīrāzī, *supra note* 324, at 2:260.

[406]Abū Yūsuf, *supra note* 53, at 266.

[407]*Ibid.*; Muhammad Hamidullah, *supra note* 373, at 148.

[408]Abū Isḥāq Ibrāhīm Ibn 'Alī al-Shīrāzī, *al-Tanbīh* (Cairo: Maṭba'at Muṣṭafā al-Bābī al-Ḥalabī, 1951), 147 [hereinafter al-Tanbīh]; al-Dasūqī, *supra note* 228, at 2:206; Ibn al-Humām, *supra note* 293, at 4:294; Mansūr Ibn Idrīs al-Buhūtī, *Kashshāf al-Qinā' 'an Matn al-Iqnā'*, 6 vols. (Cairo: Maṭba'at Anṣār al-Sunna al-Muḥammadiyya, 1947), 3: 87 [al-Buhūtī]; al-Shāfi'ī, *supra note* 21, at 4: 185; Sharf al-Dīn Ismā'īl Ibn Abī Bakr al-Muqrī, *Asnā al-Maṭālib fī Sharḥ Rawḍ al-Ṭālib*, 2 vols. (Cairo: al-Maṭba'a al-Maymaniyya, 1306 A.H.), 2:204 [hereinafter al- Muqrī]; Tuḥfat al-Muḥtāj, *supra note* 293 at 4:294.

[409]Abū Dāwūd, *supra note* 197, at 2:92; Muḥammad Ibn 'Isā al-Tirmidhī, *Sunan al-Tirmidhī*, 5 vols. (Beirut: Dār al Fikr, 1983), 4:143 [hereinafter al- Tirmidhī].

imprisoned or even killed "?[410]

6. Foreign Trade (al-Tijāra al-Khārijiyya)

It is well known that Islam emerged in Mecca, the commercial centre of Arabia, at the crossroads of international trade.[411] The Prophet Muḥammad himself was a merchant, and the *Holy Qur'ān* has made reference to the trade journeys of the Quraysh, a highbred Meccan tribe, to Yemen and Syria in winter and summer respectively.[412] The Qurashites' trade caravans and their prestige as custodians of the *Ka'ba*, the central shrine of Arabia, enabled them to obtain covenants of security and safeguard from the rulers of neighbouring countries to protect their trade journeys.[413] At a later time, foreign trade became a considerable career in Muslim society, and played a great role in the expansion of the Islamic religion and civilization. Islamic commercial law left its imprint on the European trading profession through Andalusia and Italy. Although the details of this intercourse lie outside the scope of this study, it can be said that many Islamic commercial ideas and technical expressions were introduced into the European commercial discourse during the Crusades. Furthermore, Trend claims that while Europe was shrouded in the Dark Ages, Muslims began to trade with Europe on a large scale, getting as far as Sweden. Through trade, Muslims influenced Western legal principles.[414]

---

[410]Majid Khadduri, *supra note* 50, at 244.

[411]Aḥmad Amīn, *Fajr al-Islām* (Beirut: Dār al-Kitāb al-'Arabī, 1975), 12-16; Ibn Kathīr, *supra note* 72, at 2:293; al-Ṭabarī, *supra note* 71, at 1:457.

[412]*The Holy Qur'ān*, CVI: 1-2.

[413]Abū al-Fidā' Ismā'īl Ibn Kathīr, *Tafsīr Ibn Kathīr*, 4 vols. (Beirut: Dār al-Fikr lil-Ṭibā'a wal-Nashr wal-Tawzī', 1981), 4:554-555 [hereinafter Tafsīr Ibn Kathīr]; al-Qurṭubī, *supra note* 60, at 20:137.

[414]In this respect, Le Baron Michel de Taube argues that "contre 38,000 monnaies arabes trouvées en Suède, on compte seulment 200 monnaies Byzantines découvertes dans le même pays." See Le Baron Michel de Taube, "Etudes sur le développement historique du droit international dans l'Europe Orientale," *Recueil des cours* 1:2 (1926): 395; J.B. Trend, "Spain and Portugal," in *The Legacy of Islam*, eds. Thomas Arnold and Alfred Guillaume (London: Oxford University Press, 1931), 3; Majid Khadduri, *supra note* 50, at 224; Sobhi Mahmassani, *supra note* 1, at 271-272; W. Heyd, *Histoire du commerce du Levant au moyen-âge*, 2 vols. (Leipzig: Otto Harrassowitz, 1923), 1:24-51.

However, in examining the effect of the doctrine of *jihād* on commercial intercourse with the enemy, Muslim jurists held different opinions regarding trade between *dār al-Islām* and *dār al-ḥarb*. While trading between the subjects of belligerent states usually ceases at the outbreak of war, Islamic law allows Muslims to conclude commercial agreements and exchange commodities with the subjects of *dār al-ḥarb*, with certain limitations imposed on exports and imports, for political and religious reasons.[415] Generally speaking, Muslim jurists agreed on trading with *dār al-ḥarb*,[416] except for the Malikites, who deemed that Muslims should not enter *dār al-ḥarb* to make commercial transactions, if such deals made them subject to the laws of the enemy. Furthermore, Mālik and Ibn Ḥazm advised the *Imām* to keep Muslims from entering *dār al-ḥarb* except for the performance of *jihād* or in diplomatic missionary.[417]

Muslim jurists prohibited the export of arms, riding animals, slaves, and all materials that can be used in the industry of weapons and may increase the fighting power of *dār al-ḥarb*.[418] al-Shaybānī goes so far as to prohibit the export of silk that might be used in cutting out war flags (*rāyāt al-ḥarb*), and all kinds of iron, no matter what size or usage.[419] Moreover, Abū Yūsuf advised the *Imām* to set up checkpoints (*masāliḥ*) on the borderlines of *dār al-Islām*, to apprehend contrabandists and inflict penalties upon them.[420] By contrast, al-Shāfi'ī permits the sale of *sabī* and iron to the subjects of *dār al-ḥarb*, if Muslims know for certain that

---

[415]Najīb al-Armanāzī, *supra note* 274, at 219; Sobhi Mahmassani, *supra note* 1, at 271; Wahba al-Zuḥaylī, *supra note* 182, at 512.

[416]Abū Yūsuf, *supra note* 53, at 334-338; al-Baḥr al-Zakhkhār, *supra note* 295, at 3:301; Ibn 'Ābdī n, *supra note* 227, at 3:312; al-Kāsānī, *supra note* 21, at 102; Majid Khadduri, *supra note* 50, at 224; al-Marghīnānī, *supra note* 21, at 139; Rudolph Peters, *supra note* 11, at 26; al-Siyar al-Kabīr, *supra note* 67, at7 4:1408-1409 and 1567-1574; Wahba al-Zuḥaylī, *supra note* 182, at 512-524.

[417]Ibn Ḥazm, *supra note* 21, at 7:349; Muḥammad Ibn Aḥmad Ibn Rushd, *al-Muqaddamāt al-Mumahhadāt*, 3 vols. (Cairo: Maṭba'at al-Sa'āda, 1325 A.H.), 2:285 [hereinafter al-Muqaddamāt]; al-Mudawwana, *supra note* 293, at 10:102.

[418]al-Fatāwī al-Hindiyya, *supra note* 301, at 2:197-198; al-Sarakhsī, *supra note* 21, at 88-89.

[419]al-Siyar al-Kabīr, *supra note* 67, at 4:1568.

[420]Abū Yūsuf, *supra note* 53, at 337; al-Siyar al-Kabīr, *supra note* 67, at 4:1569.

such goods will not be used for military purposes.[421]

On the other hand, most Muslim jurists permitted the export of food, cloth and agricultural products to *dār al-ḥarb*,[422] except the Malikites, who stipulated that a truce must be concluded with them first.[423] A case in point of the first position is that the Prophet Muḥammad ordered Thamāma Ibn Athāl al-Ḥanafī to put an end to the alimentary boycott imposed on the Meccans, and support them with foodstuffs in spite of being in war with Muslims.[424]

As to imports, it is worthwhile to mention here that foreign merchants were not allowed to sell forbidden commodities such as wine and pork in *dār al-Islām*. At the same time, Muslim merchants were prohibited from carrying weapons, *sabī*, or any materials which might be used for the fabrication of arms, during their visit to *dār al-ḥarb*. Furthermore, the latter are not permitted to practice *ribā* (usury), or to deal with pork, wine, or wild animals.[425] However, 'Umar Ibn al-Khaṭṭāb, the second rightly-guided Caliph imposed the *'ushūr* (tithe) duty. Accordingly, the *ḥarbī* merchants were required to pay ten percent of the value of their commercial commodities which exceeded two hundred dirhams.[426] The *Imām* has the right to increase or decrease this rate, according to the Muslim State foreign trade policy. The *Imām* is advised to invalidate *al-'ushūr* duty if the state of the *ḥarbī* merchant

[421]al-Khatīb, *supra note* 288, at 2:10; al-Shāfi'ī, *supra note* 21, at 4:198; Shams al-Dīn Muḥammad Ibn Aḥmad al-Ramlī, *Nihāyat al-Muhtāj ilā Sharḥ al-Minhāj*. 8 vols. (Cairo: al-Maṭba'a al-Bahiyya al-Miṣriyya, 1304 A.H.), 3:15 [hereinafter al-Ramlī].

[422]al-Marghīnānī, *supra note* 21, at 2:139; al-Shāfi'ī, *supra note* 21, at 7:321; al-Siyar al-Kabīr, *supra note* 67, at 4:1408.

[423]al-Mudawwana, *supra note* 293, at 10:102; al-Muqaddamāt, *supra note* 417, at 2:287-288.

[424]al-Bayhaqī, *supra note* 211, at 6:319.

[425]Abū Ḥāmid al-Ghazālī, *Iḥyā' 'Ulūm al-Dīn,* 4 vols. (Beirut: Dār al-Ma'rifa lil-Ṭibā'a wal-Nashr, 1404 A.H.), 2:65 [hereinafter Iḥyā' 'Ulūm al-Dīn].

[426]Abū Yūsuf, *supra note* 53, at 263-270; Aḥkām Ahl al-Dhimma, *supra note* 324, at 169; Ibn Sallām, *supra note* 253, at 501; al-Khatīb, *supra note* 288, at 4:247; al-Mughnī, *supra note* 21, at 10:599-600; al-Muqaddamāt, *supra note* 417, at 1:184; al-Muqrī, *supra note* 408, at 2:12; al-Shīrāzī, *supra note* 324, at 2:259; al-Wajīz, *supra note* 295, at 2:53.

does not collect such duty from Muslim merchants.[427]

[427]Abū Yūsuf, *supra note* 53, at 265-267; al-Baḥr al-Zakhkhār, *supra note* 295, at 2:223; al-Mughnī, *supra note* 21, at 8:521; al-Siyar al- Kabīr, *supra note* 67, at 5:2136.

Chapter Three
Jihād and Civilians' Personal Rights

The issue of human rights in times of war and armed disputes is one of the most fundamental human issues and, consequently, one of the most sensitive and controversial. The following chapter attempts to address the critical question: to what extent did Islamic humanitarian law contribute to the protection of civilians' personal rights? To maintain that, a number of these rights will be examined in light of the norms of Islamic and public international law, particularly, the right to life, the prohibition of torture and inhuman treatment, and the right to respect one's religious beliefs, customs and traditions.

1. Right to Life, the Prohibition of Torture and Inhuman Treatment

International humanitarian law guarantees the protection of individual human rights, whether those rights are exercised alone or in association with others. The right to life is an imperative norm of international law, which should inspire and influence all other human rights.[428] In his article "Human Rights as the Modern Tool of Revolution", Irwin Cotler concluded that "The struggle for human rights and human dignity, as Havel and Mandela have put it - separately but in solidarity -

[428] B.G. Ramcharan, ed., *The Right to Life in International Law* (Dordrecht, The Netherlands: Martinus Nijhoff Publishers, 1985), 6; Leo Kuper, *The Prevention of Genocide* (New Haven, CT: Yale University Press, 1985), 3.

is really initially and ultimately the struggle for ourselves."[429] Therefore, the international law of human rights, which is concerned with the promotion and protection of human rights must be in the forefront of the discipline, charting new courses and establishing new models.

The United Nations Charter, of 1945 made no explicit reference to the individual's right to life, but it emphasized the promotion of human rights and fundamental freedoms in the first chapter on purposes and principles.[430] In examining the other instruments of the Bill of Rights, one may find that the Universal Declaration of Human Rights, of 1948, clearly confirmed the right to life. Article 3 affirmed universal entitlement to the rights of life, liberty and security.[431] Any act of torture is declared to be an offence to human dignity, and condemned as a violation of human rights and fundamental freedoms proclaimed in the United Nations Charter and the Universal Declaration of Human Rights. Article 5 of the same declaration states that "No one shall be subjected to torture or to cruel, inhuman or degrading treatment or punishment."[432] Furthermore, this right is also confirmed in Article 6 (Part III) of the International Covenant on Civil and Political Rights, of 1966. Paragraph 1 of Article 6 declares that "every human being has the inherent right to life. This right shall be protected by law. No one shall be arbitrarily deprived of his life."[433] Paragraph 6 of this article asked the state parties to the Covenant not to delay or to prevent the abolition of capital punishment. In light of the above-mentioned statement, one may argue that Article 6 of the

---

[429]Irwin Cotler, "Human Rights as the Modern Tool of Revolution," in *Human Rights in the Twenty-First Century: A Global Challenge*, eds. Kathleen E. Mahoney and Paul Mahoney (Dordrecht, The Netherlands: Martinus Nijhoff Publishers, 1993), 20.

[430]Albert P. Blaustein, Roger S. Clark, and Jay A. Sigler, eds., *Human Rights Sourcebook* (New York: Paragon House Publishers, 1987), 8-9; United Nations Charter, *supra note* 98.

[431]*Universal Declaration of Human Rights*. G.A. Res. 217 A (III), 3 (1) U.N. GAOR Resolutions 71, U.N. Doc. A/810, 1948.

[432]*Ibid.*

[433]B.G. Ramcharan, *supra note* 428, at 30; *International Covenant on Civil and Political Rights*. G.A. Res. 2200 (XXI), 21 U.N. GAOR, Supp. (No. 16) at 52, U.N. Doc. A/6316, 1966.

International Covenant on Civil and Political Rights is limited to arbitrary deprivation of life such as by homicide, and does not guarantee any persons security against death from famine or lack of medical attention. Therefore, mere toleration of malnutrition by a state will not be regarded as a violation of the human right to life.

On the other hand, the Convention on the Prevention and Punishment of the Crime of Genocide, of 1948, was designed to prevent, as well as to punish, the crime. The definition of genocide in the Convention reflects the emphasis on punishment of the crime. It reads as follows:

> "In the present convention, genocide means any of the following acts committed with intent to destroy, in whole or in part, a national, ethnical, racial or religious group, as such:
>
> a. Killing members of the group;
> b. Causing serious bodily or mental harm to members of the group;
> c. Deliberately inflicting on the group conditions of life calculated to bring about its physical destruction in whole or in part;
> d. Imposing measures intended to prevent births within the group;
> e. Forcibly transferring children of the group to another group."[434]

According to the article cited above, the crime of genocide is defined by reference to specific acts not in general terms, but the inclusion of *intent* raises some difficulties in proof, as the denial of intent could be used as a defense. The concept of *intent* was exploited, for example, when the defence minister of the government of Paraguay, in answering to charges of genocide against the Aché Indians, replied that there was no intention to destroy them.[435]

Seeking evidence on the individual's right to life outside the United Nations, one may refer to the Charter for the International Military Tribunal that tried the major war criminals at Nuremberg specified, in Article 6, three types of crime

---

[434] *Convention on the Prevention and Punishment of the Crime of Genocide* G.A. Res. 260 A (III), 3(1) U.N. GAOR at 174, U.N. Doc. A/810, 1948.

[435] Leo Kuper, "Genocide and Mass Kilings: Illusion and Reality," in *The Right to Life in International Law*, ed. B.G. Ramcharan (Dordrecht, The Netherlands: Martinus Nijhoff Publishers, 1985), 115.

falling under the jurisdiction of the tribunal.[436] These crimes are: crimes against peace, including the waging of a war of aggression; war crimes, such as murder of the civilian population, the killing of hostages, and the destruction of cities; and crimes against humanity such as murder, extermination, and inhuman acts committed against civilian populations before or during a war.[437]

Moreover, Article 3 which is common to all four Geneva Conventions, of 1949, prohibits, at any time and in any place, violence to life and person, in particular murder of any kind, mutilation, cruel treatment and torture.[438] Article 4 of Protocol II Additional to the Geneva Conventions prohibits the same actions prohibited in Article 3.[439] Protocol I Additional to the same conventions, and relating to the protection of victims of international armed conflicts can be viewed as a convention within a convention.[440] The one hundred and two articles of this protocol are built on the four Geneva Conventions and other previous conventions, which emphasize the protection of civilian populations.[441]

However, Islamic international law considers the right to life as the most basic and supreme right which human beings are entitled to have, without distinction of any kind, based on race, colour, sex, language and religion. The right to life is a sacred right, and any transgression against it is considered a crime against the entire community.[442] This right has been emphasized in the following verses:

---

[436] Agreement for the Prosecution and Punishment of the Major War Criminals of the European Axis Powers and Charter of the International Military Tribunal, *supra note* 215.

[437] Benjamin Ferencz, "The United Nations and Human Rights Forty Years Later," in *Nuremberg Forty Years Later: The Struggle Against Injustice in Our Time*, ed. Irwin Cotler (Montreal & Kingston: McGill-Queen's University Press, 1995), 102.

[438] Adam Roberts and Richard Guelff, eds., *Documents on the Laws of War* (Oxford: The Clarendon Press, 1982), 273.

[439] Protocol II Additional to the Geneva Conventions of August 12, 1949, and Relating to the Protection of Victims of Non-International Armed Conflicst, *supra note* 140.

[440] Protocol I Additional to the Geneva Conventions of 12 August 1949, and Relating to the Protection of Victims of International Armed Conflicts, *supra note* 105.

[441] Charles A. Allan, *supra note* 218, at 19.

[442] Ahmad Farrag, "Human Rights and Liberties in Islam," in *Human Rights in a Pluralist World:*

"On that account: We ordained for the Children of Israel that if any one slew a person - unless it be for murder or for spreading mischief in the land - it would be as if he slew the whole people, and if any one saved a life, it would be as if he saved the life of the whole people."[443]

"Nor take life - which *Allāh* has made sacred - except for just cause."[444]

"Nor kill yourselves: for verily *Allāh* hath been to you Most Merciful."[445]

Islamic humanitarian law guarantees fair treatment of civilians who have not engaged in war, and prohibited random use of weapons in a manner that would affect warriors and civilians indiscriminately. Muslim fighters have been instructed to avoid civilian targets. Article 47 of the Islamic Law of Nations states that, "Whenever the Apostle of *Allāh* sent forth a detachment he said to it: Do not cheat or commit treachery, nor should you mutilate or kill children, women, or old men."[446] This obligation is supported by another tradition which states that the Prophet Muḥammad saw people gathered around something and sent a man to investigate saying: "see, what are these people collected around?" The man returned and said: "They are around a woman who has been killed." The Prophet said: "This is not one with whom fighting should have taken place." The Prophet sent a man to follow Khālid Ibn al-Walīd and said: "Tell Khālid not to kill a woman or a hired servant."[447]

Excessive killing is prohibited even when it is authorized. This principle has been expressed in the following verse: "If any one is killed wrongfully, we have given his heir authority, but let him not exceed bounds in killing."[448] Thus, Muslim

---

Individuals and Collectivities, eds., Jan Berting et al (Westport: Meckler Corporation, 1990), 137.

[443]*The Holy Qur'ān*, V:32.

[444]*Ibid.*, XVII: 33.

[445]*Ibid.*, IV: 29.

[446]Majid Khadduri, *supra note* 2, at 91.

[447]Abū Dāwūd, *supra note* 197, at 2:739.

[448]*The Holy Qur'ān*, XVII: 33.

fighters (*mujāhidūn*) are not permitted to push killing to the point where they cannot distinguish between civilians and combatants. Prophet Muḥammad instructed the Muslim fighters, dispatched against the Byzantine army, to "spare the weakness of the female sex; injure not the infants or those who are ill in bed. Refrain from demolishing the houses of the unresisting inhabitants; destroy not the means of their subsistence, nor their fruit-trees and touch not the palm, and do not mutilate bodies and do not kill children."[449]

The rightly-guided Caliphs followed the prophet's example. Abū Bakr al-Ṣiddīq, the first Muslim Caliph exhorted the Muslim army marching to Syria, to learn the following rules by heart:

> "Do not commit treachery, nor depart from the right path. You must not mutilate, neither kill a child or aged man or woman. Do not destroy a palm tree, nor burn it with fire and do not cut any fruitful tree. You must not slay any of the flock or the herds or the camels, save for your subsistence. You are likely to pass by people who have developed their lives to monastic services; leave them to that to which they have devoted their lives."[450]

Furthermore, 'Umar Ibn al-Khaṭṭāb, the second orthodox Caliph, warned the commanders of the Muslim army, he said: "Do not mutilate when you have power to do so. Do not commit excess when you triumph. Do not kill an old man or a woman or a minor, but try to avoid them at the time of the encounter of the two armies, and at the time of the heat of victory, and at the time of expected attacks."[451] By the same token, the fourth Caliph, 'Alī Ibn Abī Ṭālib, prohibited the Muslim fighters from killing those who have laid down their weapons, or fled from the battlefield. During his struggle with the Umayyads, and before the battle of Ṣaffīn, 'Alī gave his fighters the following commands, which can be considered as basic

---

[449]Karima Bennoune, "As-Salāmu 'Alaykum" Humanitarian Law in Islamic Jurisprudence," *Michigan Journal of International Law* 15:2 (Winter 1994): 624.

[450]Waldemar A. Solf, *supra note* 202, at 118; al-Shawkānī, *supra note* 192, at 7:263; al-Siyar al-Kabīr, *supra note* 67, at 1:41.

[451]'Abd Allāh Ibn Muslim Ibn Qutayba al-Dīnawarī, *Kitāb 'Uyūn al-Akhbār*, 4 vols (Cairo: Dār al-Kitāb al-'Arabī, 1957), 1:107-108 [hereinafter Ibn Qutayba]; Karima Bennoune, *supra note* 449, at 626. Shihāb al-Dīn Aḥmad Ibn 'Abd Rabbu al-Andalusī, *al-'Iqd al-Farīd* (Beirut: Dār wa Maktabat al-Hilāl, 1986), 1:79 [hereinafter Ibn 'Abd Rabbu].

rules of conduct in Islamic international humanitarian law. 'Alī said:

> "If you defeat them, do not kill a man in flight, do not finish off a wounded man, do not uncover a pudendum, or mutilate the dead, do not rip open a curtain or enter a house without permission, do not take any of their property, and do not torture or harm their women even though they may insult your leaders, and remember *Allāh*, may you will have knowledge."[452]

About the treatment of the enemy in the battlefield, Ahmed Zaki Yamani argues that Islamic humanitarian law is extremely concerned with the basic rules of the international humanitarian law. These rules are the object of many verses and traditions. The Muslim rules of war are highly practical and realistic.[453] Islamic international law of armed conflict has forbidden the breaking of promises and treaties and the separation of captive women from their children, and has called for the fair treatment of prisoners of war. Article 44 of the Islamic Law of Nations, states that, "The prisoner of war should not be killed."[454] In this sense, the Prophet Muḥammad said:

> "War prisoners are your brothers. *Allāh* has put them in your hands; so whosoever has his brother in his hands, let him give food to eat out of what he himself eats and let him give him clothes to wear out of what he himself wears, and do not impose on them a work they are not able to do themselves. If at all you give them such work, help them to carry it out."[455]

The *Holy Qur'ān*, a primary source of Islamic international law, confirms these rules in the following verse: "And they (the devotees of *Allāh*) feed the indigent, the orphaned and the captive in spite of their need and love of that food."[456]

In his book, *Kitāb al-Umm*, al-Shāfi'ī says: "Whatever is accepted by the Muslims and receives their consensus as being permissible in the Land of Islam is

---

[452]Ahmed Zaki Yamani, *supra note* 42, at 195; Nahj al-Balāgha, *supra note* 196, at 3:425.

[453]Marcel A. Boisard, *supra note* 190, at 10.

[454]Majid Khadduri, *supra note* 2, at 91.

[455]Karima Bennoune, *supra note* 449, at 633.

[456]*The Holy Qur'ān*, LXXVI: 8.

not forbidden in the land of unbelievers, and whatever is forbidden in the land of Islam, is also forbidden in the land of unbelievers. He who commits a forbidden act will receive the punishment prescribed by *Allāh* for his offence."[457] In this connection, Ahmed Zaki Yamani reported that "'Umar Ibn al-Khaṭṭāb heard that a Muslim soldier had said to a Persian combatant captive: Do not be afraid! then killed the Persian. Thereupon, 'Umar wrote to the commander of the army in these terms: "As *Allāh* is my witness, if I hear anyone has done this, I shall cut his neck.'"[458]

Nevertheless, right to life, prohibition of torture and inhuman treatment are also confirmed by contemporary Islamic human rights law. Article 1 of the Universal Islamic Declaration of Human Rights affirmed that "human life is sacred and inviolable and every effort shall be made to protect it."[459] Article 7 also emphasized the right to protection against torture. It states that "No person shall be subjected to torture in mind or body, or degraded, or threatened with injury either to himself or to anyone related to or held dear by him, or forcibly made to confess to the commission of a crime, or forced to consent to an act which is injurious to his interests."[460] The other Islamic document is the Cairo Declaration on Human Rights in Islam, of 1990. Articles 2 and 11 (a) of this declaration affirm right to life, protection from torture and inhuman treatment, while Article 3 confirms civilians' protection in time of war. Article 2 states that life is a God-given gift, and the right to life is guaranteed to every human being, and safety from bodily harm is a guaranteed right, and it is prohibited to breach it without a Sharī'a-prescribed reason.[461] Article 11 (a) maintains that human beings are born

---

[457]al-Shāfi'ī, *supra note* 21, at 7:322.

[458]Ahmed Zaki Yamani, *supra note* 42, at 202.

[459]Albert P. Blaustein, Roger S. Clark, and Jay A. Sigler, *supra note* 430, at 919.

[460]*Ibid.*, p. 920.

[461]*The Cairo Declaration on Human Rights in Islam.* (A/CONF. 157/PC/62/Add. 18) Annex to Res. No. 49/19-P, 9 June 1993. See Appendix VII: The Cairo Declaration on Human Rights in Islam".

free, and no one has the right to enslave, humiliate, oppress or exploit them.[462] Article 3 asserts that in the event of the use of force and in case of armed conflict, it is not permissible to kill non-belligerents such as old men, women and children. The wounded and the sick shall have the right to medical treatment, and prisoners of war shall have the right to be fed, sheltered and clothed. This article also prohibits the mutilation of dead bodies or the destruction of the enemy's civil properties.[463]

Ann Elizabeth Mayer criticized Article 2 and Article 11 (a). She described Article 2 as "loosely modelled on modern international law provisions."[464] She added that this article "is another instance where the authors went beyond the Islamic sources in fashioning their principles."[465] In her critique of Article 11 (a), Mayer said:

> "Article 11 (a) of the Cairo Declaration provides that no one has the right to enslave human beings - without any Islamic qualifications. This is emblematic of the selectivity with which rules taken from Islamic law have been resuscitated in Islamic human rights schemes. Slavery was a deeply ingrained feature of many Muslim societies and was extensively regulated in Islamic law."[466]

Comparing this commentary with the text of the two articles brings to our attention what was mentioned earlier that any interpretation of Islamic law out of its context is null and misleading. It is clear that Mayer has misunderstood Article 2 and distorted Article 11 (a). One may wonder about the accuracy and the obscurity of this critique. Article 11 (a) reads as follows: "Human beings are born free, and no one has the right to enslave, humiliate, oppress or exploit them, and there can be no

---

[462]*Ibid.*

[463]*Ibid.*

[464]Ann Elizabeth Mayer, "Universal Versus Islamic Human Rights: A Clash of Cultures or a Clash with a Construct?" *Michigan Journal of International Law* 15 (Winter 1994): 344.

[465]*Ibid.*

[466]*Ibid.*, p. 346.

subjugation but to God the Most High."[467] Subjugation to God does not mean, in any case, an Islamic qualification to enslave human beings. On the other hand, the institution of slavery was not established according to Islamic law. Slavery pre-dated Islam by thousands of years and has, as an institution, been the source of great suffering for Muslims, taken as war prisoners, and sold to slavery. Islamic humanitarian law regulated slavery with protective injunctions, which favoured the slave and ameliorated his status.[468] A slave is never called a slave in Islamic society but a brother. In this sense, the Prophet Muḥammad said: "They (the slaves) are your brothers, and whoever has a brother under his care, has to feed him and cloth him of the same food and cloth he eats and wears."[469] In point of fact, Islamic humanitarian law has laid down the rules regulating slavery, with an eye to its gradual disappearance.

2. Right to Respect of Religious Beliefs, Customs and Traditions

A human right, including religious liberty, is defined as the ability and freedom to perform an action, and religion is a collection of beliefs that every individual has the right to decide on and adopt.[470] Therefore, all individuals have the right to freedom of religion, including the right to choose one's religion. This right shall include the freedom of parents to ensure the religious and moral education of their children in conformity with their own convictions.[471] Contrary to the statement of Hurst Hannum that, "religion was certainly the most significant right among most groups until at least the eighteenth century,"[472] one can argue that religion is still the

---

[467]The Cairo Declaration on Human Rights in Islam, *supra note* 461.

[468]Ahmed Zaki Yamani, *supra note* 42, at 212.

[469]*Ibid.*, p. 213.

[470]Leonard Swidler, "Human Rights and Religious Liberty: From the Past to the Future," in *Religious Liberties and Human Rights in Nations and in Religions*, ed. Leonard Swidler (Philadelphia and New York: Ecumenical Press and Hippocrene Books, 1986), vii.

[471]Article 18(4) of the International Covenant on Civil and Political Rights, of 1966.

[472]Hurst Hannum, *Autonomy, Sovereignty, and Self-Determination: The Accommodation of Conflicting Rights* (Philadelphia: University of Pennsylvania Press, 1990), 50.

most significant distinction among societies, as most people still believe that religion is more than a set of beliefs, and often needs to be translated into actions.[473]

Respect for religious beliefs, in modern times, can be traced back to the Treaty of Westphalia, of 1648, which guaranteed equality of rights for both Roman Catholics and Protestants in Central Europe. In the aftermath of World War II, a new attitude towards human rights, including right to a religion, emerged. The United Nations Charter, of 1945 provides in Article 1 and 55, that universal respect shall be given to fundamental freedoms for all without distinction based on race, sex, language and religion. More concretely and without creating legal obligations, Article 18 of the Universal Declaration of Human Rights, which was adopted in Paris on 10 December 1948, states that, "everyone has the right to freedom of thought, conscience and religion; this right includes freedom to change his religion or belief, and freedom, either alone or in community with others and in public or private, to manifest his religion or belief in teaching, practice, worship and observance."[474] Moreover, Article 18 (1) of the International Covenant on Civil and Political Rights, of 1966, provides that, "everyone shall have the right to freedom of thought, conscience and religion. This right shall include freedom to have or to adopt a religion or belief of his choice, and freedom, either individually or in community with others and in public or private, to manifest his religion or belief in worship, observance, practice and teaching."[475]

A comparison of these two articles will show that the guarantee to freedom of religion in Article 18 (1) of the International Covenant on Civil and Political Rights

---

[473]For instance, many Muslims believe that *Sharī'a* is a comprehensive code, that includes ethics, worship and religious practices.

[474]Universal Declaration of Human Rights, *supra note* 431.

[475]International Covenant on Civil and Political Rights, *supra note* 433. Religiously speaking, *al-ḥijāb* (Islamic women's head cover) is considered a part of a Muslim woman's beliefs. The first controversy regarding the wearing of the *ḥijāb* in Quebec occurred in November 1993, when Quebec Judge Richard Alary asked Ms. Wafa Mousseyine to remove her *ḥijāb* in his court. In October 1994, Dania Baali, a tenth grade student at Ecole Regina Assumpta, a private Catholic girls' school, was told that she could not return to school the following year if she continued to wear the *ḥijāb*. In January 1995, a public primary school instructed parents to have their daughter remove her *ḥijāb* or change school.

was proclaimed in better terms. It clearly states that "this right shall include freedom to have and to adopt a religion or belief of his choice", not only "to manifest his religion or belief," as provided in Article 18 of the Universal Declaration of Human Rights.[476] On the other hand, it is obvious that there is an overlap between the two articles as regards protection of the right to disseminate religious ideas.[477]

In 1981, the General Assembly of the United Nations adopted the Declaration on the Elimination of all Forms of Intolerance and of Discrimination Based on Religion or Belief. The eighth articles of the Declaration confirm, in line with the previous declarations, that discrimination between human beings on the grounds of religion or belief constitutes an affront to human dignity and should be condemned as a violation of human rights. The United Nations Commission on Human Rights willingly approved the draft of the Declaration on the Rights of Persons Belonging to National or Ethnic, Religious and Linguistic Minorities, which was adopted by the General Assembly on 18 December 1992. Article 1 of the Declaration requires State Parties to encourage conditions for the promotion of the religious identity of minorities and to adopt appropriate legislation towards its realization.[478] In Article 2 (B) of Part II of the Vienna Declaration and Programme of Action on Human Rights, of 25 June 1993, the World Conference on Human Rights urged States and the international community to promote and protect the rights of persons belonging to national, ethnic, religious and linguistic minorities. The Vienna Declaration contains six paragraphs devoted specifically to racism, racial discrimination, xenophobia and other forms of intolerance.[479]

---

[476]Karl Josef Partsch, "Fundamental Principles of Human Rights: Self-Determination, Equality and Non-Discrimination," in *The International Dimensions of Human Rights*, 2 vols., ed. Karl Vasak (Westport, Connecticut: Greenwood Press, 1982), 1: 83.

[477]Brice Dickson, "The United Nations and Freedom of Religion," *International and Comparative Law Quarterly* 44:2 (April 1995): 340.

[478]*Declaration on the Rights of Persons Belonging to National or Ethinc, Religious and Linguistic Minorities*, G.A. E/1992/22, Chap. II, Section A.

[479]*Vienna Declaration and Programme of Action on Human Rights*, Doc. A/CONF, 157/24 (Part 1), 13 Oct. 1993.

Examining the documents of international law on armed conflict, one may find that the Annex to the 1907 Hague Convention IV Respecting the Laws and Customs of War on Land, the 1949 Geneva Convention IV Relative to the Protection of Civilian Persons in Times of War, as well as the 1977 Additional Protocol I and Protocol II to the same convention, have recognized and respected the individuals' rights to thought, conscience and religion. Article 46 of the Annex to the 1907 Hague Convention IV Respecting the Laws and Customs of War on Land confirms that family honour and rights, as well as religious convictions and practice, must be respected.[480] Articles 27 and 93 of the 1949 Geneva Convention IV Relative to the Protection of Civilian Persons in Time of War proclaim that protected persons are entitled, in all circumstances, to respect for their religious convictions and practices, and their manners and customs.[481] Article 53 of the 1977 Geneva Protocol I Additional to the Geneva Conventions of 12 August 1949, and Article 16 of Protocol II Additional to the same conventions, prohibit the committing of any acts of hostility directed against historic monuments, works of art or places of worship which constitute a people's cultural or spiritual heritage.[482]

In spite of these fine-sounding ideals, the extent of state violations of religious freedom remains frighteningly high. Human rights Watch World Report 1995 notes that "hatred and violence along ethnic and religious lines continued to pose the paramount threat to human rights world-wide: genocide in Rwanda; ethnic war in Bosnia; the Indian government's failure to prosecute police for participating in attacks on Muslims; violence by Islamist movements, which was, in turn, aggravated by Middle Eastern governments' denial of political freedoms; the Egyptian government's clash with Islamist militants; and the raging violence in Algeria."[483]

---

[480] Adam Roberts and Richard Guelff, *supra note* 438, at 56.

[481] *Ibid.*, 282 and 303.

[482] *Ibid.*, p. 417 and 456.

[483] *Human Rights Watch World Report 1995: Events of 1994* (New York: Human Rights Watch 1995), XIX.

However, in his book on autonomy and self-determination, Hurst Hannum concludes that: "A distinctive system of ensuring a certain degree of cultural and religious autonomy was the "*millet*" system developed by the Ottoman Empire. The *millets* generally followed religious lines, with each religious community (the most important being the Orthodox, Armenian, and Jewish) having the authority to regulate such matters as personal status and inheritance."[484] This statement can be interpreted in light of the Islamic concept of rights of non-Muslims to freedom of religious beliefs, customs and traditions. Islamic international law considers this freedom as a component of opinion and expression. Consequently, everyone has the right to choose a religion, which suits his/her personal inclinations. This freedom is guaranteed by the *Holy Qur'ān*, *Sunna*, and by the order of early Muslim Caliphs to commanders in the battlefield.[485] Religious liberty is grounded in the *Holy Qur'ān* in the following verses: "Let there be no compulsion in religion," [486] and "Wilt thou then compel mankind against their will to believe."[487]

Moreover, Islamic law respects non-Muslim customs, traditions and places of worship. In their own towns and cities, non-Muslims have full freedom to practice their customs and traditions, as well as to celebrate their holy days and communal festivals. Non-Muslim places of worship are not to be interfered with and are well-protected in times of peace and war. Furthermore, if these places are damaged or destroyed in one way or another, they should be rebuilt or repaired.[488] Jews and Christians "the People of the Book" have a respected position and special status in Islamic international law. Muslims are ordered by the *Holy Qur'ān* to treat them and argue with them gently. This issue is addressed in this Qur'anic verse: "And

---

[484]Hurst Hannum, *supra note* 472, at 50-51.

[485]Ahmad Farrag, *supra note* 442, at 137.

[486]*The Holy Qur'ān*, II: 256.

[487]*Ibid.*, X: 99.

[488]Sayyid Abul A'lā Mawdūdī, *The Islamic Law and Constitution*, trans., Khurshīd Ahmad (Lahore, Pakistan: Islamic Publications Ltd., 1960), 309.

dispute ye not with the People of the Book except with means better."[489] Moreover, in the speech cited earlier, Abū Bakr al-Ṣiddīq, instructed the Muslim fighters, saying: "...You are likely to pass by people who have devoted their lives to monastic services; leave them to that to which they have devoted their lives."[490]

Similarly, in his peace treaty with the people of *Bayt al-Maqdis* (Jerusalem), 'Umar Ibn al-Khaṭṭāb, the second Muslim Caliph, gave them a guarantee that their churches and crosses, would not be used by Muslims, or damaged or diminished in number, and that they would not be forced to abandon their faith.[491] When 'Umar visited Jerusalem to sign the peace treaty, he saw a huge building almost filled up with earth, and when he was informed that the building was a Jewish temple buried by the Roman army, he initiated removing the earth with his hands along with other Muslim soldiers until they cleaned it and asked the Jews to use it.[492] 'Amr Ibn al-'Āṣ, did the same with the Egyptians. He guaranteed that their churches and crosses, would not be damaged or interfered with.[493] Abdullahi An-Na'im affirms that the "Muslim Arabs showed promising signs of religious tolerance and political accommodation for the indigenous Coptic population."[494] In the pact issued by the Prophet Muḥammad and his successors to the people of Najrān, they affirmed that the people of Najrān "shall have the protection of *Allāh* and the guarantee of Muḥammad, the Apostle of *Allāh*, that they shall be secured in their lives, property, lands, creed, those absent and those present, their buildings and their churches. No

---

[489]Mohamed Talbi, "Religious Liberty: A Muslim Perspective," in *Religious Liberty and Human Rights in Nations and in Religions*, ed. Leonard Swidler (Philadelphia and New York: Ecumenical Press and Hippocrene Books, 1986), 186; See *The Holy Qur'ān*, XXIX: 46.

[490]Waldemar A. Solf, *supra note* 202, at 118.

[491]Zakariyya al-Birrī, "al-Islām wa Ḥuqūq al-Insān: Ḥaqq al-Ḥurriyyah" *'Ālam al-Fikr* 1:4 (January, February and March 1971), 115.

[492]*Ibid.*

[493] Zakariyya al-Birrī, *supra note* 491. See also Appendix V: The Treaty of Egypt "Mu'āhadat Ahl Miṣr".

[494]Abdullahi Ahmed An-Na'im, "Religious Freedom in Egypt under the Shadow of the Islamic *Dhimma* System," in *Religious Liberty and Human Rights in Nations and in Religions*, ed. Leonard Swidler (Philadelphia and New York: Ecumenical Press and Hippocrene Books, 1986), 50.

bishop or monk shall be displaced from his parish or monastery and no priest shall be forced to abandon his priestly life. All their belongings little or much, remain theirs."[495]

On the other hand, Articles 10 and 13 of the Universal Islamic Declaration of Human Rights, of 1981, affirms that religious rights of non-Muslim minorities are governed by the Qur'anic principle: "There is no compulsion in religion", and those minorities have the choice whether to be governed in respect of their civil and personal matters by Islamic law or by their own laws. According to his or her religious beliefs, every person has the right to freedom of conscience and worship.[496] Article 10 of the Cairo Declaration on Human Rights in Islam emhasized the prohibition of exercising any form of compulsion on anyone to convert him or her to another religion or belief.[497]

To this end, one may conclude that Islamic humanitarian law, under the doctrine of *jihād*, has affirmed and protected all personal individual rights, for all people, without distinction as to race, sex, language or religion. Islamic law which rests on two universal human principles, *al-'adl* (justice) and *al-iḥsān* (kindness), has recognized equality and justice as two sides of the same coin, and concluded that all rights become of little value when any of those who have a right cannot secure a remedy.[498] Accordingly, it must be emphasized that all personal individual

---

[495]Majid Khadduri, *supra note* 2, at 279-280; Muhammad Hamidullah, *supra note* 253, at 145. See also Appendix II: The Pact of Najrān "'Ahd Najrān".

[496]Albert P. Blaustein, Roger S. Clark and Jay A. Sigler, *supra note* 430 at 920-921. See also Appendix VI: Universal Islamic Declaration of Human Rights.

[497]The Cairo Declaration on Human Rights in Islam, *supra note* 461.

[498]Lateef Adegbite, "Human Rights in Islamic Law," *The Journal of Islamic and Comparative Law* 7 (1977): 9. Furthermore, human rights in Islamic international law are based on the premise that these rights are considered necessary (*ḍarūrāt*) and essential to the preservation of world public order. These rights include: respect of religious beliefs, customs and traditions (*ḥifẓ al-dīn*); right to life, and prohibition of torture and inhuman treatment (*ḥifẓ al-nafs*); children's right to life, custody and education (*ḥifẓ al-nasl*); the right to individual ownership and private property (*ḥifẓ al-māl*); and the right to freedom of thought, opinion and expression (*ḥifẓ al-ᶜaql*). These rights are protected by (*al-ḥudūd*), which are penalties established by *Allāh* and left a judge no discretionary authority.

See Abū Ḥāmid al-Ghazālī, *Shifā' al-Ghalīl fī Bayān al-Shabah wal-Mukhīl wa Masālik al-Ta'līl*, ed. Ḥamad al-Kubaisī (Baghdād: Maṭba'at al-Irshād, 1971). 160; Abū Isḥāq al-Shāṭibī, *al-Muwāfaqāt fī Usūl al- Sharī'a*, ed. Muḥammad 'Abdullāh Darrāz, 4 vols. (Beirut: Dār al-Ma'rifa,

rights are not realized through the Islamic principle of equality alone, but are also accompanied by a system of legal and administrative rules, which are designed to ensure their application and implied that any violation of these rights should be brought before a judge.[499]

n.d.), 1: 38; Abū al-Ma'ālī al-Juwaynī, *al-Burhān fī Usūl al-Fiqh*, ed. 'Abdul 'Aẓīm al-Dīb, 2 vols. (al-Qāhira: Dār al-Anṣār, 1400 A.H.), 2: 1151; Aḥmad al-Raysūnī, *Naẓariyyat al-Maqāṣid 'ind al-Imām al-Shāṭibī* (Beirut: al-Mu'ssasa al-Jāmi'iyya lil-Dirāsāt wal-Nashr wal-Tawzī, 1992), 139-141; Hammādī al-'Ubaydī, *al-Shāṭibī wa Maqāṣid al-Sharī'a* (Tripoli, Libya: Manshūrāt Kulliyyat al-Da'wa al-Islāmiyya, 1992), 123-129.

[499]Abdur Rahman O. Olayiwola, "Human Rights in Islam," *The Islamic Quarterly* 36:4 (1992): 272.

Chapter Four
Is Jihād a Just War?

The word *jihād* might be one of the most misinterpreted terms in the history of Islamic legal discourse. However, discussion of the doctrine of *jihād* as *bellum justum* cannot easily proceed without first giving a clear definition of this term within its historical context. Therefore, this chapter will examine chronologically the relevant primary sources of both Islamic and public international law.

1. Just War in Western Legal Discourse

It is a well-known fact that a distinction between just and unjust war has been made since antiquity. Even primitive people have recognized that if war was waged under certain conditions, and with certain methods, it would be a just war; and if it were waged under different circumstances, it could be unjust.[500] The term *bellum justum* has existed in the works of the Greek philosophers Plato and Aristotle, while ancient Roman used *jus fetiale*.[501] Aristotle, for his part, concluded that war should be waged only for the sake of peace. He outlined three cases:[502] self-defense; to establish hegemony over those who would thereby be benefited; and to set up

[500]Hasan Moinuddin, *supra note* 50, at 26; William Ballis, *The Legal Position of War Changes in Its Practice and Theory from Plato to Vattel* (The Hague, The Netherlands: Martinus Nijhoff Publishers, 1937), 1.

[501]Josef L. Kunz, *supra note* 93, at 530; William Ballis, *supra note* 500, at 21.

[502]William Ballis, *supra note* 500, at 19.

political control over those nations that deserve to be enslaved.[503]

Nevertheless, the mediaeval concept of international relations has changed considerably from the form it took in ancient Greece and Rome. In the mediaeval times, the doctrine of *bellum justum* was painted with a theological brush, and developed by Saint Augustine and Saint Thomas Aquinas, who held that a just war was one which had a *causa justa.*[504] Influenced by the divine law,[505] Saint Aquinas mentioned three criteria for a just war: the authority of the prince; the just cause; and the right intent.[506] Furthermore, he distinguished seven kinds of war, four of which were just and three unjust. The just wars are: *bellum romanum*, waged by believers against infidels; *bellum judicale*, waged by the believers who have the authority of a judge; *bellum licitum*, waged on the authority of a prince; and *bellum necessarium*, waged by believers in self-defense. The unjust wars are: *bellum praesumptuosum*, waged by rebels; *bellum temerarium*, waged by believers against legal authority; and *bellum voluntarium*, waged by believers on their own authority.[507] In similar terms, Franciscus de Victoria stated three unjust causes of war: differences in religion, extension of empires, and personal ambitions of princes.[508]

At a later period, the concept of just war was secularized and extracted from its theological soil by Gentili, Grotius and the *jus gentium* writers of the seventeenth

---

[503]W.L. Newman, *The Politics of Aristotle*, 4 vols. (Oxford: The Clarendon Press, 1887), 1:328.

[504]Joan D. Tooke, *The Just War in Aquinas and Grotius* (London: S.P.C.K., 1965), 10; Lisa Sowle Cahill, *supra note* 26, at 384; M.H. Keen, *The Laws of War in the Late Middle Ages* (London: Routledge & Kegan Paul, 1965), 66; Paul Ramsey, "The Just War According to St. Augustine," in *Just War Theory*, ed. Jean Bethke Elshtain (New York: New York University Press, 1992), 8.

[505]*The Holy Scriptures*, Deuteronomy 20:10.

[506]A. Vanderpol, *La doctrine scolastique du droit de la guerre* (Paris: A Pedone, 1925), 56; G. Butler and S. Maccoby, *The Development of International Law* (London: Longmans, Green & Co., 1926), 4.

[507]C.L. Lange, *Histoire de l'internationalisme* (Kristiana: H. Aschenhoug & Co., 1919), 44; Ernest Nys, *Les origines du droit international* (Bruxelles and Paris: Alfred Castaigne and Thorin & Fils, 1894), 102; Thomas Aquinas, *Summa Theologica*, trans. Fathers of the English Dominican Province (New York: Benziger Brothers, 1917), 40; William Ballis, *supra note* 500, at 50.

[508]Franciscus de Victoria, *De Indis et de jure belli relectiones*, trans. H.F. Wright (Washington, D.C.: Carnegie Institution, 1917), 170.

and eighteenth centuries.[509] Hugo Grotius, a distinguished writer on the subject of war during the seventeenth century, led a legal reform movement. He argued that war was a legal right, while to preceding writers it was simply a historical fact. In his book *De jure belli ac pacis*, Grotius reached this idea by fusing natural law with the *jus gentium*.[510] According to him, there are three just causes of war: defense of self, recovery of property, and inflicting of punishment. In other words, Gtotius' justification of war was mainly based on the fundamental morality of self-defense. Thus, just war could be either a war of self-defense against the *injustus aggressor* or a war of execution to enforce one's right.[511]

By the twentieth century, following the Hague Conventions of 1899 and 1907, the Covenant of the League of Nations, of 1919, the Kellogg-Briand Pact (Pact of Paris), of 1925, and the United Nations Charter, of 1945, legal developments came to represent a new trend in the concept of just war. Writers divorced the *bellum justum* doctrine from natural law, and unanimously introduced it into the norms of positive international law, as represented by the above treaties.[512] Consequently, the terms just and unjust were replaced by legal and illegal; the concept of war was replaced by "the threat or use of force"; and peace and security were emphasized more than justice.[513]

---

[509]H. Kelsen and Robert Tucker, *Principles of International Law* (New York: Holt, Reinhart and Winston, 1966), 30; I. Brownlie, *International Law and the Use of Force by States* (Oxford: The Clarendon Press, 1963), 9; Lisa Sowle Cahill, *supra note* 26, at 394-396.

[510]Benedict Kingsbury and Adam Roberts, "Introduction: Grotian Thought in International Relations," in *Hugo Grotius and International Relations*, eds. Hedley Bull, Benedict Kingsbury, and Adam Roberts (Oxford: The Clarendon Press, 1990), 16-26; Hamilton Vreeland, *Hugo Grotius: The Father of the Modern Science of International Law* (New York: Oxford University Press, 1917), 171; Lord McNair and A. D. Watts, *supra note* 106, at 3; Michael Walzer, *Just and Unjust Wars: A Moral Argument with Historical Illustrations* (New York: Basic Books, Inc., Publishers, 1977), 168; William Ballis, *supra note* 500, at 110.

[511]Joan D. Tooke, *supra note* 504, at 219; Josef L. Kunz, *supra note* 93, at 530; Peter Haggenmacher, *Grotius et la doctrine de la guerre juste* (Paris: Presses Universitaires de France, 1983), 148-151; Robert L. Holmes, "Can War Be Morally Justified? The Just War Theory," in *Just War Theory*, ed. Jean Bethke Elshtain (New York: New York University Press, 1992), 202.

[512]D.W. Bowett, *Self-Defense in International Law* (Manchester: Manchester University Press, 1958), 7; Joan D. Tooke, *supra note* 504, at 232; Josef L. Kunz, *supra note* 93, at 532.

[513]Hans Kelsen, *The Law of the United Nations: A Critical Analysis of its Fundamental Problems*

As a matter of fact, war was not declared unlawful under the Covenant of the League of Nations. It was classified into legal and illegal wars instead of being categorized into just and unjust wars, according to the classical doctrine under natural law. The right to take military action against a state, which has resorted to illegal war, is embodied in Article (16) of the Covenant. In this case, the action is taken against an illegal belligerent not an *injustus aggressor*. [514] Article (1) of the Kellogg-Briand Pact condemned, in the name of the High Contracting Parties, recourse to war for the solution of international controversies, and renounced it as an instrument of national policy in their relations with one another.[515]

However, the failure of the Covenant of the League of Nations and the Kellogg-Briand Pact to maintain international peace and security, suggested to the drafters of the United Nations Charter that renunciation of all kinds of war was not possible. Although Article 2 (paragraph 4) of the Charter prohibited the threat or use of force against the territorial integrity or political independence of any state, Article (51) of the same Charter stated that force can be resorted to in the exercise of the right of self-defence. Hence, under this Article, force can legally be used against an armed attack until the Security Council takes the necessary measures. It is clear from this Article, as well as from Article 1 (paragraph 1) of the same Charter that the main purpose is to maintain international peace and security, not to achieve and maintain justice.[516] Generally speaking, the Charter definitely distinguished between legal

---

(New York: F.A. Praeger, 1950), 732; Josef L. Kunz, *supra note* 93, at 533; Yahuda Melzer, *Concepts of Just War* (Leyden, The Netherlands: Sijthoff International Publishing Company, 1975), 17.

[514]Hans Kelsen and Robert Tucker, *supra note* 509, at 34; I. Brownlie, *supra note* 509, at 57; Josef L. Kunz, *supra note* 93, at 532; L. Oppenheim, *supra note* 91, at 2:133; Myres Smith McDougal, *Law and Minimum World Order: The Legal Regulation and International Coercion* (New Haven: Yale University Press, 1961), 138.

[515]D.W. Bowett, *supra note* 512, at 133; Hans Kelsen and Robert Tucker, *supra note* 509; at 37; I. Brownlie, *supra note* 509, at 34; L. Oppenheim, *supra note* 91, at 2:157; Leon Friedman, *supra note* 97, at 1:468.

[516]Hans Kelsen, *supra note* 513, at 733; Louis Henkin, "Force, Intervention, and Neutrality in Contemporary International Law," *Procceding of the American Society of International Law* (1963): 155; Robert W. Tucker, "The Interpretation of War," *The International Law Quarterly* 4:1 (1951): 21.

and illegal wars, and gave the member states, by exercising their right of individual or collective self-defense, the right to resort to a justified war.[517] In light of the foregoing analysis, one may understand that the concept of war as *bellum justum* has existed in the Western legal discourse, both classical and modern, under different terms. Just war, in the Western legal discourse, can be either a war of self-defense against the *injustus aggressor* or a war waged for *causa justa*.

2. Jihād as a Just War

To this end, two questions come to mind: was *jihād* the *bellum justum* of Islam? and if so, can a *jihād* be waged by contemporary Muslim States, although they are members of the United Nations?

Historically speaking, Ibn Khaldūn used the terms "just" and "unjust" to distinguish between wars. According to him, wars could be either *ḥurūb jihād wa 'adl* (just wars) or *ḥurūb baghī* (unjust wars).[518] Unlike mediaeval Western doctors, Muslim jurists did not justify wars for such worldly purposes as territorial expansion, imposing their religion on unbelievers, or supporting a particular social regime.[519] The classical sources of Islamic legal theory maintain that all kinds of warfare are outlawed except the *jihād*, which is an exceptional war waged by Muslims to defend the freedom of religious belief for all humanity, and constitutes a deterrent against aggression, injustice and corruption.[520] This does not mean,

---

[517]Josef L. Kunz, *supra note* 100, at 876.

[518]'Abd al-Raḥmān Ibn Khaldūn, *supra note* 22, at 271.

[519]Among wars, which were justified by Saint Thomas Aquinas, was a war waged by believers against infidels. Furthermore, sixteenth century writers claimed that, under natural law and the *jus gentium*, that a just war can be waged to enforce a natural right including the right to travel and to conduct trade. According to Josef L. Kunz, it is exactly the natural right that ultimately justified the conquest of America. At a later time, Franciscus de Victoria rejected the arguments advanced by the Spanish Emperor's legislators in justifying the slaughter of the Indians and the occupation of their land. Those legislators claimed that the Indians belonged to a race lower than the Spanish, and consequently, there was no reason why the Spaniards should not occupy their land. See Franciscus de Victoria, *supra note* 508, at 116-165; Gerhard von Glahn, *supra note* 95, at 38; Josef L. Kunz, *supra note* 93, at 532; L. Oppenehim, *supra note* 91, at 1:104.

[520]Muḥammad Abū Zahra, *supra note* 182, at 18; Rasā'il Ibn Taymiyya, *supra note* 21, at 123; Rudolph Peters, *supra note* 11, at 122; Sobhi Mahmassani, *supra note* 1, at 279.

however, that Muslims have never waged unjust wars. The reason for this can be found in the conduct of Muslim commanders, not in the norms of Islamic law.[521]

There is considerable support for the belief that the norms of international humanitarian law adopted in more recent international agreements were in fact endorsed by Islamic international law fifteen centuries ago. In this connection, Ernest Nys argues that the early Spaniards derived their notion of the rules of war from Islamic Law, particularly, the rules included in *Las siete partidas*, written under the patronage of King Alphonse X, by the the Castilian jurists Ruiz, Martinez and Roland between 1256 and 1265. This document described as a monument to legal science, deals with the laws of war, legislation, politics and penal law.

Moreover, one can trace the influence of Islamic law on public international law by examining its impact on the works of early European philosophers and godfathers of public international law. Alfred Guillaume asserts that Thomas Aquinas was very familiar with the Arabic legal works, and drew heavily from them in composing his *Summa Theologica*. Aquinas was most influenced by the works of al-Ghazālī and Ibn Rushd. In a lecture to the Academy of Political Science, at the Hague in 1926, Le Baron Michel de Taube stated that "les diverses institutions dans la civilisation du Moyen âge européen portent une empreinte indélébile sinon de leur origine purement et simplement orientale, du moins de leur forte dépendance des institutions militaires analogues de l'Orient musulman." Furthermore, Scott argues that the ideas expressed in "*De jure belli ac pacis libritres*," by the Dutch jurist Hugo Grotius, were taken from the Spanish jurists Francisco de Victoria and Francisco Suárez. In turn, the latter derived their ideas from Islamic law, as they themselves acknowledged.[522]

---

[521]Hasan Moinuddin, *supra note* 50, at 28; Marcel A. Boisard, *supra note* 190, at 6; Rudolph Peters, *supra note* 11, at 123.

[522]Alfred Guillaume, "Philosophy and Theology," in *The Legacy of Islam*, eds. Thomas Arnold and Alfred Guillaume (London: Oxford University Press, 1931), 273-281; A. Nussbaum, *A Concise History of the Law of Nations* (New York: Macmillan, 1954), 52; C.G. Weeramantry, *Islamic Jurisprudence: An International Perspective* (London: Macmillan, 1988), 157; Ernest Nys, *supra note* 507, at 209; J.B. Scott, *Classics of International Law* (New York: Oceana Publications, 1939), 17-21; Le Baron Michel de Taube, *supra note* 414, at 384; Marcel A. Boisard, "On the Probable Influence of Islam on Western Public and International Law," *International Journal of Middle East*

Moreover, Islamic international law regulates conduct during *jihād* on the basis of certain humane principles, compatible with those upon which modern international conventions are based. These rules include: preparedness, fortification, reciprocity, avoidance of non-military elements,[523] treatment and exchange of prisoners of war,[524] protection of civilians during war, as well as peaceful settlements, treaties and neutrality. In other words, Islamic international law outlines a clear and firm distinction between combatants and non-combatants in times of war.[525] Muslim soldiers are instructed to regard as 'neutral' places of worship, residential areas, and medical personnel. Furthermore, they are strictly forbidden the following: waging *jihād* until all peaceful options have been exhausted;[526] using poisoned weapons or weapons of mass destruction;[527] delivering a *coup de grâce* to the wounded;[528] killing an enemy *hors de combat*;[529] and mutilating dead bodies.[530]

Although it would be hard to dispute the fact that the idea of just war existed

---

Studies 2 (1980): 445.

Generally speaking, however, the contributions made by Islamic law have been marginalized by Western jurists involved in the development of public international law. This phenomenon was noted by Marcel A. Boisard, who argues that "there are many explanations for the general refusal of European authors to recognise their borrowings from the Muslim World. We must first mention human vanity. The most general explanation aside from the fact that most European writers of the time never referred to their sources - lies in the religious prejudice, even fanaticism of a West that could not admit to itself that it owed anything to the 'infidel'. This prejudice prevented any just appraisal of the contribution of Islamic culture." Marcel A. Boisard, *op. cit.*, 446.

[523]al-Kāsānī, *supra note* 21, at 7:100-102; al-Marghīnānī, *supra note* 21, at 2:144; al-Siyar al-Kabī r, *supra note* 67 at 1:38-45.

[524]Ibn Ḥanbal, *supra note* 402, at 4:152.

[525]al-Bukhārī, *supra note* 66, at 4:21; Ibn Ḥanbal, *supra note* 402, at 3:152; Ibn Rushd, *supra note* 21, at I:304; al-Kurdi, *supra note* 32, at 109; al-Mughnī, *supra note* 21, at 10:542.

[526]al-Sarakhsī, *supra note* 21, at 10:31; al-Siyar al-Kabīr, *supra note* 67, at 1:78.

[527]Marcel A. Boisard, *supra note* 190, at 13.

[528]Nahj al-Balāgha, *supra note* 196, at 3:425.

[529]*Ibid.*

[530]Abū Dāwūd, *supra note* 197, at 2:59; al-Shawkānī, *supra note* 192, at 7:262.

before Islam, one has no difficulty seeing that this notion has been developed and refined by Muslim jurists. It becomes evident from the preceding study that *jihād*, in the form of armed struggle, must be just in its causes, defensive in its initiative, decent in its conduct and peaceful in its conclusion.[531] Hence, as a defensive war, *jihād* can be exercised individually or collectively by contemporary Muslim States, since such type of war is definitely sanctioned by the norms of international law, particularly the United Nations Charter.

[531] John Kelsay, "Religion, Morality, and the Governance of War: The Case of Classical Islam," *Religious Ethics* 18:2 (Fall 1990): 135; Marcel A. Boisard, *supra note* 190, at 7.

Conclusion

This thesis has shown that peace is the rule and war is the exception in the doctrine of *jihād*, and that no obligatory state of war exists between Muslims and the rest of the world. Nor is *jihād* to be waged until the world has either accepted the Islamic faith or submitted to the power of the Islamic State. Furthermore, there is no exact equivalent in Islamic legal discourse to the concept of "holy war" in Western Christendom, nor is there resemblance between the concept of *jihād*, as a collective religious duty, and the Christian concept of crusade. Thus, the description of *jihād* as "holy war" is most misleading.

Jihād is a defensive war launched with the aim of establishing justice, equity and protecting basic human rights. Accordingly, Islamic humanitarian law strictly lays down a number of humane rules compatible with those established by international humanitarian law governing the conduct of war and the treatment of enemy persons and property.

It has also been shown that the dividing of the world into *dār al-Islām* and *dār al-ḥarb* by Muslim jurists, was dictated by particular events and did not necessitate a permanent state of hostility between these territories. Basing themselves on the doctrine of *jihād*, Muslim jurists tried to develop an Islamic theory of international relations, in the modern sense of the term, to regulate inter-state relations between *dār al-Islām* and other territories in times of peace and war. In this respect, Islamic law insists on honouring treaties even above honouring religious solidarity. In other words, if the *Imām* concludes a treaty with the enemy, this treaty is binding upon all

Muslims, who are thus prohibited from assisting their fellow believers if this assistance is in violation of a treaty of mutual alliance.

Moreover, since the beginning of the seventh century, Islamic international law has played a significant role in protecting the personal, economic, judicial and political rights of civilians during armed conflicts. It has introduced a human revolution, consisting of a number of human principles, as early as fourteen centuries before the drafting of the Universal Declaration of Human Rights in 1948, and eight centuries before the appearance of Grotius, the godfather of European international law. These claims have been acknowledged by a number of European scholars who have emphasized the fact that Islamic international law has made great contributions to international humanitarian law. Indeed, occasionally the substantive postulates of Islamic humanitarian law exceed the norms decreed by the Hague and the Geneva Conventions. Consequently, the principles of human rights used in international humanitarian law are not only the product of Western civilization, but also the experiences and teachings of non-European peoples, whose traditions have also made great contributions.

In sum, by carrying this study to its conclusion we find that there is a unique relationship between *jihād* and the notion of just war. Thus, *jihād* should be recognized as the *bellum justum* of Islam, and Lewis-Huntington's notion of "Muslim bloody borders" should be seen as inaccurate and groundless.

Appendices

Appendix I

The Treaty of Medina *(Ṣaḥīfat al-Madīnah)* [532]

IN THE NAME OF ALLAH, MOST COMPASSIONATE, MOST MERCIFUL

1. This agreement of Allāh's Prophet Muḥammad (S.A.W.) shall apply to the migrants, Quraysh, the citizens of Yathrib (*al-Madīnah*) who have accepted Islam and all such people who are in agreement with the above mentioned bodies and side with them in *Jihād*.

2. Those who are a party to this agreement shall be treated as a body separate from all those who are not a party to this agreement.

3. The Quraysh migrants are in themselves a party and as in the past; shall be responsible for the payment of blood-money (*Fidyah*) on behalf of their criminals and shall themselves get their prisoners freed, after the payment of ransom. All this process shall be in accordance with the principles of belief (*Imān)* and justice.

4. Banū 'Awf shall be responsible for their own tribe and shall jointly pay their blood-money (*Fidyah*) in accordance with article 3 and shall themselves be responsible for getting their prisoners freed after paying ransom. All this work shall be completed in conformity with the principle of honesty and justice.

---

[532] al-Ansāb, *supra note* 373, at 1:286; al-Bukhārī, *supra note* 66, at 3:49; Ibn Hishām, *supra note* 67, at 2:106-108; Ibn Isḥāq, *supra note* 84, at 198; Ibn Kathīr, *supra note* 72, at 3:224-226; Khadduri, *supra note* 50, at 206-209; al-Maqrīzī, *supra note* 253, at 1:49, 104 and 107; Muhammad Hamidullah, "The First Written Constitution of the World," *Islamic Review* (1941):442-448; Reuben Levy, *The Social Structure of Islam* (Cambridge, UK: Cambridge University Press, 1979), 273-275; *The Treaty of Medina,* online: Islamic Gateway <http://www.ummah.org.uk/science/letters.htm>(Access date: 8 November 2000).

5. Banū al-Ḥārith shall be responsible for their own tribe and shall jointly pay their blood-money (*Fidyah*) in accordance with article 3 and shall themselves be responsible for getting their prisoners freed after paying ransom. All this work shall be completed in conformity with the principle of honesty and justice.

6. Banū Sā'idah shall be responsible for their own tribe and shall jointly pay their blood-money (*Fidyah*) in accordance with article 3 and shall themselves be responsible for getting their prisoners freed after paying ransom. All this work shall be completed in conformity with the principle of honesty and justice.

7. Banū Jusham shall be responsible for their own tribe and shall jointly pay their blood-money (*Fidyah*) in accordance with article 3 and shall themselves be responsible for getting their prisoners freed after paying ransom. All this work shall be completed in conformity with the principle of honesty and justice.

8. Banū al-Najjār shall be responsible for their own tribe and shall jointly pay their blood-money (*Fidyah*) in accordance with article 3 and shall themselves be responsible for getting their prisoners freed after paying ransom. All this work shall be completed in conformity with the principle of honesty and justice.

9. Banū 'Amr Ibn 'Awf shall be responsible for their own tribe and shall jointly pay their blood-money (*Fidyah*) in accordance with article 3 and shall themselves be responsible for getting their prisoners freed after paying ransom. All this work shall be completed in conformity with the principle of honesty and justice.

10. Banū al-Nabīt shall be responsible for their own tribe and shall jointly pay their blood-money (*Fidyah*) in accordance with article 3 and shall themselves be responsible for getting their prisoners freed after paying ransom. All this work shall be completed in conformity with the principle of honesty and justice.

11. Banū al-Aws shall be responsible for their own tribe and shall jointly pay their blood-money (*Fidyah*) in accordance with article 3 and shall themselves be responsible for getting their prisoners freed after paying ransom. All this work shall be completed in conformity with the principle of honesty and justice.

12. If from amongst the Muslims, an indigent person is guilty of an offence, in which blood-money (*Fidyah*) becomes due or he is taken prisoner and is unable to pay ransom; it shall be incumbent on other Muslims to pay blood-money or ransom on his behalf and get him freed, in order that virtue and sympathy in the mutual relationship of the Muslims may be created.

13. No Muslim shall be hostile to the slave set free by another Muslim.

14. It shall be the duty of the Muslims to oppose openly every such person as created mischief and riot and troubles human beings or forcibly wants to grab something and resorts to oppression. All the Muslims shall remain mutually united in punishing such a person, even if he is the son of anyone of them.

15. No Muslim shall have the right of killing another Muslim in exchange of an infidel (who is at war) or assist a person who is at war with the Muslims.

16. The promise of Allāh, responsibility and protection are all one and the same. This means that if a Muslim gives refuge to someone, it shall be incumbent on all Muslims to honour it; although the Muslim providing the refuge may be a plebeian. All the Muslims are brethren amongst themselves, as compared to others.

17. It is incumbent on all the Muslims to help and extend sympathetic treatment to the Jews who have entered into an agreement with us. Neither an oppression of any type should be perpetrated on them nor should their enemy be helped against them.

18. The truce of all the Muslims shall be one: When there is a war in the way of Allah; none of the Muslims leaving aside other Muslims, shall enter into a peace treaty with an enemy, unless the treaty in one and the same for all the Muslims.

19. All the groups who participate in war along with us, shall be afforded an opportunity to rest by turns.

20. The provision of subsistence to the dependants of the Muslim who get martyred in the way of Allāh, shall be the responsibility of all the Muslims.

21. No doubt all the Allāh-fearing and devout Muslims are on the right path and are the followers of the best way of life.

22. Neither shall any non-Muslim who is a party to this agreement, provide refuge to the life and property of any Quraysh nor shall assist any non-Muslim against a Muslim.

23. If someone murders a Muslim and there is a proof against him, the murderer shall be punished. But if the next of kin is prepared to accept blood-money (*Fidyah*), the murderer could be set free after the payment of blood-money. It shall be obligatory on all the Muslims to observe this injunction without any exception. Nothing other than the prescribed injunctions shall be acceptable.

24. For a Muslim, who after accepting the treaty, has agreed to abide by it and he believes in Allāh and the Day of Judgement, it would neither be permissible to

create a new thing or practice, nor would it be right for him to have dealings with such a person as does not respect this treaty. Whoever infringes this injunction, the curse and wrath of Allāh shall descend on him on the Day of Judgement, and no excuse and request for forgiveness shall be accepted from him, in this respect.

25. When there arises a mutual difference about anything in this agreement, the matter shall be referred for a decision to Allāh and Muḥammad (S.A.W.).

26. After the treaty, it shall be obligatory on the Jews to render financial assistance to the Muslims when they are at war with an enemy.

27. The Jews of Banū ʻAwf, who are a party to this agreement and are the supporters of the Muslims, shall adhere to their religion and the Muslims to theirs. Excepting religious matters, the Muslims and Jews shall be regarded as belonging to a single party. If anyone from amongst them commits an outrage or breaks a promise or is guilty of a crime, he shall deserve punishment for his crime.

28. The Jews of Banū al-Najjār, who are a party to this agreement and are the supporters of the Muslims, shall adhere to their religion and the Muslims to theirs. Excepting religious matters, the Muslims and the Jews shall be regarded as belonging to a single party. If anyone from amongst them commits an outrage or breaks a promise or is guilty of a crime, he shall deserve punishment for his crime.

29. The Jews of Banū al-Ḥārith, who are party to this agreement and are the supporters of the Muslims, shall adhere to their religion and the Muslims to theirs. Excepting religious matters, the Muslims and the Jews shall be regarded as belonging to a single party. If anyone from amongst them commits an outrage or a breaks promise or is guilty of a crime, he shall deserve punishment for his crime.

30. The Jews of Banū Sāʻidah, who are a party to this agreement and are the supporters of the Muslims, shall adhere to their religion and the Muslims to theirs. Excepting religious matters, the Muslims and the Jews shall be regarded as belonging to a single party. If anyone from amongst them commit an outrage or breaks a promise or is guilty of a crime, he shall deserve punishment for his crime.

31. The Jews of Banū Jusham, who are a party to this agreement and are the supporters of the Muslims shall adhere to their religion and the Muslims to theirs. Excepting religious matters, the Muslims and Jews shall be regarded as belonging to a single party. If anyone from amongst them commit an outrage or breaks promise or is guilty of a crime, he shall deserve punishment for his crime.

32. The Jews of Banū al-Aws, who are a party to this agreement and are the supporters of the Muslims, shall adhere to their religion and the Muslims to theirs.

Excepting religious matters, the Muslims and Jews shall be regarded as belonging to a single party. If anyone from amongst them commits an outrage or breaks promise or is guilty of a crime, he shall deserve punishment for his crime.

33. The Jews of Banū Tha'labah, who are a party to this agreement and are the supporters of the Muslims, shall adhere to their religion and the Muslims to theirs. Excepting religious matters, the Muslims and Jews shall be regarded as belonging to a single party. If anyone from amongst them commits an outrage or breaks a promise or is guilty of a crime, he shall deserve punishment for his crime.

34. The Jews of Banū Jafnah, who are a party to this agreement and are the supporters of the Muslims, shall adhere to their religion and the Muslims to theirs. Excepting religious matters, the Muslims and the Jews shall be regarded as belonging to a single party. If anyone from amongst them commits an outrage or breaks promise or is guilty of a crime, he shall deserve punishment for his crime.

35. The Jews of Banū al-Shuṭaybah, who are a party to this agreement and are the supporters of the Muslims, shall adhere to their religion and the Muslims to theirs. Excepting religious matters, the Muslims and the Jews shall be regarded as belonging to a single party. If anyone from amongst them commits an outrage or breaks a promise or is guilty of a crime, he shall deserve punishment for his crime.

36. The subordinate branches of the above mentioned tribes shall have the same rights as are enjoyed by the original branches.

37. None of the treaty makers shall take any military action, without the permission of Muḥammad (S.A.W.).

38. No hindrance shall be created in the requital or avenging of an injury or a blow. Whoever commits a breach of promise, shall deserve punishment for it and whoever abides most faithfully by this agreement, Allāh will help him.

39. If a third community wages war against the Muslims and Jews treaty makers, they will have to fight unitedly. They shall help each other mutually and there shall be mutual goodwill and faithfulness. The Jews shall bear their expenses of war and the Muslim their expenses.

40. It is incumbent on the parties to the agreement to treat each other sincerely and to wish each other well. None shall subject the other to oppression and injustice and the oppressed shall be helped.

41. The Jews shall share the expenses along with the Muslims as long as they fight jointly.

42. The plain of Yathrib, which is surrounded by hills, shall be a *ḥaram* (haven) for the treaty makers.

43. The same treatment shall be meted out to a refugee, to, which a person giving the refuge, is entitled; he shall not be harmed. A refuge shall abide by this agreement and he shall not be permitted to break a promise.

44. Nobody shall be provided a refuge without the permission of the people of that place.

45. If there is any occurrence or difference of opinion amongst the treaty makers, which might result in a breach of peace, the matter shall be referred, for a decision, to Allāh and Muḥammad, the Prophet of Allāh (S.A.W.). Allāh shall be with him, who abides most by the treaty.

46. None shall provide protection to the Quraysh of Mecca or any of their helpers.

47. If Yathrib *(Madīnah)* is invaded, the Muslims and the Jews both shall put up a joint defence.

48. If the Muslims make a peace treaty with some one, the Jews shall abide by it. And if the Jews make peace with somebody, it shall be obligatory on the Muslims to extend similar co-operation to the Jews. However, in the case of a religious war of a party, it shall not be the responsibility of the other party to co-operate in it.

49. In the case of an invasion of *Madīnah*, every party will have to defend the part, which is in front of it.

50. The helpers of the Aws tribe shall have the same rights, as are enjoyed by the parties to this treaty, provided they too show their loyalty. Whoever adheres to this treaty most, Allāh is his supporter and helper.

51. If anyone of the parties to this treaty, has to go out of *Madīnah*, on account of the exigency of war, it shall be entitled to peace and protection. And whoever stays in *Madīnah*, shall also be entitled to peace. Neither shall anybody be oppressed nor breach of promise shall be permissible for him. Whoever will respect this agreement with his heart and will abide by it, Allāh and His Prophet (S.A.W.) are his protectors.

Appendix II

The Pact of Najran *('Ahd Najrān)* [533]

IN THE NAME OF ALLAH, MOST COMPASSIONATE, MOST MERCIFUL

1. Although Prophet Muḥammad (S.A.W.), had the power to take a share from their produce, gold, silver, weapons and slaves, he treated the people generously and leaving aside all these things, he fixed for them two thousand *hullas* of the value of one *Auqia* each, annually-one thousand (to be supplied) in the month of *Rajab* and one thousand in the month of *Ṣafar*.

2. Each Hulls shall be of the value of one *Auqia* and whichever is of more or less value, shall be accounted for accordingly.

3. If instead of *Hullas*, something like armours or horses or riding camels are given it shall be accepted in accordance with its evaluation.

4. It shall be obligatory on the people of Najrān to arrange for the stay of my workers. But they will have to pay taxes within one month. They should not be made to stay far more than a month.

5. If due to a rebellion in Yemen we have to wage war, the people of Najrān will have to lend 30 armours, 20 horses and 30 camels. If any of the animals are lost, the people of Najrān shall be provided substitutes.

6. The lives of the people of Najrān and its surrounding area, their religion, their land, property, cattle and those of them who are present or absent, their messengers and their places of worship are under the protection of Allāh and

---

[533] *The Pact of Najrān,* online: Islamic Gateway <http://www.ummah.org.uk>(Access date: 16 November 2000); Ibn Sallām, *supra note* 253, at 198.

guardianship of His Prophet. Their present state shall neither be interfered with, nor their rights meddled with, nor their idols deformed. No *Usquf* (Bishop) *Rāhib* shall be removed from his office. The intention being that no change in whatever state every one is; shall be made (status quo shall be maintained).

7. Neither the people shall be punished for any past crime or murder, nor shall they be compelled to do military service. Neither shall *'Ushr* be imposed on them, expelled from their homeland nor any army shall enter their area.

8. If any one of the people of Najrān demands his rights, justice shall be done between the plaintiff and respondent. Neither oppression shall be allowed to be perpetrated on them, nor shall they be permitted to oppress any one.

9. Whoever from the people of Najrān takes interest alter the conclusion of the pact, shall be excluded from my assurance.

10. No one from the people of Najrān shall be implicated in the crime of someone else.

11. Whatever has been written in this pact, Allāh and Muḥammad His Prophet (S.A.W.) are guarantors for it, unless there is an order from Allāh, in this connection, and as long as the people of Najrān remain faithful and adhere to the conditions which have been made for them, except that some one compels them to do otherwise. Witness 'Uthmān Ibn 'Affān. Mu'ayqib wrote that and was present.

Appendix III

The Farewell-Pilgrimage Sermon *(Khuṭbat Ḥijjat al-Wadā')*[534]

(This Sermon was delivered on the Ninth Day of Dhū al-Ḥijjah 10 A.H. in the 'Uranah Valley of mount 'Arafāt)

IN THE NAME OF ALLAH, MOST COMPASSIONATE, MOST MERCIFUL

Praise be to Allāh, whom we seek help from, and repent to, seeking his help against our evil inclinations and acts. Whoever Allāh will guide none can mislead, and whoever He misleads, none can guide. I bear witness that there is no God but Allāh, the One with no partner, and bear witness that Muḥammad is His servant and messenger.

I call upon you (on people), to be pious, and obey Allāh, and I'll begin with what is of benefit to you.

Oh People! Lend me your ears, for I don't know whether after this year (pilgrimage), I'll ever be amongst you in this situation again. Therefore, listen to what I am saying to you carefully and take these words to those who could not be present here today.

---

[534] Abū Bakr Muḥammad Ibn al-Ṭayyib al-Bāqillānī, *I'jāz al-Qur'ān* (Beirut: Mu'assat al-Kutub al-Thaqāfiyya, 1986), 149-150; Abū 'Uthmān 'Amr Ibn Baḥr al-Jāḥiẓ, *al-Bayān wal-Tabyīn*, 5th ed., 4 vols. (Cairo: Maṭba'at al-Khānjī, 1985), 2:31-33; al-Bayhaqī, *supra note* 211, at 5:8; Ibn Hishām, *supra note* 67, at 4:183-184; al-Maqrīzī, *supra note* 253, at 1:522-523; Muḥammad Ibn Sa'd Ibn Manī' al-Zuhrī, *Kitāb al-Ṭabaqāt al-Kabīr*, 9 vols. (Leiden, The Netherlands: E. J. Brill, 1325 A. H.), 2/1:131-134; al-Ya'qūbī, *supra note* 280, at 2: 122-123.

Oh People! Just as this day, this month, and this city are sacred to you, so are the life, honour, and property of your brother Muslims, a sacred trust until you meet your Lord. Have I conveyed the message? Oh Allāh, be witness!

Return the goods entrusted to you, to their rightful owners. Usury is waived henceforth, but your wealth remains yours, without wronging or being wronged. This is Allāh's decree, and the first usury to be abolished is the usury of my uncle Abū al-'Abbās Ibn 'Abd al-Muṭṭalib.

The blood of those killed before Islam is waived, and the first one whom this will be applied to is the blood of 'Āmir Ibn Rabī'a Ibn al-Ḥārith Ibn 'Abd al- Muṭṭalib, who was nursed by Banū Sa'd and killed by Banū Hudhayl. Have I conveyed the message? Oh Allāh, be witness!

The rites of pagan Arabia are waived except for *Sidāna* (serving Holy Ka'ba), and *Siqāya* (offering drinking water to pilgrims).

Deliberate murder is to be punished by death, but if not deliberate (resulting from a stone or a rod) a ransom of as when one hundred camels should be paid whoever asks for more, he is of the ways of infidels. Have I conveyed the message? Oh Allāh, be witness!

Oh People! Satan has no hope of being worshipped in this land of yours, but he is satisfied to be obeyed in other matters of mean deeds. You should therefore guard your faith against him.

Oh People! Violating the sacred months, in which violence is prohibited, is verily excess in infidelity that misleads infidels. They make it lawful in one year, and prohibit it in another, deviating from the term set by Allāh. They make lawful what Allāh hath prohibited, and prohibit what Allāh hath made lawful. Time has wheeled around as when Allāh created the skies and earth. The term of months with Allāh is twelve, four of which are sacred. Three months of them (*Dhu al-Qi'da, Dhu al-Ḥijja*, and *Muḥarram*) are subsequent, and (*Rajab Modar*) that comes between *Jamāda* and *Sha'bān*. Have I conveyed the message? Oh Allāh, be witness!

Oh People! You owe your women rights, and they owe you too. They should let no one between your sheets, invite none to your homes without your consent. They should not commit adultery. If they did, Allāh permits you to abandon them, and chastise them but not violently. If they changed (to the better) and become obedient, you have to provide for their subsistence and clothes in fairness and kindness. Therefore, fear Allāh when dealing with women and treat them kindly for they are your partners and committed helpers. You have taken them as a trust from Allāh, and intercourse with them has been made permissible by the words of Allāh. Have I conveyed the message? Oh Allāh, be witness!

Oh People! Your slaves should be treated kindly, be fed of your food, and dressed as you do. If they commit a sin that you can not forgive, get rid of them, and do not torture them.

Oh People! Believers are but brothers. Nothing shall be legitimate to a Muslim, which belongs to a fellow Muslim, unless given willingly. Have I conveyed the message? Oh Allāh, be witness!

Avoid apostasy when I am no more among you, lest you should kill each other. If you adhere to what I have left to you (The *Qur'ān* and the *Sunna*), you will never go astray. Have I conveyed the message? Oh Allāh, be witness!

Oh People! You have but one God, and you descend from one father, Adam, who is from dust. No one has superiority over another except in piety. An Arab has no superiority over a non-Arab but in piety. Have I conveyed the message? Oh Allāh, be witness! The Prophet's Companions replied, "Yes, You have conveyed the message and fulfilled your mission". The Prophet said, " Then pass my words to others who could not be present here today."

Oh People! Allāh hath allocated to each inheritor his lot of inheritance. No will could be awarded to an inheritor. In all cases, a will should not exceed the third. A boy follows his father, and a tart is to be stoned. Whoever chooses a lineage other than that of his father, or follows other than his folk, he will be cursed by Allāh, His angels, and all people. Neither his council nor his judgement will be accepted. And peace be upon you!

Appendix IV

The Treaty of Jerusalem (*Mu'āhadat Ahl Īliyā'*) [535]

IN THE NAME OF ALLAH, THE
COMPASSIONATE, THE MERCIFUL

This what the servant of Allāh, 'Umar, Commander of the Faithful, gave to the people of Īliyā'(Jerusalem) in pledge of security:

He gave them security for their persons, goods, churches, crosses, and its sick and its sound, and all of its religion. Their churches shall not be impoverished or destroyed; nor shall be diminished, neither of its appurtenances nor of its crosses nor of anything of its provisions; and they shall not be forced against their faith; and not one of them shall be harmed.

And none of the Jews shall dwell with them in Jerusalem.

And [it is binding] on the people of Jerusalem that they pay the poll-tax as the people of al-Madā'in pay it;

And that they expel the Romans and robbers from Jerusalem: and whosoever of them goes forth, he shall be safe as to his person and property until they reach their place of safety. Whosoever of them stays, he shall be safe and on him [is binding] the like of that which [is binding] on the people of Jerusalem, a poll-tax.

And whosoever of the people of Jerusalem prefers to go away, himself and his property, along with the Romans, and leave their churches and crosses, they shall be safe in person and churches and crosses until they reach their place of safety.

---

[535] Stanley Lane-Poole, "The First Mohammedan Treaties with Christians" in *Proceedings of the Royal Irish Academy*, vol. 24 (Dublin: The Royal Irish Academy, 1904), 232-234; al-Ya'qūbī, *supra note* 280, at 2:167.

And whosoever of the people of the land was in it [Jerusalem] before the fighting, if he wish to settle, on him [is binding] the like as what [is binding] on the people of Jerusalem, a poll-tax, and if he wishes to depart with the Romans or to return to his own people, nothing shall be taken from them [i.e. in poll-tax] until the harvest is reaped. And for what is in this writing [stands] the pledge and warranty of Allāh, and the warranty of the Caliphs, and the warranty of the faithful, provides they pay what is due of the poll-tax. Witnesses to that, Khālid Ibn al-Walīd, and 'Amr Ibn al-'Aṣ, and 'Abd al-Raḥmān Ibn 'Awf. Mu'āwiya Ibn Abī-Sufyān wrote and was present in 15 A.H.

Appendix V

The Treaty of Egypt *(Mu'āhadat Ahl Miṣr)*[536]

IN THE NAME OF ALLAH, THE COMPASSIONATE, THE MERCIFUL

This is what 'Amr Ibn al-'Āṣ granted the people of Miṣr in pledge of security for their persons and their religion and their goods, and their churches and their crosses and their land and their waters: there shall not be taken from them anything of this, nor diminished.

And the garrisons shall not settle among them.

And [it is binding] upon the people of Miṣr that they pay the poll-tax when they come into this treaty of peace and the overflow of their river has subsided- fifty millions.

And [binding] on them is what their robbers commit.

And if any of them refuse [to come into this Treaty], the sum of the taxes shall be cut down for them [who are liable for it] in proportion to them: and our obligation towards those that refuse is quit.

And if their river has less than its full rise, then the sum [of taxation] shall be reduced for them in proportion.

And whosoever of the Romans and garrisons shall come into their Treaty, for him is the like as for them, and on him is the like [obligation] as on them.

---

[536] Alfred J. Butler, *The Arab Conquest of Egypt and the Last Thirty Years of the Roman Domination* (Oxford: Oxford Clarendon Press, 1902), 365; al-Qalqashandī, *supra note* 266, at 13:323-324; Stanley Lane-Poole, *supra note* 535, at 229-231.

And whosoever refuses and chooses to go away, he shall be safe till he reaches his place of security or departs from our dominion.

What is [laid] upon them is by thirds, at every third drawing a third of what is [laid] upon them.

For what is in this writing [stands] the pledge and warranty of Allāh, and the warranty of His Prophet, and the warranty of the Khalīfa, the Commander of the Faithful, and the Warranties of the Faithful.

And [it is prescribed] for the garrisons who consent [to this Treaty], that they shall assist with so many head and so many horse that they be not plundered or hindered from commerce to and from. Witness al-Zubayr and ʻAbd Allāh and Muḥammad his sons. Wardān wrote that and was present.

Appendix VI

Universal Islamic Declaration of Human Rights[537]

21 Dhū al-Qi'dah 1401 A. H.
19 September 1981 A. D.

CONTENTS

---

[537] Albert P. Blaustein, *supra note* 430 at 917-926; *Universal Islamic Declaration of Human Rights* (London: Islamic Council of Europe, 1981); *Universal Islamic Declaration of Human Rights,* online: Al-Hewar Center <http://www.al-hewar.com> (Access date: 13 November 2000).

"This is a declaration for mankind, a guidance and
instruction to those who fear Allāh."
(Qur'ān, Āl-'Imrān 3:138)

FOREWORD

Islam gave to mankind an ideal code of human rights fourteen centuries ago. These rights aim at conferring honour and dignity on mankind and eliminating exploitation, oppression and injustice.

Human rights in Islam are firmly rooted in the belief that Allāh, and Allāh alone, is the Law Giver and the Source of all human rights. Due to their Divine origin, no ruler, government, assembly or authority can curtail or violate in any way the human rights conferred by Allāh, nor can they be surrendered.

Human rights in Islam are an integral part of the overall Islamic order and it is obligatory on all Muslim governments and organs of society to implement them in letter and in spirit within the framework of that order.

It is unfortunate that human rights are being trampled upon with impunity in many countries of the world, including some Muslim countries. Such violations are a matter of serious concern and are arousing the conscience of more and more people throughout the world.

I sincerely hope that this *Declaration of Human Rights* will give a powerful impetus to the Muslim peoples to stand firm and defend resolutely and courageously the rights conferred on them by Allāh.

This *Declaration of Human Rights* is the second fundamental document proclaimed by the Islamic Council to mark the beginning of the 15th Century of the Islamic era, the first being the *Universal Islamic Declaration* announced at the International Conference on The Prophet Muḥammad (peace and blessings be upon him) and his Message, held in London from 12 to 15 April 1980.

The *Universal Islamic Declaration of Human Rights* is based on the *Qur'ān* and the *Sunnah* and has been compiled by eminent Muslim scholars, jurists and representatives of Islamic movements and thought. May Allāh reward them all for their efforts and guide us along the right path.

Salem Azzam
Secretary General

Paris 21 Dhū al- Qi'dah 1401
19th September 1981

"O mankind! We created you from a mail and female, and made you into nations and tribes, that ye may know each other. Verily the most honoured of you in the sight of Allāh is the most righteous of you. And Allāh has full knowledge and is well acquainted."
(Qur'ān, al-Ḥujurāt 49:13)

PREAMBLE

WHEREAS the age-old human aspiration for a just world order wherein people could live, develop and prosper in an environment free from fear, oppression, exploitation and deprivation, remains largely unfulfilled;

WHEREAS the Divine Mercy unto mankind reflected in its having been endowed with super-abundant economic sustenance is being wasted, or unfairly or unjustly withheld from the inhabitants of the earth;

WHEREAS Allāh has given mankind through His revelations in the Holy *Qur'ān* and the *Sunnah* of His Blessed Prophet Muḥammad an abiding legal and moral framework within which to establish and regulate human institutions and relationships;

WHEREAS the human rights decreed by the Divine Law aim at conferring dignity and honour on mankind and are designed to eliminate oppression and injustice;

WHEREAS by virtue of their Divine source and sanction these rights can neither be curtailed, abrogated or disregarded by authorities, assemblies or other institutions, nor can they be surrendered or alienated;

Therefore we, as Muslims, who believe

a) in Allāh, the Beneficent and Merciful, the Creator, the Sustainer, the Sovereign, the sole Guide of mankind and the Source of all Law;

b) in the Vicegerency *(Khilāfah)* of man who has been created to fulfil the Will of Allāh on earth;

c) in the wisdom of Divine guidance brought by the Prophets, whose mission found its culmination in the final Divine message that was conveyed by the Prophet Muḥammad (Peace be upon him) to all mankind;

d) that rationality by itself without the light of revelation from Allāh can neither be a sure guide in the affairs of mankind nor provide spiritual nourishment to the human soul, and, knowing that the teachings of Islam represent the quintessence of Divine guidance in its final and perfect form, feel duty-bound to remind man of the high status and dignity bestowed on him by Allāh;

e) in inviting all mankind to the message of Islam;

f) that by the terms of our primeval covenant with Allāh our duties and obligations have priority over our rights, and that each one of us is under a bounden duty to spread the teachings of Islam by word, deed, and indeed in all gentle ways, and to make them effective not only in our individual lives but also in the society around us;

g) in our obligation to establish an Islamic order:

i) wherein all human beings shall be equal and none shall enjoy a privilege or suffer a disadvantage or discrimination by reason of race, colour, sex, origin or language;

ii) wherein all human beings are born free;

iii) wherein slavery and forced labour are abhorred;

iv) wherein conditions shall be established such that the institution of family shall be preserved, protected and honoured as the basis of all social life;

v) wherein the rulers and the ruled alike are subject to, and equal before, the Law;

vi) wherein obedience shall be rendered only to those commands that are in consonance with the Law;

vii) wherein all worldly power shall be considered as a sacred trust, to be exercised within the limits prescribed by the Law and in a manner approved by it, and with due regard for the priorities fixed by it;

viii) wherein all economic resources shall be treated as Divine blessings bestowed upon mankind, to be enjoyed by all in accordance with the rules and the values set out in the *Qur'ān* and the *Sunnah;*

ix) wherein all public affairs shall be determined and conducted, and the authority to administer them shall be exercised after mutual consultation *(Shūra)* between the believers qualified to contribute to a decision which would accord well with the Law and the public good;

x) wherein everyone shall undertake obligations proportionate to his capacity and shall be held responsible pro rata for his deeds;

xi) wherein everyone shall, in case of an infringement of his rights, be assured of appropriate remedial measures in accordance with the Law;

xii) wherein no one shall be deprived of the rights assured to him by the Law except by its authority and to the extent permitted by it;

xiii) wherein every individual shall have the right to bring legal action against anyone who commits a crime against society as a whole or against any of its members;

xiv) wherein every effort shall be made to

(a) secure unto mankind deliverance from every type of exploitation, injustice and oppression,

(b) ensure to everyone security, dignity and liberty in terms set out and by methods approved and within the limits set by the Law;

Do hereby, as servants of Allāh and as members of the Universal Brotherhood of Islam, at the beginning of the Fifteenth Century of the Islamic Era, affirm our commitment to uphold the following inviolable and inalienable human rights that we consider are enjoined by Islam.

I. Right to Life

a) Human life is sacred and inviolable and every effort shall be made to protect it. In particular no one shall be exposed to injury or death, except under the authority of the Law.

b) Just as in life, so also after death, the sanctity of a person's body shall be inviolable. It is the obligation of believers to see that a deceased person's body is handled with due solemnity.

II. Right to Freedom

a) Man is born free. No inroads shall be made on his right to liberty except under the authority and in due process of the Law.

b) Every individual and every people has the inalienable right to freedom in all its forms—physical, cultural, economic and political—and shall be entitled to struggle by all available means against any infringement or abrogation of this right; and every oppressed individual or people has a legitimate claim to the support of other individuals and/or peoples in such a struggle.

III. Right to Equality and Prohibition against Impermissible Discrimination

a) All persons are equal before the Law and are entitled to equal opportunities and protection of the Law.

b) All persons shall be entitled to equal wage for equal work.

c) No person shall be denied the opportunity to work or be discriminated against in any manner or exposed to greater physical risk by reason of religious belief, colour, race, origin, sex or language.

IV. Right to Justice

a) Every person has the right to be treated in accordance with the Law, and only in accordance with the Law.

b) Every person has not only the right but also the obligation to protest against injustice; to recourse to remedies provided by the Law in respect of any unwarranted personal injury or loss; to self-defence against any charges that are preferred against him and to obtain fair adjudication before an independent judicial tribunal in any dispute with public authorities or any other person.

c) It is the right and duty of every person to defend the rights of any other person and the community in general (*Ḥisbah*).

d) No person shall be discriminated against while seeking to defend private and public rights.

e) It is the right and duty of every Muslim to refuse to obey any command, which is contrary to the Law, no matter by whom it may be issued.

V. Right to Fair Trial

a) No person shall be adjudged guilty of an offence and made liable to punishment except after proof of his guilt before an independent judicial tribunal.

b) No person shall be adjudged guilty except after a fair trial and after reasonable opportunity for defence has been provided to him.

c) Punishment shall be awarded in accordance with the Law, in proportion to the seriousness of the offence and with due consideration of the circumstances under which it was committed.

d) No act shall be considered a crime unless it is stipulated as such in the clear wording of the Law.

e) Every individual is responsible for his actions. Responsibility for a crime cannot be vicariously extended to other members of his family or group, who are not otherwise directly or indirectly involved in the commission of the crime in question.

VI. Right to Protection against Abuse of Power

Every person has the right to protection against harassment by official agencies. He is not liable to account for himself except for making a defence to the charges made against him or where he is found in a situation wherein a question regarding suspicion of his involvement in a crime could be *reasonably* raised

VII. Right to Protection against Torture

No person shall be subjected to torture in mind or body, or degraded, or threatened with injury either to himself or to anyone related to or held dear by him, or forcibly made to confess to the commission of a crime, or forced to consent to an act which is injurious to his interests.

VIII. Right to Protection of Honour and Reputation

Every person has the right to protect his honour and reputation against calumnies, groundless charges or deliberate attempts at defamation and blackmail.

IX. Right to Asylum

a) Every persecuted or oppressed person has the right to seek refuge and asylum. This right is guaranteed to every human being irrespective of race, religion, colour and sex.

b) *Al-Masjid al-Ḥarām* (the sacred house of Allāh) in Mecca is a sanctuary for all Muslims.

X. Rights of Minorities

a) The Qur'anic principle "There is no compulsion in religion" shall govern the religious rights of non-Muslim minorities.

b) In a Muslim country religious minorities shall have the choice to be governed in respect of their civil and personal matters by Islamic Law, or by their own laws.

XI. Right and Obligation to Participate in the Conduct and Management of Public Affairs

a) Subject to the Law, every individual in the community *(Ummah)* is entitled to assume public office.

b) Process of free consultation *(Shūra)* is the basis of the administrative relationship between the government and the people. People also have the right to choose and remove their rulers in accordance with this principle.

XII. Right to Freedom of Belief, Thought and Speech

a) Every person has the right to express his thoughts and beliefs so long as he remains within the limits prescribed by the Law. No one, however, is entitled to disseminate falsehood or to circulate reports, which may outrage public decency, or to indulge in slander, innuendo or to cast defamatory aspersions on other persons.

b) Pursuit of knowledge and search after truth is not only a right but a duty of every Muslim.

c) It is the right and duty of every Muslim to protest and strive (within the limits set out by the Law) against oppression even if it involves challenging the highest authority in the state.

d) There shall be no bar on the dissemination of information provided it does not endanger the security of the society or the state and is confined within the limits imposed by the Law.

e) No one shall hold in contempt or ridicule the religious beliefs of others or incite public hostility against them; respect for the religious feelings of others is obligatory on all Muslims.

XIII. Right to Freedom of Religion

Every person has the right to freedom of conscience and worship in accordance with his religious beliefs.

XIV. Right to Free Association

a) Every person is entitled to participate individually and collectively in the religious, social, cultural and political life of his community and to establish institutions and agencies meant to enjoin what is right *(Ma'rūf)* and to prevent what is wrong *(Munkar)*.

b) Every person is entitled to strive for the establishment of institutions where under an enjoyment of these rights would be made possible. Collectively, the community is obliged to establish conditions so as to allow its members full development of their personalities.

XV. The Economic Order and the Rights Evolving Therefrom

a) In their economic pursuits, all persons are entitled to the full benefits of nature and all its resources. These are blessings bestowed by Allāh for the benefit of mankind as a whole.

b) All human beings are entitled to earn their living according to the Law.

c) Every person is entitled to own property individually or in association with others. State ownership of certain economic resources in the public interest is legitimate.

d) The poor have the right to a prescribed share in the wealth of the rich, as fixed by *Zakāh*, levied and collected in accordance with the Law.

e) All means of production shall be utilised in the interest of the community *(Ummah)* as a whole, and may not be neglected or misused.

f) In order to promote the development of a balanced economy and to protect society from exploitation, Islamic Law forbids monopolies, unreasonable restrictive trade practices, usury, the use of coercion in the making of contracts and the publication of misleading advertisements.

g) All economic activities are permitted provided they are not detrimental to the interests of the community *(Ummah)* and do not violate Islamic laws and values.

XVI. Right to Protection of Property

No property may be expropriated except in the public interest and on payment of fair and adequate compensation.

XVII. Status and Dignity of Workers

Islam honours work and the worker and enjoins Muslims not only to treat the worker justly but also generously. He is not only to be paid his earned wages promptly, but is also entitled to adequate rest and leisure.

XVIII. Right to Social Security

Every person has the right to food, shelter, clothing, education and medical care consistent with the resources of the community. This obligation of the community extends in particular to all individuals who cannot take care of themselves due to some temporary or permanent disability.

XIX. Right to Found a Family and Related Matters

a) Every person is entitled to marry, to found a family and to bring up children in conformity with his religion, traditions and culture. Every spouse is entitled to such rights and privileges and carries such obligations as are stipulated by the Law.

b) Each of the partners in a marriage is entitled to respect and consideration from the other.

c) Every husband is obligated to maintain his wife and children according to his means.

d) Every child has the right to be maintained and properly brought up by its parents, it being forbidden that children are made to work at an early age or that any burden is put on them which would arrest or harm their natural development.

e) If parents are for some reason unable to discharge their obligations towards a child it becomes the responsibility of the community to fulfil these obligations at public expense.

f) Every person is entitled to material support, as well as care and protection, from his family during his childhood, old age or incapacity. Parents are entitled to material support as well as care and protection from their children.

g) Motherhood is entitled to special respect, care and assistance on the part of the family and the public organs of the community *(Ummah)*.

h) Within the family, men and women are to share in their obligations and responsibilities according to their sex, their natural endowments, talents and inclinations, bearing in mind their common responsibilities toward their progeny and their relatives.

i) No person may be married against his or her will, or lose or suffer diminution of legal personality on account of marriage.

XX. Rights of Married Women

Every married woman is entitled to:

a) live in the house in which her husband lives;

b) receive the means necessary for maintaining a standard of living which is not inferior to that of her spouse, and, in the event of divorce, receive during the statutory period of waiting *('Iddah)* means of maintenance commensurate with her husband's resources, for herself as well as for the children she nurses or keeps, irrespective of her own financial status, earnings, or property that she may hold in her own rights;

c) seek and obtain dissolution of marriage *(Khul'ah)* in accordance with the terms of the Law. This right is in addition to her right to seek divorce through the courts.

d) inherit from her husband, her parents, her children and other relatives according to the Law;

e) strict confidentiality from her spouse, or ex-spouse if divorced, with regard to any information that he may have obtained about her, the disclosure of which could prove detrimental to her interests. A similar responsibility rests upon her in respect of her spouse or ex-spouse.

XXI. Right to Education

a) Every person is entitled to receive education in accordance with his natural capabilities.

b) Every person is entitled to a free choice of profession and career and to the opportunity for the full development of his natural endowments.

XXII. Right of Privacy

Every person is entitled to the protection of his privacy.

XXIII. Right to Freedom of Movement and Residence

a) In view of the fact that the World of Islam is veritably *Ummah Islāmiyyah,* every Muslim shall have the right to freely move in and out of any Muslim country.

b) No one shall be forced to leave the country of his residence, or be arbitrarily deported therefrom without recourse to due process of Law.

EXPLANATORY NOTES

1. In the above formulation of Human Rights, unless the context provides otherwise:

a) the term 'person' refers to both the male and female sexes.

b) the term 'Law' denotes the *Sharī'ah,* i.e. the totality of ordinances derived from the *Qur'ān* and the *Sunnah* and any other laws that are deduced from these two sources by methods considered valid in Islamic jurisprudence.

2. Each one of the Human Rights enunciated in this declaration carries a corresponding duty.

3. In the exercise and enjoyment of the rights referred to above every person shall be subject only to such limitations as are enjoined by the Law for the purpose of securing the due recognition of, and respect for, the rights and the freedom of others and of meeting the just requirements of morality, public order and the general welfare of the Community *(Ummah).*

The Arabic text of this Declaration is the original.

GLOSSARY OF ARABIC TERMS

ḤISBAH: Public vigilance, an institution of the Islamic State enjoined to observe and facilitate the fulfilment of right norms of public behaviour. The "*Ḥisbah*" consists in public vigilance as well as an opportunity to private individuals to seek redress through it.

'IDDAH: The waiting period of a widowed or divorced woman during which she is not to re-marry.

KHALĪFAH: The vicegerency of man on earth or succession to the Prophet, transliterated into English as the Caliphate.

KHUL'AH: Divorce a woman obtains at her own request.

MA'RŪF: Good act.

MUNKAR: Reprehensible deed.

SHARĪ'AH: Islamic law.

SUNNAH: The example or way of life of the Prophet (peace be upon him), embracing what he said, did or agreed to.

UMMAH ISLĀMIYYA: World Muslim community.

ZAKĀH: The 'purifying' tax on wealth, one of the five pillars of Islam obligatory on Muslims.

REFERENCES

Note: The Roman numerals refer to the topics in the text. The Arabic numerals refer to the Chapter and the Verse of the *Qur'ān*, i.e. 5:32 means Chapter 5, Verse 32.

I

1. Qur'ān, al-Mā'idah 5:32.
2. Ḥadīth narrated by Muslim, Abū Dāwūd,Tirmidhī, Nasā'ī.
3. Ḥadīth narrated by Bukhārī.

II

4. Ḥadīth narrated by Bukhārī, Muslim.
5. Sayings of Caliph 'Umar.
6. Qur'ān, al-Shūra 42:41.
7. Qur'ān, al-Ḥajj 22:41.

III

8. From the Prophet's address.
9. Ḥadīth narrated by Bukhārī, Muslim, Abū Dāwūd, Tirmidhī , Nasā'ī.
10. From the address of Caliph Abū Bakr.
11. From the Prophet's farewell address.
12. Qur'ān, al-Aḥqāf 46:19.
13. Ḥadīth narrated by Aḥmad.
14. Qur'ān, al-Mulk 67:15.
15. Qur'ān, al-Zalzalah 99:7-8.

IV

16. Qur'ān, al-Nisā' 4:59.
17. Qur'ān, al-Mā'idah 5:49.
18. Qur'ān, al-Nisā' 4:148.
19. Ḥadīth narrated by Bukhārī, Muslim, Tirmidhī .
20. Ḥadīth narrated by Bukhārī, Muslim.
21. Ḥadīth narrated by Muslim, Abū Dāwūd, Tirmidhī , Nasā'ī.
22. Ḥadīth narrated by Bukhārī, Muslim, Abū Dāwūd, Tirmidhī , Nasā'ī.
23. Ḥadīth narrated by Abū Dāwūd, Tirmidhī .
24. Ḥadīth narrated by Bukhārī, Muslim, Abū Dāwūd, Tirmidhī, Nasā'ī.
25. Ḥadīth narrated by Bukhārī.

V

26. Ḥadīth narrated by Bukhārī, Muslim.
27. Qur'ān, al-Isrā' 17:15.
28. Qur'ān, al-Aḥzāb 33:5.
29. Qur'ān, al-Ḥujurāt 49:6.
30. Qur'ān, al-Najm 53:28.
31. Qur'ān, al-Baqarah 2:229.
32. Ḥadīth narrated by al-Bayhaqī, al-Ḥākim.
33. Qur'ān, al-Isrā' 17:15.
34. Qur'ān, al-Ṭūr 52:21.
35. Qur'ān, Yūsuf 12:79.

VI

36. Qur'ān, al-Aḥzāb 33:58.

VII

37. Ḥadīth narrated by Bukhārī, Muslim, Abū Dāwūd, Tirmidhī , Nasā'ī.
38. Ḥadīth narrated by Ibn Mājah.

VIII

39. From the Prophet's farewell address.
40. Qur'ān, al-Ḥujurāt 49:12.
41. Qur'ān, al-Ḥujurāt 49:11.

IX

42. Qur'ān, al-Tawba 9:6.
43. Qur'ān, Āl-'Imrān 3:97.
44. Qur'ān, al-Baqarah 2:125.
45. Qur'ān, al-Ḥajj 22:25.

X

46. Qur'ān, al-Baqarah 2:256.

47. Qur'ān, al-Mā'idah 5:42.
48. Qur'ān, al-Mā'idah 5:43.
49. Qur'ān, al-Mā'idah 5:47.

XI

50. Qur'ān, al-Shūra 42:38.
51. Ḥadīth narated by Aḥmad.
52. From the address of Caliph Abū Bakr.

XII

53. Qur'ān, al-Aḥzāb 33:60-61.
54. Qur'ān, Saba' 34:46.
55. Ḥadīth, narrated by Tirmidhī , Nasā'ī.
56. Qur'ān, al-Nisā' 4:83.
57. Qur'ān, al-An'ām 6:108.

XIII

58. Qur'ān, al-Kāfirūn 109:6.

XIV

59. Qur'ān, Yūsuf 12:108.
60. Qur'ān, Āl-'Imrān 3:104.
61. Qur'ān, al-Mā'idah 5:2.
62. Ḥadīth narrated by Abū Dāwūd, Tirmidhī, Nasā'ī , Ibn Mājah.

XV

63. Qur'ān, al-Mā'idah 5:120.
64. Qur'ān, al-Jāthiyah 45:13.
65. Qur'ān, al-Shūra 26:183.
66. Qur'ān, al-Isrā' 17:20.
67. Qur'ān, Hūd 11:6.
68. Qur'ān, al-Mulk 67:15.
69. Qur'ān, al-Najm 53:48.
70. Qur'ān, al-Ḥashr 59:9.
71. Qur'ān, al-Ma'ārij 70:24-25.
72. Sayings of Caliph Abū Bakr.
73. Ḥadīth narrated by Bukhārī, Muslim.
74. Ḥadīth narrated by Muslim.
75. Ḥadīth narrated by Muslim, Abū Dāwūd, Tirmidhī , Nasā'ī.
76. Ḥadīth narrated by Bukhārī, Muslim, Abū Dāwūd, Tirmidhī , Nasā'ī.
77. Qur'ān, al-Muṭṭaffifīn 83:1-3.
78. Ḥadīth narrated by Muslim.
79. Qur'ān, al-Baqarah 2:275.
80. Ḥadīth narrated by Bukhārī, Muslim, Abū Dāwūd, Tirmidhī , Nasā'ī.

XVI

81. Qur'ān, al- Baqarah 2:188.
82. Ḥadīth narrated by Bukhārī.
83. Ḥadīth narrated by Muslim.
84. Ḥadīth narrated by Muslim, Tirmidhī.

XVII

85. Qur'ān, al-Tawbah 9:105.
86. Ḥadīth narrated by Abū Ya'lā, Majma' al-Zawā'id.
87. Ḥadīth narrated by Ibn Mājah.
88. Qur'ān, al-Aḥqāf 46:19.
89. Qur'ān, al-Tawbah 9:105.
90. Ḥadīth narrated by Ṭabarānī, Majma' al-Zawā'id.
91. Ḥadīth narrated by Bukhārī.

XVIII

92. Qur'ān, al-Aḥzāb 33:6.

XIX

93. Qur'ān, al-Nisā' 4:1.
94. Qur'ān, al-Baqarah 2:228.
95. Ḥadīth narrated by Bukhārī, Muslim, Abū Dāwūd, Tirmidhī , Nasā'ī.
96. Qur'ān, al-Rūm 30:21.
97. Qur'ān, al-Ṭalāq 65:7.
98. Qur'ān, al-Isrā' 17:24.
99. Ḥadīth narrated by Bukhārī, Muslim, Abū Dāwūd, Tirmidhī .
100. Ḥadīth narrated by Abū Dāwūd.
101. Ḥadīth narrated by Bukhārī, Muslim.
102. Ḥadīth narrated by Abū Dāwūd, Tirmidhī.
103. Ḥadīth narrated by Aḥmad, Abū Dāwūd.

XX

104. Qur'ān, al-Ṭalāq 65:6.
105. Qur'ān, al-Nisā' 4:34.
106. Qur'ān, al-Ṭalāq 65:6.
107. Qur'ān, al-Ṭalāq 65:6.
108. Qur'ān, al-Baqarah 2:229.
109. Qur'ān, al-Nisā' 4:12.
110. Qur'ān, al-Baqarah 2:237.

XXI

111 Qur'ān, al-Isrā' 17:23-24.
112. Ḥadīth narrated by Ibn Mājah.
113. Qur'ān, Āl-'Imrān 3:187.

114. From the Prophet's farewell address.
115. Ḥadīth narrated by Bukhārī, Muslim.
116. Ḥadīth narrated by Bukhārī, Muslim, Abū Dāwūd, Tirmidhī.

XXII

117. Ḥadīth narrated by Muslim.
118. Qur'ān, al-Ḥujurāt 49:12.
119. Ḥadīth narrated by Abū Dāwūd, Tirmidhī.

XXIII

120. Qur'ān, al-Mulk 67:15.
121. Qur'ān, al-An'ām 6:11.
122. Qur'ān, al-Nisā' 4:97.
123. Qur'ān, al-Baqarah 2:217.
124. Qur'ān, al-Ḥashr 59:9.

Appendix VII

The Cairo Declaration on Human Rights in Islam[538]

United Nations

General Assembly

Distr.
GENERAL

A/CONF.157/PC/62/Add.18
9 June 1993

ENGLISH
Original: ARAB, ENGLISH AND FRENCH

WORLD CONFERENCE ON HUMAN RIGHTS
Preparatory Committee
Fourth Session
Geneva, 19 April – 7 May 1993
Item 5 on the Provisional agenda

STATUS OF PREPARATION OF PUBLICATIONS, STUDIES AND DOCUMENTS FOR THE WORLD CONFERENCE

---

[538] *The Cairo Declaration on Human Rights in Islam.* (A/CONF.157/PC/62/Add.18) Annex to Res. No. 49/19-P, 9 June 1993; *The Cairo Declaration on Human Rights in Islam*, online: Organization of the Islamic Conference <http://www.oic-oci.org>(Access date: 20 November 2000).

Note by the Secretariat

Addendum

Contribution of the Organization of the Islamic Conference

The attention of the Preparatory Committee is drawn to the attached contribution submitted by Dr. N. S. Tarzi, the Ambassador of the Organization of the Islamic Conference to the Office of the United Nations at Geneva. The contribution consists of the Cairo Declaration on Human Rights in Islam, which was adopted on 5 August 1990, and also resolution 41/21-P of the Twenty-First Islamic Conference of Foreign Ministers (Session of Islamic Unity and Co-operation for Peace, Justice and Progress) held in Karachi from 25 to 29 April 1993. In this resolution, it was requested that the Cairo Declaration and the resolution be considered as a contribution of the Organization of the Islamic Conference to the World Conference on Human Rights.

RESOLUTION NO. 49/19-P
ON THE CAIRO DECLARATION ON HUMAN RIGHTS IN ISLAM

The Nineteenth Islamic Conference of Foreign Ministers (Session of Peace, Interdependence and Development), held in Cairo, Arab Republic of Egypt, from 9-14 Muḥarram 1411H (31 July to 5 August 1990),

Keenly aware of the place of mankind in Islam as vicegerent of Allāh on Earth;

Recognizing the importance of issuing a Document on Human Rights in Islam that will serve as a guide for Member States in all aspects of life;

Having examined the stages through which the preparation of this draft Document has, so far, passed and the relevant report of the Secretary General;

Having examined the Report of the Meeting of the Committee of Legal Experts held in Tehran from 26 to 28 December 1989;

Agrees to issue the Cairo Declaration on Human Rights in Islam, which will serve as a general guidance for Member States in the field of human rights.

بسم الله الرحمن الرحيم

The Organisation of the Islamic Conference

ANNEX TO
RES. No. 49/19 – P

THE CAIRO DECLARATION ON HUMAN RIGHTS IN ISLAM

ANNEX TO

RES. NO. 49/19-P

THE CAIRO DECLARATION ON HUMAN RIGHTS IN ISLAM

The Member States of the Organization of the Islamic Conference,

Reaffirming the civilizing and historical role of the Islamic *Ummah* which God made the best nation that has given mankind a universal and well-balanced civilization in which harmony is established between this life and the hereafter and knowledge is combined with faith; and the role that this *Ummah* should play to guide a humanity confused by competing trends and ideologies and to provide solutions to the chronic problems of this materialistic civilization.

Wishing to contribute to the efforts of mankind to assert human rights, to protect man from exploitation and persecution, and to affirm his freedom and right to a dignified life in accordance with the Islamic *Sharī'ah.*

Convinced that mankind which has reached an advanced stage in materialistic science is still, and shall remain, in dire need of faith to support its civilization and of a self motivating force to guard its rights;

Believing that fundamental rights and universal freedoms in Islam are an integral part of the Islamic religion and that no one as a matter of principle has the right to suspend them in whole or in part or violate or ignore them in as much as they are binding divine commandments, which are contained in the Revealed Books of God and were sent through the last of His Prophets to complete the preceding divine messages thereby making their observance an act of worship and their neglect or violation an abominable sin, and accordingly every person is individually responsible - and the *Ummah* collectively responsible - for their safeguard.

Proceeding from the above-mentioned principles,

Declare the following:

ARTICLE I

(a) All human beings form one family whose members are united by submission to God and descent from Adam. All men are equal in terms of basic human dignity and basic obligations and responsibilities, without any discrimination on the grounds of race, colour, language, sex, religious belief, political affiliation, social status or other considerations. True faith is the guarantee for enhancing such dignity along the path to human perfection.

(b) All human beings are God's subjects, and the most loved by Him are those who are most useful to the rest of His subjects, and no one has superiority over another except on the basis of piety and good deeds.

ARTICLE 2

(a) Life is a God-given gift and the right to life is guaranteed to every human being. It is the duty of individuals, societies and states to protect this right from any violation, and it is prohibited to take away life except for a *Sharī'ah* prescribed reason.

(b) It is forbidden to resort to such means as may result in the genocidal annihilation of mankind.

(c) The preservation of human life throughout the term of time willed by Allāh is a duty prescribed by *Sharī'ah*.

(d) Safety from bodily harm is a guaranteed right. It is the duty of the state to safeguard it, and it is prohibited to breach it without a *Sharī'ah*-prescribed reason.

ARTICLE 3

(a) In the event of the use of force and in case of armed conflict, it is not permissible to kill non-belligerents such as old man, women and children. The wounded and the sick shall have the right to medical treatment; and prisoners of war shall have the right to be fed, sheltered and clothed. It is prohibited to mutilate dead bodies. It is a duty to exchange prisoners of war and to arrange visits or reunions of the families separated by the circumstances of war.

(b) It is prohibited to fell trees, to damage crops or livestock, and to destroy the enemy's civilian buildings and installations by shelling, blasting or any other means.

ARTICLE 4

Every human being is entitled to inviolability and the protection of his good name and honour during his life and after his death. The state and society shall protect his remains and burial place.

ARTICLE 5

(a) The family is the foundation of society, and marriage is the basis of its formation. Men and women have the right to marriage, and no restrictions stemming from race, colour or nationality shall prevent them from enjoying this right.

(b) Society and the State shall remove all obstacles to marriage and shall facilitate marital procedure. They shall ensure family protection and welfare.

ARTICLE 6

(a) Woman is equal to man in human dignity, and has rights to enjoy as well as duties to perform; she has her own civil entity and financial independence, and the right to retain her name and lineage.

(b) The husband is responsible for the support and welfare of the family.

ARTICLE 7

(a) As of the moment of birth, every child has rights due from the parents, society and the state to be accorded proper nursing, education and material, hygienic and moral care. Both the fetus and the mother must be protected and accorded special care.

(b) Parents and those in such like capacity have the right to choose the type of education they desire for their children, provided they take into consideration the interest and future of the children in accordance with ethical values and the principles of the *Sharī'ah*.

(c) Both parents are entitled to certain rights from their children, and relatives are entitled to rights from their kin, in accordance with the tenets of the *Sharī'ah*.

ARTICLE 8

Every human being has the right to enjoy his legal capacity in terms of both obligation and commitment, should this capacity be lost or impaired, he shall be represented by his guardian.

ARTICLE 9

(a) The question for knowledge is an obligation and the provision of education is a duty for society and the State. The State shall ensure the availability of ways and means to acquire education and shall guarantee educational diversity in the interest of society so as to enable man to be acquainted with the religion of Islam and the facts of the Universe for the benefit of mankind.

(b) Every human being has the right to receive both religious and worldly education from the various institutions of, education and guidance, including the family, the school, the university, the media, etc., and in such an integrated and balanced manner as to develop his personality, strengthen his faith in Allāh and promote his respect for and defence of both rights and obligations.

ARTICLE 10

Islam is the religion of unspoiled nature. It is prohibited to exercise any form of compulsion on man or to exploit his poverty or ignorance in order to convert him to another religion or to atheism.

ARTICLE 11

(a) Human beings are born free, and no one has the right to enslave, humiliate, oppress or exploit them, and there can be no subjugation but to Allāh the Most-High.

(b) Colonialism of all types being one of the most evil forms of enslavement is totally prohibited. Peoples suffering from colonialism have the full right to freedom and self-determination. It is the duty of all States and peoples to support the struggle of colonized peoples for the liquidation of all forms of colonialism and occupation, and all States and peoples have the right to preserve their independent identity and exercise control over their wealth and natural resources.

ARTICLE 12

Every man shall have the right, within the framework of *Sharī'ah*, to free movement and to select his place of residence whether inside or outside his country and if persecuted, is entitled to seek asylum in another country. The country of refuge shall ensure his protection until he reaches safety, unless asylum is motivated by an act which *Sharī'ah* regards as a crime.

ARTICLE 13

Work is a right guaranteed by the State and Society for each person able to work. Everyone shall be free to choose the work that suits him best and which serves his interests and those of society. The employee shall have the right to safety and security as well as to all other social guarantees. He may neither be assigned work beyond his capacity nor be subjected to compulsion or exploited or harmed in any way. He shall be entitled - without any discrimination between males and females - to fair wages for his work without delay, as well as to the holidays allowances and promotions which he deserves. For his part, he shall be required to be dedicated and meticulous in his work. Should workers and employers disagree on any matter, the State shall intervene to settle the dispute and have the grievances redressed, the rights confirmed and justice enforced without bias.

ARTICLE 14

Everyone shall have the right to legitimate gains without monopolization, deceit or harm to oneself or to others. Usury *(ribā)* is absolutely prohibited.

ARTICLE 15

(a) Everyone shall have the right to own property acquired in a legitimate way, and shall be entitled to the rights of ownership, without prejudice to oneself, others or to society in general. Expropriation is not permissible except for the requirements of public interest and upon payment of immediate and fair compensation.

(b) Confiscation and seizure of property is prohibited except for a necessity dictated by law.

ARTICLE 16

Everyone shall have the right to enjoy the fruits of his scientific, literary, artistic or technical production and the right to protect the moral and material interests stemming therefrom, provided that such production is not contrary to the principles of *Sharī'ah*.

ARTICLE 17

(a) Everyone shall have the right to live in a clean environment, away from vice and moral corruption, an environment that would foster his self-development and it is incumbent upon the State and society in general to afford that right.

(b) Everyone shall have the right to medical and social care, and to all public amenities provided by society and the State within the limits of their available resources.

(c) The State shall ensure the right of the individual to a decent living which will enable him to meet all is requirements and those of his dependants, including food, clothing, housing, education, medical care and all other basic needs.

ARTICLE 18

(a) Everyone shall have the right to live in security for himself, his religion, his dependants, his honour and his property.

(b) Everyone shall have the right to privacy in the conduct of his private affairs, in his home, among his family, with regard to his property and his relationships. It is not permitted to spy on him, to place him under surveillance or to besmirch his good name. The State shall protect him from arbitrary interference.

(c) A private residence is inviolable in all cases. It will not be entered without permission from its inhabitants or in any unlawful manner, nor shall it be demolished or confiscated and its dwellers evicted.

ARTICLE 19

(a) All individuals are equal before the law, without distinction between the ruler and the ruled.

(b) The right to resort to justice is guaranteed to everyone.

(c) Liability is in essence personal.

(d) There shall be no crime or punishment except as provided for in the *Sharī'ah*.

(e) A defendant is innocent until his guilt is proven in a fair trial in which he shall be given all the guarantees of defence.

ARTICLE 20

It is not permitted without legitimate reason to arrest an individual, or restrict his freedom, to exile or to punish him. It is not permitted to subject him to physical or psychological torture or to any form of humiliation, cruelty or indignity. Nor is it permitted to subject an individual to medical or scientific experimentation without his consent or at the risk of his health or of his life. Nor is it permitted to promulgate emergency laws that would provide executive authority for such actions.

ARTICLE 21

Taking hostages under any form or for any purpose is expressly forbidden.

ARTICLE 22

(a) Everyone shall have the right to express his opinion freely in such manner as would not be contrary to the principles of the *Sharī'ah*.

(b) Everyone shall have the right to advocate what is right, and propagate what is good, and warn against what is wrong and evil according to the norms of Islamic *Sharī'ah*.

(c) Information is a vital necessity to society. It may not be exploited or misused in such a way as may violate sanctities and the dignity of Prophets, undermine moral and ethical values or disintegrate, corrupt or harm society or weaken its faith.

(d) It is not permitted to arouse nationalistic or doctrinal hatred or to do anything that may be an incitement to any form or racial discrimination.

ARTICLE 23

(a) Authority is a trust; and abuse or malicious exploitation thereof is absolutely prohibited, so that fundamental human rights may be guaranteed.

(b) Everyone shall have the right to participate, directly or indirectly in the administration of his country's public affairs. He shall also have the right to assume public office in accordance with the provisions of *Sharī'ah*.

ARTICLE 24

All the rights and freedoms stipulated in this Declaration are subject to the Islamic *Sharī'ah*.

ARTICLE 25

The Islamic *Sharī'ah* is the only source of reference for the explanation or clarification of any of the articles of this Declaration.

Cairo, 14 Muḥarram 1411 H
5 August 1990

RESOLUTION NO. 41/21-P. ON COORDINATION AMONG MEMBER STATES IN THE FIELD OF HUMAN RIGHTS

The Twenty-First Islamic Conference of Foreign Ministers (Session of Islamic Unity and Co-operation for Peace, Justice and Progress), held in Karachi, Islamic Republic of Pakistan from 4 to 8 Dhū al-Qi'dah 1413H (25-29 April 1993),

Bearing in mind the objectives of the Charter of OIC and the "Cairo Declaration on Human Rights in Islam" to promote and encourage respect for human rights and fundamental freedoms for all in accordance with Islamic values and teachings as well as the Charter of the United Nations and the Universal Declaration on Human Rights;

Mindful of the Islamic values on human rights, the supreme place of mankind in Islam as vicegerent of Allāh on earth and accordingly the great importance that is being attached by the Islamic thought to promote and encourage respect for human rights;

Aware that the increasing importance of human rights throughout the world calls for further intensification of the efforts of the Islamic *Ummah* and Islamic organizations in order to take appropriate initiatives at the national, regional and international levels for the promotion and protection of human rights;

Emphasizing the significance of the World Conference on Human rights, which provides an invaluable opportunity to review all aspects of human rights and ensure a just and balanced approach thereto;

Recognizing the contribution that can be made to the World Conference by Islamic countries on the basis of the valuable guidelines contained in the "Cairo Declaration on Human Rights in Islam";

Believing that the respect of human rights is an integral part of Islam;

Bearing in mind the existence of different constitutional and legal systems among OIC Member States and various international or regional human rights instruments to which they are parties;

Reaffirming the principles of respect for national sovereignty, territorial integrity and non-interference in the internal affairs of states;

Recognizing that the promotion and protection of human rights should be encouraged by co-operation and consensus, and not through confrontation and the imposition of incompatible values;

Reiterating the interdependence and indivisibility of economic, social, cultural, civil and political rights, and the inherent interrelationship between development, democracy, universal enjoyment of all human rights, and social justice which must be addressed in an integrated and balanced manner;

Considering that Development is a comprehensive economic, social, cultural and political process, which aims at the constant improvement of the well-being of the entire population and of all individuals on the basis of their active, free and meaningful participation;

Recalling that the international community has a duty to fulfil its commitment to eradicate poverty, which is a major obstacle to any effort aimed at sustainable development and the full realization of human rights;

1. **Reaffirms** its commitment to the principles contained in the Charter of the OIC as well as the "Cairo Declaration on Human Rights in Islam" as general guidelines and the Charter of the United Nations.

2. **Emphasizes** the principles of respect for national sovereignty and territorial integrity as well as non-interference in the internal affairs of states, and the non-use of human rights as an instrument of political or economic pressure.

3. **Reiterates** that all countries, large and small, have the right to determine their political systems, control and freely utilize their resources, and freely pursue their economic, social and cultural development.

4. **Stresses** the necessity of achieving universality, objectivity, and non-selectivity in the application of human rights standards and instruments.

5. **Recognizes** that while human rights are universal in nature, they must be considered in the context of a dynamic and evolving process of international norm-setting, taking into account the various historical, cultural and religious backgrounds and the principal legal systems.

6. **Emphasizes** the necessity to rationalize the United Nations human rights mechanism in order to enhance its effectiveness and efficiency and avoid duplication of tasks and multiple parallel mechanisms.

7. **Reaffirms** the interdependence and indivisibility of economic, social, cultural, civil and political rights, and the need to give equal emphasis to all categories of human rights.

8. **Expresses** concern over violation of human rights, including manifestations of racial discrimination, racism, apartheid, colonialism, foreign aggression and occupation, and the establishment of illegal settlements in occupied territories, as well as the recent resurgence of intolerance, neo-nazism, xenophobia and ethnic cleansing.

9. **Reiterates** that self-determination is a principle of international law and a universal right recognized by the United Nations for peoples under alien or colonial domination or foreign occupation, by virtue of which they can freely determine their political status and freely pursue their economic, social and cultural development, and that its denial constitutes a grave violation of human rights.

10. **Stresses** that the right to self-determination is applicable to peoples under alien or colonial domination or foreign occupation, and should not be used to undermine the territorial integrity, national sovereignty and political independence of States.

11. **Strongly** reaffirms its support for the legitimate struggle of the Palestinian people to restore their national and inalienable rights to self-determination and independence, and demands an immediate end to the grave violations of human rights in the Palestinian, Syrian *Golān* and other occupied Arab territories including Jerusalem as well as the immediate withdrawal of Israeli forces from all occupied territories.

12. **Reaffirms** its support for the legitimate struggle of the people of South Africa for the total eradication of Apartheid and their right to establish a non-racial democratic system.

13. **Reaffirms** its support for the fundamental human rights of the people of Jammu and Kashmir, including their right to self-determination and calls for an immediate end to the violations of their human rights.

14. **Condemns** the genocide being perpetrated against the people of Bosnia-Herzegovina and calls for urgent action by the international community to halt the massive violations of their human rights.

15. **Reaffirms** its strong commitment, in accordance with article 6 of the "Cairo Declaration on Human Rights in Islam", to the promotion and protection of the rights of women.

16. Recognizes the rights of the child and the mother to enjoy special protection and also the right of every child due from parents, society and the state to be accorded proper nursing, education and material, hygienic and moral care.

17. Urges the international community to give priority to the rendering of appropriate assistance to children who are victims of hunger, disease, drought, and armed conflicts and to allocate adequate resources for this purpose.

18. Requests the Secretary General to co-ordinate effectively the participation of the member states in the World Conference on Human Rights, and report to the Twenty-Second Islamic Conference of Foreign Ministers, the progress in implementation of the present resolution.

19. Requests also the Secretary General to transmit this resolution along with the "Cairo Declaration on Human Rights in Islam" to the Secretary General of the World Conference on Human Rights as a contribution of OIC to the Conference.

Glossary

Ahdname: Ottoman written pact, treaty or charter.

Ahl al-Kitāb: People of the Scriptures. Refers to Jews and Christians, and may also include other non-Muslims who believe in a revealed Scripture.

Amān: Protection, pledge of security or safe conduct.

Bay'a: Homage paid to the *Imām* by recognizing his authority, offered by a certain number of people acting individually or collectively.

Bayt al-māl: Muslim public treasury.

Bulūgh al-takālīf: Legal capacity, reaching the age at which one can rightfully engage in a particular undertaking or transaction under the law.

Bāghī: (pl. *bughāt*), rebels.

Dār al-'adl: Territory of justice, refers to *dār al-Islām.*

Dār al-'ahd: Territory of covenant, refers to lands linked by a peace treaty with *dār al-Islām.*

Dār al-ḍīfān: Guesthouse.

Dār al-ḥarb: Territory of war, land of the enemy.

Dār al-ḥiyād: Territory of neutrality.

Dār al-Islām: Territory of Islam, in which the laws of Islam prevail.

Sources: 'Alī Ibn Muḥammad al-Jurjānī, *Kitāb al-Ta'rīfāt* (Beirut: Maktabat Lubnān, 1990); *The Encyclopaedia of Islam* (Leiden, The Netherlands: Brill, 1987); Muḥammad Rawwās Qal'ajī and Ḥāmid Ṣādiq Qunaibī, *Mu'jam Lughat al-Fuqahā': Dictionary of Islamic Legal Terminology* (Beirut: Dār al- Nafā'is, 1985); Sayed Hassan Amin, *Arabic-English Dictionary of Legal Terms* (Glasgow: Royston, 1990); Sir James Redhouse, *New Redhouse Turkish-English Dictionary* (Istanbul: Redhouse Press, 1987).

Dār al-jawr: Territory of injustice, refers to *dār al-ḥarb.*

Dār al-salām: Territory of peace, refers to *dār al-Islām.*

Dār al-ṣulh: Territory of truce, and peace with *dār al-Islām* by concluding a peace treaty and paying tribute to the latter.

Da'wah: The mission of Islam.

Dhimma: Covenant of protection given to non-Muslims living in Muslim territory, particularly the *Ahl al-Kitāb.*

Dhimmī: (pl. *dhimmīs*), protected people, the beneficiaries of the *dhimma* covenant.

Farḍ 'ayn: Individual obligation or duty, which must be fulfilled by every Muslim individual, like performing ritual prayer and fasting *Ramaḍān.*

Farḍ kifāya: Collective obligation or duty, the carrying out of which by a sufficient number of individual Muslims exempts the rest of the community from performing it, such as funeral prayer, and returning greetings.

Fatḥ: Victory (literally "opening") or conquest of a country.

Fay': War booty gained from the enemy without fighting.

Ḥajj: The greater pilgrimage to Mecca during the season of the pilgrimage. The *ḥajj* is the fifth of the five pillars of Islam.

Ḥaram Ḥijāz: The sacred land of *Ḥijāz*, which is between Tuhāma and Najd in the Arabian Peninsula.

al-Ḥaramayn al-Sharīfayn: The two noble sanctuaries of Mecca and Medina and surroundings.

Hijra: The emigration of the Prophet Muḥammad from Mecca to Medina. It is calculated that this began on July 16, 622 A.D., and it serves as day one of the Muslim calendar.

Ḥadd: (pl. *ḥudūd*), punishments stipulated in the *Qur'ān.* The *Ḥadd* is the right of *Allāh* (*ḥaqq Allāh*), which cannot be waived once the case has been brought before the Judge.

Ḥudaybiya: A small village located on the edge of the sacred territory of Mecca, where Prophet Muḥammad concluded a treaty of peace with the Meccans' leadership in 6 A. H.

Ḥaqq: (pl. *ḥuqūq*), rights. *Ḥuqūq al-'ibād* are the rights of people guaranteed by Islamic law, regardless of race, sex or religion.

Ījāb: Offer.

Imām: Community leader or head of a Muslim state. It is also used to describe the leader of congregational prayer or an eminent Muslim jurist or scholar.

Jizya: Poll tax, tribute, head tax levied on non-Muslims (adult, male and free) living in the territory of Islam.

Ka'ba: The most holy Islamic shrine in Mecca. It is *Bayt Allāh al-Ḥarām* (the sacred house of *Allāh,* the sacred mosque). Muslims throughout the whole world turn their faces in the direction of the *Ka'ba* when they perform their prayers.

Karmathians: *Qarāmiṭa*, the followers of Ḥamdān Qarmaṭ, an *Ismā'īlī* leader from Kūfa in Iraq. After Ḥamdān's revolt against the leadership and his subsequent disappearance, the term *Qarāmiṭa* was generally used for those *Ismā'īlī* groups who joined his revolution and consequently refused to recognize the claim of the Fatimid caliphs to the Imamate.

Kharāj: Land tax.

Kharijite: (pl. *Kharijites*), the oldest religious sect of Islam, after applied to those regarded as rebels, separatists or dissidents.

al-Khulafā' al-Rāshidūn: Rightly-guided caliphs (Abū Bakr al-Ṣiddīq, 'Umar Ibn al Khaṭṭāb, 'Uthmān Ibn 'Affān and 'Alī Ibn Abī Ṭālib).

Mamlūk: Slave.

Masāliḥ: Checkpoints on the borders of *dār al-Islām.*

Millet system: Official division of Ottoman society along religious lines: Orthodox, Armenian, Jewish and Muslim millets. Later in the nineteenth century, the Orthodox and Armenian millets were further divided.

Mu'āhada: Treaty, pact.

Mufādāh: Ransoming, paying ransom.

Muhādana: Conclusion of a truce, making peace (with).

Muḥālafa: Alliance, confederation.

Muḥāribūn: Highway robbers.

Murtadd: Apostate.

Muṣālaḥa: Reconciliation.

Musālama: Peacemaking.

Musta'min: The enemy granted safeguard in *dār al-Islām.*

Mustaḥab: Desirable.

Mustaḥaq: Deserved, rightful.

Muwāda'a: Peace treaty, peace making.

Muwālāh: Adherence.

Nabdh: Renunciation, discarding.

Najrān: A major urban center in the Arabian Peninsula in ancient times. In 630 A.D., a delegation from Najrān came to Medina to meet with the Prophet Muḥammad, and consequently, the Prophet granted them the so-called *'Ahd Najrān* (the Pact of Najrān, see appendix II).

Naqīb: Tribal chief, community leader, head of a tribe.

Nāqūs: Bell

People of the book: See *Ahl al-Kitāb.*

Qabūl: Acceptance.

Qiṣāṣ: Retaliation, the Law of Equality (between crime and punishment).

Quraysh: The major Meccan tribe, into which the prophet Muḥammad was born.

Rasūl: Messenger, apostle.

Rāya: (pl. *rāyāt*), flags.

Ribā: Usury, interest on a loan, any pre-agreed excess paid or received over and above the principle in a loan contract.

Sabī: Captivity.

Safīr: Ambassador

Sha'ām: The greater Syria. It can also denote Damascus, the capital of Syria.

al-Sharī'a: Islamic law.

Shī'a: Literally "adherents" or "party", it refers to the movement that favors a privileged position for the Family of the Prophet Muḥammad (*Ahl al-Bayt*) in the political and religious leadership of the Muslim nation.

Shī'ī: Follower of the *Shī'a* sect.

Ṣulḥ: Reconciliation, settlement, compromise.

Sunnī: Muslim followers of the tradition of the Prophet Muḥammad, believing that *Khilāfa* (succession) to the political and religious leadership of the Muslim nation should be by election.

Taḥkīm: Arbitration.

Thaqīf: The tribe that controlled the walled city of al-Ṭā'if in the Arabia.

Uḥud: Mountain in the region of the Medina.

'Umra: Minor pilgrimage to Mecca at any time in the year.

'Ushūr: Tithe, tax levied on lands held in absolute ownership.

Wazīr: Minister.

al-Zunnār: Girdle, band worn around the waist.

Bibliography

I. Primary Sources

Abū Shāma, 'Abd al-Raḥmān Ibn Ismā'īl. *Kitāb al-Rawḍatayn fī Akhbār al-Dawlatayn.* 2 vols. Cairo: Maṭba'at Lajnat al-Ta'līf wal-Tarjama wal-Nashr, 1956.

al-'Adawī, 'Alī al-Ṣa'īdī. *Ḥāshiya 'alā Kifāyat al-Ṭālib al-Rabbānī li-Risālat Ibn Abī Zayd al-Qayrawānī fī Madhhab Mālik.* 2 vols. Cairo: al-Maṭba'a al-Azhariyya al-Miṣriyya, 1309 A.H.

'Ālimkīr, Abū al-Muẓaffar Muḥyī al-Dīn Ūrānk. *al-Fatāwī al-Hindiyya wa Tu'raf bil-Fatāwī al-'Ālimkīriyya.* 6 vols. Cairo: al-Maṭba'a al-Azhariyya bi-Būlāq, 1310 A.H.

al-Andalusī, Shihāb al-Dīn Aḥmad Ibn 'Abd Rabbu. *al-'Iqd al-Farīd.* Beirut: Dār wa Maktabat al-Hilāl, 1986.

Aquinas, Thomas. *Summa Theologica.* Translated by Fathers of the English Dominican Province. New York: Benziger Brothers, 1917.

al-'Asqalānī, Aḥmad Ibn 'Alī Ibn Ḥajar. *Fatḥ al-Bārī bi-Sharḥ Ṣaḥīḥ al-Bukhārī.* 13 vols. Beirut: Dār al-Ma'rifa, n.d.

al-Awzā'ī, 'Abd al-Raḥmān Abū 'Amr. "Kitāb Siyar al-Awzā'ī." In *Kitāb al-Umm.* 7 vols. Edited by Abū 'Abd Allāh Muḥammad Ibn Idrīs al-Shāfi'ī. Cairo: al-Hay'a al-Miṣriyya al-'Āmma lil-Kitāb, 1987.

al-'Aynī, Badr al-Dīn Maḥmūd Ibn Aḥmad. *'Umdat al-Qārī -Sharḥ Ṣaḥīḥ al-Bukhārī.* 25 vols. Cairo: al-Maṭba'a al-Munīriyya, 1348 A.H.

al-Baghdādī, 'Abd al-Qāhir. *al-Farq Bayn al-Firaq.* Beirut: Dār al-Ma'rifa lil-Ṭibā'a wal-Nashr, n.d.

al-Baghdādī, Shihāb al-Dīn al-Sayyid Maḥmūd al-Alūsī. *Rūḥ al-Ma'ānī fī Tafsīr al-Qur'ān al-'Aẓīm wal-Sab' al-Mathānī.* 29 vols. Beirut: Dār Iḥyā' al-Turāth al-'Arabī, 1980.

al-Bājī, Abū al-Walīd Sulaymān Ibn Khalaf. *al-Muntaqā Sharḥ Muwaṭṭ' Imām Dār al-Hijra.* 7 vols. Cairo: Maṭba'at al-Sa'āda, 1332 A.H.

al-Balādhurī, Aḥmad Ibn Yaḥyā. *Ansāb al-Ashrāf.* 5 vols. Jerusalem: Hosta'at Sefarim, 1938.

_______. *Kitāb Futūḥ al-Buldān.* Beirut: Dār al-Nashr lil-Jāmi'iyyīn, 1957.

al-Bāqillānī, Abū Bakr Muḥammad Ibn al-Ṭayyib. *I'jāz al-Qur'ān.* Beirut: Mu'assasat al-Kutub al-Thaqāfiyya, 1986.

al-Bayhaqī, Abū Bakr Aḥmad Ibn al-Ḥusayn. *al-Sunan al-Kubrā.* 10 vols. Ḥaydar Abād, India: Maṭba'at Majlis Dā'irat al-Ma'ārif al-'Uthmaniyya, 1925.

Brown, Lesley, ed. *The New Shorter Oxford English Dictionary on Historical Principles.* 2 vols. Oxford: The Clarendon Press, 1993.

al-Buhūtī, Manṣūr Ibn Idrīs, *Kashshāf al-Qinā' 'an Matn al-Iqnā'.* 6 vols. Cairo: Maṭba'at Anṣār al-Sunna al-Muḥammadiyya, 1947.

al-Bukhārī, Abū 'Abd Allāh Muḥammad Ibn Ismā'īl. *Ṣaḥīḥ al-Bukhārī.* 8 vols. Beirut: Dār al-Fikr lil-Ṭibā'a wal-Nashr, 1981.

al-Dahlawī, Shāh Walī Allāh. *Ḥujjat Allāh al-Bāligha.* 2 vols. Beirut: Dār al-Ma'rifa, n.d.

al-Dīnawarī, 'Abd Allāh Ibn Muslim Ibn Qutayba. *Kitāb 'Uyūn al-Akhbār.* 4 vols. Cairo: Dār al-Kitāb al-'Arabī, 1957.

al-Dusūqī, Muḥammad Ibn Aḥmad Ibn 'Arafa. *Ḥāshiyya 'alā al-Sharḥ al-Kabīr lil-Dardīr.* 4 vols. Cairo: Maṭba'at Muṣṭafā Muḥammad, 1373 A.H.

al-Farrā', Abū Ya'lā. *al-Aḥkām al-Sulṭāniyya.* Cairo: Maṭba'at Muṣṭafā al-Bābī al-Ḥalabī, 1938.

al-Ghazālī, Abū Ḥāmid. *Iḥyā' 'Ulūm al-Dīn.* 4 vols. Beirut: Dār al-Ma'rifa lil-Ṭibā'a wal-Nashr, 1404 A.H.

_______. *Shifā' al-Ghalīl fī Bayān al-Shabah wal-Mukhīl wa Masālik al-Ta'līl.* Edited by Ḥamad al-Kubaisī. Baghdād: Maṭba'at al-Irshād, 1971.

al-Ghazālī, Abū Ḥāmid. *al-Wajīz fī Fiqh Madhhab al-Imām al-Shāfi'ī.* 2 vols. Cairo: Maṭba'at al-Ādāb wal-Mu'ayyad, 1899.

Grotius, Hugo. *De jure belli ac pacis libri tres*. Amstelodami: Apud Viduam Abrahami Asomeren, 1701.

_______. *Prolegomena to the Law of War and Peace*. New York: The Liberal Arts Press, 1957.

Ḥamīdullāh, Muḥammad. *Majmū'at al-Wathā'iq al-Siyāsiyya lil-'Ahd al-Nabawī wal-Khilāfa al-Rāshida.* Beirut: Dār al-Irshād, 1969.

al-Haytamī, Aḥmad Ibn Ḥijr. *Tuḥfat al-Muḥtāj ilā Sharḥ al-Minhāj*. 8 vols. Cairo: Maṭba'at Muṣṭafā al-Bābī al-Ḥalabī, 1933.

al-Haythamī, Nūr al-Dīn 'Alī Ibn Abī Bakr. *Majma' al-Zawā'id wa Manba' al-Fawā'id.* 10 vols. Cairo: Maktabat al-Qudsī, 1353 A.H.

Heyd, W. *Histoire du commerce du Levant au moyen âge*. 2 vols. Leipzig: Otto Harrassowitz, 1923.

The Holy Qur'ān. Cairo: Dār al-Shurūq, 1977.

The Holy Scriptures: A Jewish Bible According to the Masoretic Text. Tel Aviv: Shalom Publishing House, 1970.

Ibn 'Abd al-Ḥakam, Abū al-Qāsim 'Abd al-Raḥmān. *Futūḥ Miṣr wa Akhbāruhā.* Cairo: Maktabat Madbūlī, 1991.

Ibn 'Abd Rabbu, Shihāb al-Dīn Aḥmad. *Al-'Iqd al-Farīd*. Beirut: Dār wa Maktabat al-Hilāl, 1986.

Ibn 'Ābidīn, Muḥammad Amīn. *Radd al-Muḥtār 'alā al-Durr al-Mukhtār.* 5 vols. Cairo: al-Maṭba'a al-Amīriyya, 1326 A.H.

Ibn Abī al-Ḥadīd, 'Izz al-Dīn. *Kitāb Nahj al-Balāgha*. 4 vols. Beirut: Dār al-Ma'rifa, n.d.

Ibn Anas, Mālik. *al-Mudawwana al-Kubrā*. 5 vols. Cairo: Maṭba'at al-Sa'āda, 1323 A.H.

Ibn al-Ash'ath, Abū Dāwūd Sulaymān. *Sunan Abī Dāwūd*, 2 vols. Beirut: Dār al-Janān, 1988.

Ibn al-Athīr, Abū al-Ḥasan 'Alī. *al-Kāmil fī al-Tārīkh*. 12 vols. Beirut: Dār al-Kutub al-'Ilmiyya, 1987.

Ibn al-Bazzāz, Muḥammad Ibn Shihāb. "al-Fatāwī al-Bazzāziyya aw al-Jāmi' al-Wajīz." In *al-Fatāwī al Hindiyya wa Tu'raf bil-Fatāwī al-'Ālimkīriyya*. 6 vols. Cairo: al-Maṭba'a al-Amīriyya bi-Būlāq, 1310 A.H.

Ibn al-Farrā', Abū 'Alī al-Ḥusayn Ibn Muḥammad. *Kitāb Rusul al-Mulūk wa-man Yaṣluḥ lil-Risāla wal-Safāra*. Edited by Ṣalāḥ al-Dīn al-Munajjid. Cairo: Lajnat al-Ta'līf wal-Tarjama wal-Nashr, 1947.

Ibn al-Hajjāj, Abū al-Ḥusayn Muslim. *Ṣaḥīḥ Muslim*. 5 vols. Beirut: Mu'assasat 'Izz al-Dīn lil-Ṭibā'a wal-Nashr, 1987.

Ibn Ḥanbal, Aḥmad Ibn Muḥammad. *al-Musnad* 6 vols. Beirut: al-Maktab al-Islāmī, 1969.

Ibn Ḥazm, Abū Muḥammad 'Alī. *al-Faṣl fī al-Milal wal-Ahwā' wal-Niḥal*. 5 vols. Beirut: Dār al-Jīl, 1985.

_______. *al-Īṣāl fī al-Muḥallā bil-Āthār*. 12 vols. Beirut: Dār al-Kutub al-'Ilmiyya, 1988.

Ibn Hishām, Abū Muḥammad 'Abd al-Malik. *al-Sīra al-Nabawiyya*. 4 vols. Beirut: Dār al-Jīl, 1987.

Ibn al-Humām, Muḥammad Ibn 'Abd al-Wāḥid. *Fatḥ al-Qadīr Sharḥ al-Hidāya lil-Marghīnānī*. 10 vols. Beirut: Dār al-Fikr, 1990.

Ibn Ibrāhīm, Abū Yūsuf Ya'qūb. *Kitāb al-Kharāj*. Beirut: Dār al-Ḥadātha, 1990.

Ibn Isḥāq, Muḥammad. *Sīrat Rasūl Allāh*. Translated by A. Guillaume. Karachi, Pakistan: Oxford University Press, 1955.

Ibn Kathīr, Abū al-Fidā' al-Ḥāfiẓ. *al-Bidāya wal-Nihāya*. 14 vols. Beirut: Maktabat al-Ma'ārif, n.d.

_______. *Tafsīr Ibn Kathīr*. 4 vols. Beirut: Dār al-Fikr lil-Ṭibā'a wal-Nashr wal-Tawzī', 1981.

Ibn Khaldūn, 'Abd al-Raḥmān. *Muqaddimat Ibn Khaldūn*. Beirut: Dār al-Qalam, 1984.

Ibn Khurradādhbih, Abū al-Qāsim 'Abd Allāh. *al-Masālik wal-Mamālik*. Edited by Michel Jan de Goeje. Leiden, The Netherlands: E.J. Brill, 1889.

Ibn Manẓūr, Muḥammad. *Lisān al-'Arab al-Muḥīṭ*. 3 vols. Beirut: Dār Lisān al-'Arab, n.d.

Ibn al-Murtaḍā, Aḥmad Ibn Yaḥyā. *al-Baḥr al-Zakhkhār al-Jāmi' li-Madhāhib 'Ulamā' al-Amṣār*. 5 vols. Beirut: Mu'assasat al-Risāla, 1975.

Ibn Nujaym, Zayn al-Dīn Ibn Ibrāhīm. *al-Baḥr al-Rā'iq Sharḥ Kanz al-Daqā'iq*. 8 vols. Cairo: Maṭba'at Muṣṭafā al-Bābī al-Ḥalabī, 1334 A.H.

Ibn Qayyim al-Jawziyya, Shams al-Dīn. *Aḥkām Ahl al-Dhimma*. 2 vols. Damascus: Maṭba'at Jāmi'at Dimashq, 1961.

_______. *I'lām al-Muwaqqi'īn 'an Rabb al-'Ālamīn*. 4 vols. Cairo: al-Maktaba al-Tijāriyya al-Kubrā, 1955.

Ibn Qayyim al-Jawziyya, Shams al-Dīn. *Zād al-Ma'ād fī Hudā Khayr al-'Ibād*. 2 vols. Cairo: Maṭba'at Muṣṭafā al-Bābī al-Ḥalabī, 1950.

Ibn Qudāma, Muwaffaq al-Dīn and Ibn Qudāma, Shams al-Dīn 'Abd al-Raḥmān. *al-Mughnī wa Yalīhi al-Sharḥ al-Kabīr*. 12 vols. Beirut: Dār al-Kitāb al-'Arabī, 1983.

Ibn Rushd, Abū al-Walīd Muḥammad. *Bidāyat al-Mujtahid wa Nihāyat al-Muqtaṣid*. 2 vols. Beirut: Dār al-Ma'rifa, 1986.

Ibn Rushd, Muḥammad Ibn Aḥmad. *al-Muqaddamāt al-Mumahhadāt*, 3 vols. Cairo: Maṭba'at al-Sa'āda, 1325 A.H.

Ibn Sallām, Abū 'Ubayd al-Qāsim. *Kitāb al-Amwāl*. Beirut: Dār al-Ḥadātha, 1988.

Ibn Shaddād, Bahā' al-Dīn Yūsuf. *al-Nawādir al-Sulṭāniyya wal-Maḥāsin al-Yūsufiyya*. Cairo: al-Dār al-Miṣriyya lil-Ta'līf wal-Tarjama, 1962.

Ibn Taghrībirdī, Jamāl al-Dīn Yūsuf. *al-Nujūm al-Zāhira fī Mulūk Miṣr wal-Qāhira*. 12 vols. Cairo: Maṭba'at Dār al-Kitāb, 1930.

Ibn al-Ṭaqṭaqī, Muḥammad Ibn 'Alī Ibn Ṭabāṭabā. *al-Fakhrī fī al-Ādāb al-Sulṭāniyya wal-Duwal al-Islāmiyya*. Cairo: Maṭba'at Muḥammad 'Alī Ṣubayh, n.d.

Ibn Taymiyya, Shams al-Islām Aḥmad. "Qā'ida fī Qitāl al-Kuffār." In *Majmū'at Rasā'il Ibn Taymiyya*, pp. 115-146. Edited by Muḥammad Ḥāmid al-Faqī. Cairo: Maṭba'at al-Sunna al-Muḥammadiyya, 1949.

Ibn Taymiyya, Shams al-Islām Aḥmad. *al-Siyāsa al-Shar'iyya fī Iṣlāḥ al-Rā'ī wal-Ra'iyya*. Beirut: Dār al-Kutub al-'Arabiyya, 1966.

Ibn Wāṣil, Jamāl al-Dīn Muḥammad. *Mufarrij al-Kurūb fī Akhbār Banī Ayyūb*. 5 vols. Cairo: Maṭba'at Jāmi'at Fu'ād al-Awwal, 1953-1972.

al-Jāḥiẓ, Abū 'Uthmān 'Amr Ibn Baḥr. *al-Bayān wal-Tabyīn*, 5th. ed., 4 vols. Cairo: Maktabat al-Khānjī, 1985.

Johnes, F. Liewellyn. *Military Occupation of Alien Territory in Time of Peace: Transactions of the Grotius Society*. London: Macmillan, 1923.

al-Juwaynī, Abū al-Ma'ālī. *al-Burhān fī Usūl al-Fiqh*. Edited by 'Abd al-'Aẓīm al-Dīb. 2 vols. Cairo: Dār al-'Urūba lil-Ṭibā'a wal-Nashr, 1400 A.H.

______. *Ghiyāth al-Umam fī Iltiyāth al-Ẓulam*. Alexandria, Egypt: Dār al-Da'wa lil-Ṭab' wal-Nashr, 1979.

al-Kalbī, Muḥammad Ibn Aḥmad Ibn 'Abd Allāh. *al-Qawānīn al-Fiqhiyya*. Tunus: Maṭba'at al-Nahḍa, 1334 A.H.

al-Kāsānī, 'Alā' al-Dīn. *Kitāb Badā'i' al-Ṣanā'i' fī Tartīb al-Sharā'i'*. 7 vols. Cairo: al-Maṭba'a al-Jamāliyya, 1910.

al-Khatīb, Muḥammad al-Sharbīnī. *Mughnī al-Muḥtāj ilā Sharḥ al-Minhāj*. 4 vols. Cairo: Maṭba'at Muṣṭafā al-Bābī al-Ḥalabī, 1933.

al-Khirshī, Abū 'Abd Allāh Muḥammad. *Fatḥ al-Jalīl 'alā Mukhtaṣar al-'Allāma Khalīl*. 8 vols. Cairo: Maṭba'at Būlāq, 1299 A.H.

Le Bon, Gustave. *La civilisation des Arabes*. Paris: Librarie de Firmin-Didot, 1884.

______. *Les premières civilisations*. Paris: C. Marpon et E. Flammarion, 1889.

al-Maghribī, Abū 'Abd Allāh Muḥammad. *Kitāb Mawāhib al-Jalīl li-Sharḥ Mukhtaṣar Khalīl*. 6 vols. Beirut: Dār al-Fikr, 1992.

al-Maqrīzī, Taqī al-Dīn Aḥmad Ibn 'Alī. *Imtā' al-Asma'*. Cairo: Maṭba'at Lajnat al-Ta'līf wal-Tarjama wal-Nashr, 1941.

______. *Kitāb al-Khiṭaṭ al-Maqrīziyya*. 4 vols. Cairo: Maṭba'at al-Nīl, 1325 A.H.

______. *al-Sulūk li-Ma'rifat Duwal al-Mulūk*. 4 vols. Cairo: Maṭba'at Lajnat al-Ta'līf wal-Tarjama wal-Nashr, 1957.

al-Marghīnānī, Shaykh al-Islām Burhān al-Dīn. *al-Hidāya Sharḥ Bidāyat al-Mubtadā*, 2 vols. Beirut: al-Maktaba al-Islāmiyya, n.d.

Mas-Latrie, Louis de. *Relations et commerce de l'Afrique septentrionale ou Magreb avec les nations Chrétiennes ou moyen-âge*. Paris: Firmin-Didot, 1886.

al-Mas'ūdī, Abū Ḥasan 'Alī Ibn al-Ḥusayn. *Kitāb al-Tanbīh wal-Ishrāf*. 8 vols. Leiden, The Netherlands: E.J. Brill, 1967.

_______. *Murūj al-Dhahab wa Ma'ādin al-Jawhar*. 4 vols. Beirut: Dār al-Fikr, 1973.

al-Māwardi, Abū al-Ḥasan 'Alī. *Adab al-Dunyā wal-Dīn*. Mecca: Dār al-Bāz lil-Nashr, 1987.

al-Māwardi, Abū al-Ḥasan 'Alī. *al-Aḥkām al-Sulṭāniyya wal-Wilāyāt al-Dīniyya*. Cairo: Dār al-Fikr, 1983.

al-Muqrī, Sharaf al-Dīn Ismā'īl Ibn Abī Bakr. *Asnā al-Maṭālib fī Sharḥ Rawḍ al-Ṭālib*, 2 vols. Cairo: al-Maṭba'a al-Maymaniyya, 1306 A.H.

al-Nasā'ī, Abū 'Abd al-Raḥmān Aḥmad Ibn Shu'ayb. *Sunan al-Nasā'ī*. 8 vols. Cairo: al-Maktaba al-Tijāriyya al-Kubrā, 1930.

al-Nawawī, Muḥyī al-Dīn Yaḥyā Ibn Sharaf al-Dīn. *Minhāj al-Ṭālibīn*. London: W. Thacker & Co., 1914.

al-Naysābūrī, Abū al-Ḥusayn Muslim Ibn al-Ḥajjāj. *Ṣaḥīḥ Muslim*, 5 vols. Beirut: Mu'ssasat 'Izz al- Dīn lil-Ṭibā'a wal-Nashr, 1987.

Newman, W.L. *The Politics of Aristotle*. 4 vols. Oxford: The Clarendon Press, 1887.

New World Translation of the Holy Scriptures. New York: International Bible Students Association, 1984.

Nys, Ernest. *Les origines du droit international*. Bruxelles and Paris: Alfred Castaigne & Thorin & Fils, 1894.

Oppenheim, L. *International Law*. 2 vols. Revised by Hersch Lauterpacht. London: Longmans, Green & Co., Inc., 1952.

al-Qaffāl al-Shāshī, Abū Bakr Muḥammad Ibn Aḥmad. *Ḥilyat al-'Ulamā' fī Ma'rifat Madhāhib al-Fuqahā'*. 8 vols. Amman: Maktabat al-Risāla al-Ḥadītha, 1988.

al-Qafṣī, Muḥammad Ibn ‘Abd Allāh. *Lubāb al-Lubāb*. Tūnus: al-Maṭba‘a al-Tūnusiyya, 1346 A.H.

al-Qalqashandī, Aḥmad Ibn ‘Alī. *Subḥ al-A‘shā fī Ṣinā‘at al-Inshā*. 14 vols. Beirut: Dār al-Kutub al-‘Ilmiyya, 1987.

al-Qannūjī, Ṣiddīq Ibn Ḥasan. al-Rawḍa al-Nadiyya Sharḥ al-Durar al-Bahiyya lil-Shawkānī. 6 vols. Cairo: al-Maṭba‘a al-Munīriyya, 1941.

al-Qarāfī, Aḥmad Ibn Idrīs Ibn ‘Abd al-Raḥmān. *al-Furūq*. 4 vols. Cairo: Maṭba‘at Muṣṭafā al-Bābī al-Ḥalabī, 1344 A.H.

al-Qurashī, Yaḥyā Ibn Ādam. *Kitāb al-Kharāj*. Beirut: Dār al-Ḥadātha, 1990.

al-Qurtubī, Abū ‘Abd Allāh Muḥammad. *al-Jāmi‘ li-Aḥkām al-Qur’ān*. 20 vols. Beirut: Dār al-Kutub al-‘Ilmiyya, 1988.

al-Ramlī, Shams al-Dīn Muḥammad Ibn Aḥmad. *Nihāyat al-Muḥtāj ilā Sharḥ al-Minhāj*. 8 vols. Cairo: al-Maṭba‘a al-Bahiyya al-Miṣriyya, 1304 A.H.

al-Rāzī, Fakhr al-Dīn. *al-Tafsīr al-Kabīr*. 32 vols. Beirut: Dār Iḥyā’ al-Turāth al-‘Arabī, 1980.

al-Rāzī, Muḥammad Ibn Abī Bakr. *Mukhtār al-Ṣiḥāḥ*. Beirut: Maktabat Lubnān, 1988.

Ridā, Aḥmad. *Mu‘jam Matn al-Lugha*. 5 vols. Beirut: Dār Maktabat al-Ḥayāt, 1958.

al-Ṣan‘ānī, Muḥammad Ibn Ismā‘īl. *Subul al-Salām Sharḥ Bulūgh al-Marām min Jam‘ Adillat al-Aḥkām*. 4 vols. Beirut: Dār Maktabat al-Ḥayāt, 1989.

al-Sarakhsī, Muḥammad Ibn Aḥmad. *Sharḥ Kitāb al-Siyar al-Kabīr li-Muḥammad Ibn al-Ḥasan al-Shaybānī*. 5 vols. Cairo: Maṭba‘at Sharikat al-I‘lānāt al-Sharqiyya, 1971-1972.

_______. *Kitāb al-Mabsūṭ*. 30 vols. Cairo: Maṭba‘at al-Sa‘āda, 1324 A.H.

al-Ṣāwī, Aḥmad. *Bulghat al-Sālik li-Aqrab al-Masālik*. 2 vols. Beirut: Dār al-Fikr lil-Ṭibā‘a wal-Nashr, 1980.

al-Shāfi‘ī, Muḥammad Ibn Idrīs. *Kitāb al-Umm*. 7 vols. Cairo: al-Hay’a al-Miṣriyya al-‘Āmma lil-Kitāb, 1987.

al-Shahrastānī, Abū al-Fatḥ Muḥammad ‘Abd al-Karīm. *al-Milal wal-Niḥal*. Beirut: Dār al-Fikr lil-Ṭibā‘a wal-Nashr, n.d.

al-Shāṭibī, Abū Isḥāq. *al-Muwāfaqāt fī Usūl al-Sharī'a*. Edited by Muḥammad 'Abd Allāh Darrāz. 4 vols. Beirut: Dār al-Ma'rifa, n.d.

al-Shawkānī, Muḥammad Ibn 'Alī. *Nayl al-Awṭār Sharḥ Muntaqā al-Akhbār min Aḥādīth Sayyid al-Akhyār*. 8 vols. Cairo: Maṭba'at Muṣṭafā al-Bābī al-Ḥalabī, 1952.

al-Shaybānī, Muḥammad Ibn al-Ḥasan. *Kitāb al-Siyar*. Edited by Majīd Khaddūrī. Beirut: al-Dār al-Muttaḥida lil-Nashr, 1975.

al-Shīrāzī, Abū Isḥāq Ibrāhīm Ibn 'Alī. *al-Muhadhdhab*. 2 vols Cairo: Maṭba'at Muṣṭafā al-Bābī al-Ḥalabī, , 1343 A.H.

_______. *al-Tanbīh*. Cairo: Maṭba'at Muṣṭafā al-Bābī al-Ḥalabī,-, 1951.

al-Suhaylī, Abū al-Qāsim 'Abd al-Raḥmān Ibn Aḥmad al-Khath'amī. *al-Rawḍ al-Anaf fī Sharḥ al-Sīra al-Nabawiyya li-Ibn Hishām*. 7 vols. Cairo: al-Maṭba'a al-Jamāliyya, 1914.

al-Ṭabarī, Abū Ja'far Muḥammad Ibn Jarīr. *Kitāb Ikhtilāf al-Fuqahā'*. Edited by Joseph Schacht. Leiden, The Netherlands: E.J. Brill, 1933.

_______. *Tārīkh al-Ṭabarī: Ṭārīkh al-Umam wal-Mulūk*. 6 vols. Beirut: Mu'ssast 'Izz al-Dīn lil-Ṭibā'a wal-Nashr, 1987.

al-Ṭarīhī, Fakhr al-Dīn, *Majma' al-Baḥrayn*. 6 vols. Beirut: Dār wa Maktabat al-Hilāl, 1985.

al-Tirmidhī, Muḥammad Ibn 'Isā. *Sunan al-Tirmidhī*, 5 vols. Beirut: Dār al-Fikr, 1983.

de Vattle, Emmerich. *Le droit de gens, ou principes de la loi nautrelle, appliques à la conduite et aux affairs de nations et des souverains*. Paris: Chez Janet et Cotelle, 1820.

de Victoria, Franciscus. *De Indis et de jure belli relectiones*. Translated by H.F. Wright. Washington, D.C.: Carnegie Institution, 1917.

Vreeland, Hamilton. *Hugo Grotius: The Father of the Modern Science of International Law*. New York: Oxford University Press, 1917.

al-Ya'qūbī, Aḥmad Ibn Abī Ya'qūb Ibn Ja'far. *Tārīkh al-Ya'qūbī*. 3 vols. al-Najaf, Iraq: al-Maktaba al-Murtaḍawiyya, 1964.

al-Zamakhsharī, Abū al-Qāsim. *Asās al-Balāgha*. Beirut: Dār al-Ma'rifa lil-Ṭibā'a wal-Nashr, n.d.

al-Zawzanī, Abū 'Abd Allāh al-Ḥusayn Ibn Aḥmad. *Sharḥ al-Mu'allaqāt al-Sab'*. Beirut: Dār al-Qāmūs al-Hadīth, n.d.

al-Zirikl, Khayr al-Dīn. *al-A'lām: Qāmūs Tarājim li-Ashhar al-Rijāl wal-Nisā' min al-'Arab wal-Musta'ribīn wal-Mustashriqīn*. 8 vols. Beirut: Dār al-'Ilm lil-Malāyīn, 1980.

al-Zuhrī, Muḥammad Ibn Sa'd Ibn Manī'. *Kitāb al-Ṭabaqāt al-Kabīr*. 9 vol. Leiden, The Netherlands: E. J. Brill, 1325 A.H. Reprinted in 14 vols. Cairo: Dār al-Taḥrīr, 1388 A.H.

Secondary Sources

Abdel Haleem, Harfiya et al. eds. *The Crescent and the Cross: Muslim andd Christian Approaches to War and Peace.* New York: St. Martin's Press, 1998.

Abou El Fadl, Khalid. "Ahkām al-Bughāt: Irregular War and the Law of Rebellion in Islam." In *Cross, Crescent, and Sword: The Justification and Limitation of War in Western and Islamic Tradition*, pp. 149-176. Edited by James Turner Johnson and John Kelsay. Westport, CT: Greenwood Press, 1990.

_________. "The Use and Abuse of 'holy war'". *Ethics & International Affairs* 14 (2000): 133-140.

Abū-'Īd, 'Ārif Khalīl. *al-'Alāqāt al-Khārijiyya fī dawlat al-Khilāfa.* Kuwait: Dār al-Arqam, 1983.

Abu-Sahlieh, Sami A. Aldeeb. *Les Musulmans face aux droits de l'homme: religion & droit & politique étude et documents*. Bochum, Germany: Winkler, 1994.

Abū Sharī'a, Ismā'īl Ibrāhīm. *Naẓariyyat al-Ḥarb fī al-Sharī'a al-Islāmiyya.* Kuwait: Maktabat al-Falāḥ, 1981.

Abu Sulayman, Abdul Hamid. "Al-dhimmah and Related Concepts in Historical Perspective." *Journal of the Institute of Muslim Minority Affairs* 9 (Jannuary 1988): 8-29.

_________. *The Islamic Theory of International Relatione: New Directions for Islamic Methodology and Thought.* Herndon, Virginia: International Institute of Islamic Thought, 1987.

Abu Sulayman, Abdul Hamid. *Towards an Islamic Theory of International Relations: New Directions for Methodology and Thought.* Herndon, Virginia: The International Institute of Islamic Thought, 1993.

Abū Zahra, Muḥammad. *Naẓariyyat al-Ḥarb fī al-Islām*. Cairo: Wazārat al-Awqāf, 1961.

Adegbite, Lateef. "Human Rights in Islamic Law." *The Journal of Islamic and Comparative Law* 7 (1977): 1-12.

Adeney, Bernard T. *Just War, Political Realism, and Faith*. Metuchen, N.J.: The American Theological Library Association, 1988.

Algase, Roger C. "Protection of Civilian Lives in Warfare: A Comparison between Islamic Law and Modern International Law Concerning the Conduct of Hostilities." *Revue de droit pénel militaire et de droit de la guerre* 16:2-3 (1977): 245-261.

Ali, Moulavi Cheragh. *A Critical Exposition of the Popular Jihād*. New Delhi, India: Idarah-I Adabiyat-I Delli, 1884.

Allen, Charles A. "Civilian Starvation and Relief during Armed Conflict: The Modern Humanitarian law." *Georgia Journal of International & Comparative Law* 19:1 (Spring 1989): 1-85.

'Amāra, Muḥammad. *al-Islām wa Ḥuqūq al-Insān:Ḍarūrāt lā Ḥuqūq*. 'Ālam al-Ma'rifa, no. 89. Kuwait: al-Majlis al-Waṭanī lil-Thaqāfa wal-Funūn wal-Ādāb, 1985.

Amīn, Aḥmad. *Fajr al-Islām*. Beirut: Dār al-Kitāb al-'Arabī, 1975.

Amjad-Ali, Charles. "Text and Interpretation: Superfluity on Issues of Human Rights in Islam." *Al-Mushir* 36:3 (1994): 69-84.

Anderson, J.N.D. "The Significance of Islamic Law in the World Today." *American Journal of International Law* 9 (1960): 187-198.

Anderson, J.N.D. and Coulson, N.J. "The Moslem Ruler and Contractual Obligations." *New York University Law Review* 33: 11 (November 1958): 917-933.

An-Na'im, Abdullahi Ahmed. "Religious Freedom in Egypt under the Shadow of the Islamic Dhimma System." In *Religious Liberty and Human Rights in Nations and in Religions*, pp. 43-59. Edited by Leonard Swidler. Philadelphia and New York: Ecumenical Press and Hippocrene Books, 1986.

Armanāzī, Najīb. *al-Shar' al-Dawlī fī al-Islām*. London: Riad El-Rayyes Books, 1990.

Arnold, Thomas W. *The Preaching of Islam: A History of the Propagation of the Muslim Faith.* Lahore, Pakistan: Muhammad Ashraf Publications, 1961.

Arzt, Donna E. "The Treatment of Religious Dissidents under Classical and Contemporary Islamic Law." In *Religious Human Rights in Global Perspective: Religious Perspectives*, pp. 387-453. Edited by John Witte, Jr. and Johan D. van der Vyver. The Hague, The Netherlands Martinus Nijhoff Publishers, 1996.

Badr, Gamal M. "A Survey of Islamic International Law." *American Society of International Law: Proceedings of the 76th Annual Meeting* (1982): 56-61.

Baehr, P.R. "Some Observations on Islam and Human Rights." *Recht van de Islam* 15 (1998): 69-73.

Bainton, Roland H. *Christian Attitudes Toward War and Peace: A Historical Survey and Critical Re-evaluation.* New York: Abingdon Press, 1961.

Ballis, William. *The Legal Position of War Changes in Its Practice and Theory from Plato to Vattel.* New York: Garland Publishing, Inc., 1973.

al-Banna, Ḥasan. *al-Jihād fī Sabīl Allāh.* Cairo: Maktabat al-Turāth al-Islāmī, n.d.

Barber, Benjamin. *Jihād vs. McWorld.* New York: Times Books, a Division of Random House, Inc., 1995.

Bassiouni, M. Cherif. "Sources of Islamic Law, and the Protection of Human Rights in the Islamic Criminal Justice System." In *The Islamic Criminal Justice System*, pp. 3-53. Edited by M. Cherif Bassiouni. New York: Oceana Publications, Inc., 1982.

_______. "The Commission of Experts Established Pursuant to Security Council Resolution 780: Investigating Violations of International Humanitarian law in the Former Yugoslavia." *Criminal Law Forum* 5: 2-3 (1994): 279-340.

Beeston, A. F. *Warfare in Ancient South Arabia.* London: Luzac, 1976.

Bannerman, Patrick. *Islam in Perspective: A Guide to Islamic Society, Politics and Law.* London: Routledge, 1988.

Bennoune, Karima. "As-Salāmu 'Alaykum? Humanitarian Law in Islamic Jurisprudence". *Michigan Journal of International Law* 15: 2 (Winter 1994): 605-643.

Berman, Nathaniel. "Sovereignty in Abeyance: Self-determination and International Law." *Wisconsin International Law Journal* 7:1 (Fall 1988): 51-105.

Bertsch, Margaret Elizabeth. "Counter-Crusade: A Study of Twelfth Century 'Jihad' in Syria and Palestine." Ph.d.diss., The University of Michigan, 1951.

al-Birrī, Zakariyya. "al-Islām wa Ḥuqūq al-Insān: Ḥaqq al-Ḥurriyyah" *'Ālam al-Fikr* 1:4 (January, February and March 1971):105-134.

Blaustein, Albert P., et al., eds. *Human Rights Sourcebook.* New York: Paragon House Publishers, 1987.

Boisard, Marcel. *Jihād: A Commitment to Universal Peace.* Indianapolis, Indiana: American Trust Publications, 1988.

_______. *Humanism in Islam.* Indianapolis, Indiana: American Trust Publications, 1988.

_______. "The Conduct of Hostilities and the Protection of the Victims of Armed Conflicts in Islam." *Hamdard Islamicus* 1: 2 (Autumn 1978): 3-17.

_______. "On the Probable Influence of Islam on Western Public and International Law." *International Journal of Middle Eastern Studies* 11 (1980): 429-450.

Bonner, Michael David. *Aristocratic Violence and Holy War: Studies in the Jihad and the Arab Byzantine Frontier.* Washington, D.C.: American Oriental Society, 1996.

Bosworth, C.E. "The Concept of Dhimma in Early Islam." In *Christians and Jews in the Ottoman Empire: The Functioning of a Plural Society.* vol. 1, pp. 37-51. Edited by Benjamin Braude and Bernard Lewis. New York: Holmes & Meier Publishers, Inc., 1982.

Boven, T. van. "Human Rights in Islamic States." *Recht van de Islam* 15(1998): 59-67.

Bowett, D. W. *Self-Defense in International Law.* Manchester: Manchester University Press, 1958.

Brownlie, Ian. *International Law and the Use of Force by States.* Oxford: The Clarendon Press, 1963.

Brownlie, Ian. *Basic Documents on Human Rights.* Oxford: Clarendon Press, 1981.

Buchanan, Alen E. "The Right to Self-determination: Analytical and Moral Foundations." *Arizona Journal of International and Comparative Law* 8:2 (Fall 1991): 41-50.

Bueren, Geraldine van. "The International Legal Protection of Children in Armed Conflicts." *International and Comparative Law Quarterly* 43:4 (October 1994): 809-826.

Bull, Hedley; Kingsbury, Benedict; and Roberts, Adam. *Hugo Grotius and International Relations*. Oxford: The Clarendon Press, 1990.

Butler, Alfred J. The Arab Conquest of Egypt and the Last Thirty Years of the Roman Dominion. Oxford, UK: Oxford Clarendon Press, 1902

Butler, G. and Maccoby, S. *The Development of International Law*. London: Longmans, Green & Co., 1926.

Cahill, Lisa Sowle. "Non-resistance, Defense, Violence, and the Kingdom in Christian Tradition." *Interpretation* 38:4 (October 1984): 380-397.

Carroll, Robert. "War in the Hebrew Bible." In *War and Society in the Greek World*, pp. 25-44. Edited by John Rich and Graham Shipley. New York: Routledge, 1993.

Chinkin, Christine. "Rape and Sexual Abuse of Women in International Law." *European Journal of International Law* 5 (1994): 326-341.

Conrad, Gerhard. "Combatant and Prisoner of War in Classical Islamic Law." *Revue de droit pénel militaire et de droit de la guerre* 20 (1981): 269-307.

Cooper, J. P. *Human Rights Towards an Islamic Framework*. London: Gulf Centre for Strategic Studies, 1994.

Cotler, Irwin. "Human Rights as the Modern Tool of Revolution." In *Human Rights in the Twenty-First Century: A Global Challenge*, pp. 7-20. Edited by Kathleen E. Mahoney and Paul Mahoney. Dordrecht, The Netherlands: Martinus Nijhoff Publishers, 1993.

_______. ed. *Nuremberg Forty Years Later: The Struggle Against Injustice in Our Time*. Montreal and Kingston: McGill-Queen's University Press, 1995.

Cotler, Irwin and Eliadis, F. Pearl, eds. *International Human Rights Law, Theory and Practice*. Montreal: The Canadian Human Rights Foundation, 1992.

Coulson, Noel. "The State and the Individual in Islamic Law." *The International and Comparative Law Quarterly* 6 (1957): 49-60.

Cowdrey, H. E. "The Genesis of the Crusades: The Springs of Western Ideas of Holy War." In *The Holy War*, pp. 9-32. Edited by Thomas Patrick Murphy. Columbus, Ohio: Ohio State University Press, 1976.

Crouzet, Maurice. *Histoire général des civilisations.* 7 vols. Paris: Presses Universitaires de France, 1986.

Dajani-Shakeel, Hadia and Messier, Ronald A., eds. *The Jihad and its Times.* Ann Arbor, Michigan: Center for Near Eastern and North African Studies, The University of Michigan, 1991.

El-Dakkak, Said. "International Humanitarian Law Lies between the Islamic Concept and Positive International Law." *International Review of Red Cross* 275 (March-April 1990): 101-114.

Davis, Joyce. *Between Jihad and Salaam: Profiles in Islam.* New York: St. Martin's Press, 1997.

Delupis, Ingrid. *International Law and the Independent State.* Glasgow: The University Press, 1974.

de Taube, Le Baron Michel. "Etudes sur le développement historique du droit international dans l'Europe Orientale." Recueil des cours 1:2 (1926): 44-535.

Dickson, Brice. "The United Nations and Freedom of Religion." *International and Comparative Law Quarterly* 44: 2 April 1995): 327-357.

Donner, Fred M. *The Early Islamic Conquests*. Prinnceton: Princeton University Press, 1981.

________. The Sources of Islamic Conceptions on War." In *Just War and Jihad: Historical and Theoretical Perspectives on War and Peace in Western and Islamic Traditions*, pp. 31-69. Edited by John Kelsey and James Turner Johnson. Westport, CT: Greenwood Press, 1991.

Edward, J. Jurji. "The Islamic Theory of War." *The Moslem World* 30 (1940): 332-342.

Elahi, Maryam. "The Rights of the Child under Islamic Law: Prohibition of the Child Soldier." *Columbia Human Rights Law Review* 19:2 (Spring 1988): 259-279.

Elshtain, Jean Bethke, ed. *Just War Theory.* New York: New York University Press, 1992.

Emerson, Steven. "Political Islam Promotes Terrorism." In *Islam: Opposing Viewpoints*, pp. 157-163. Edited by Paul A. Winters. San Diego: Greenhaven Press, Inc., 1995.

The Encyclopaedia of Islam. 2nd ed. s.v. "Amān," by Joseph Schacht.

_______. 2nd ed. s.v. "Cyprus," by R. Hartmann.

_______. 2nd ed. s.v. "Dār al-'Ahd," by Halil Inalcik..

_______. 2nd ed. s.v. "Dār al-Ḥarb," by A. Abdel.

_______. 2nd ed. s.v. "Dār al-Islām," by A. Abdel.

_______. 2nd ed. s.v. "Dār al-Ṣulḥ" by D.B. Macdonald and A. Abdel.

_______. 2nd ed. s.v. "Dhimma," by C. Cahen.

_______. 2nd ed. s.v. "Djihad," by D.B. Macdonald.

_______. 2nd ed. s.v. "Ghiyār," by M. Perlman.

_______. 2nd ed. s.v. "Ḥakam," by E. Tyan.

_______. 2nd ed. s.v. "Hudna," by Majid Khadurri.

Encyclopaedia Judaica, 2nd ed. s.v. "Byzantine Empire."

Encyclopedia of Public International Law, 6th ed., s.v. "International Law, Islamic," by Majid Khadduri.

Faizar, Rizwis. "Muhammad and thhe Medinan Jews: A Comparison of the Texts of Ibn Ishaq's Kitāb Sīrat Rasūl Allāh with al-Wāqidī's Kitāb al-Maghāzī." *IJMES* 28 (1996): 463-489.

Farrag, Ahmad. "Human Rights and Liberties in Islam." In *Human Rights in a Pluralist World: Individuals and Collectivities*, pp. 13-44. Edited by Jan Berting et al. Westport: Meckler Cororation, 1990.

Faruqi, Isma'il R. "The Rights of Non-Muslims under Islam: Social and Cultural Aspects." In *Muslim Communities in Non-Muslim States*, pp. 43-66. London: Islamic Council of Europe, 1980.

Fauchille, Paul. *Traité de droit international public*. 2 vols. Paris: Rousseau, 1921.

Ferencz Benjamin. "The United Nations and Human Rights Forty Years Later." In *Nuremberg Forty Years Later: The Struggle Against Injustice in our Time*, pp. 97-114. Edited by Irwin Cotler. Montreal & Kingston: McGill-Queen's University Press, 1995.

Firestone, Reuven. "Conceptions of Holy War in Biblical and Qur'ānic Traditions." *Journal of Reigionns Ethics* 24:1 (Spring 1996): 99-123.

________. "Conceptions of Holy War in the Scriptures of Judaism and Islam." *Journal of Religious Ethics* 24 (Spring 1996): 801-824.

________. "Disparity and Resolution in the Qur'anic Teachings on War: A Re-evoluation of a Traditional Problem." *JNES* 55 (1977): 1-19.

________. "The Failure of a Jewish Program of Public Satire in the Squares of Medina." *Judaim* 46 (Winter 1997): 438-452.

________. *Jihad: The Origins of Holy War in Islam*. New York: Oxford University Press, 1999.

Francisse, A. E., "Status of Women in Islam and Their Right to Choose Spouses." *Hamdard Islamicus* 18:1 (1995): 111-117.

Fregosi, Paul. *Jihad in the West: Muslim Conquests from the 7th to the 21st Centuries*. Amherst, N.Y.: Prometheus Books, 1998.

Friedman, Leon. *The Law of War: A Documentary History*. 2 vols. New York: Random House, 1972.

Furnish, Victor Paul. "War and Peace in the New Testament." *Interpretation* 38:4 (October 1984) 363-379.

Garaudy, Roger. *Promesses de l'Islam*. Paris: Éditions du Seuil, 1979.

Gardner, W. "Jihād." *The Moslem World* 2:1 (January 1912): 347-357.

Gendler, Everette E. "War and the Jewish Tradition." In *Contemporary Jewish Ethics*, 189-210. Edited by Menachem Marc Kellner. New York: Sanhedrin Press, 1979.

al-Ghunaimi, Mohammad Talaat. *The Muslim Conception of International Law and the Western Approach*. The Hague, The Netherlands: The Hague Martinus Nijhoff, 1969.

Gil, Moshe. "The Constitution of Medina: A Reconsideration." *Israel Oriental Studies* 4 (1974): 44-66.

Gil, Moshe. "The Origin of the Jews of Yathrib." *JSAI* 4 (1984): 203-223

Glahn, Gerhard von. *Law Among Nations: An Introduction to Public International Law*. New York: The Macmillan Company, 1970.

_______. *The Occupation of Enemy Territory: A Commentary on the Law and Practice of Belligerent Occupation*. Minneapolis: University of Minnesota Press, 1957.

Glenn, H. Patrick. *Legal Traditions of the World: Sustainable Diversity in Law*. New York: Oxford University Press, 2000.

Graber, Doris Appel. *The Development of the Law of Belligerent Occupation, 1863-1914: A Historical Survey*. New York. Columbia University Press, 1949.

Grawford, James. *The Creation of States in International Law*. Oxford: The Clarendon Press, 1979.

Greig, D.W. "Reciprocity, Proportionality, and the Law of Treaties." *Virginia Journal of International Law* 34 (Winter 1994): 295-403.

Grinstein, Joseph. "Jihad and the Constitution: The First Amendment Implications of Combating Religiously Motivated Terrorism." *The Yale Law Journal* 105:5 (March 1996): 1347-1381.

Guillaume, Alfred. "Philosophy and Theology." In *The Legacy of Islam*, pp. 239-283. Edited by Thomas Arnold and Alfred Guillaume. London: Oxford University Press, 1931.

Haddad, Wadi Zaidan. "Ahl al-Dhimma in an Islamic State: The Teaching of Abū al-Ḥasan al-Māwardī's al-Aḥkām al-Sulṭāniyya." *Islam and christian-Muslim Relations* 7:2 (1996): 169-180.

Haggenmacher, Peter. *Grotius et la doctrine de la guerre juste*. Paris: Presses Universitaires de France, 1983.

Hall, William. *A Treatise on International Law*. Oxford: The Clarendon Press, 1924.

_______. *International Law*. Oxford: The Clarendon Press, 1924

Hallaq, Wael B. "On Inductive Corroboration, Probability and Certainty in Sunni-Legal Thought." In *Islamic Law and Jurisprudence*, pp. 3-31. Edited by N. Heer. Seattle: University of Washington Press, 1990.

Halliday, Fred. *Islam and the Myth of Confrontation: Religion and Politics in the Middle East*. London: J.B. Tauris Publishers, 1996.

Hamidullah, Muhammad. "Administration of Justice in Early Islam." *Islamic Culture* 9 (1937): 163-171.

_______. *Muslim Conduct of State*, 4th ed. Lahore, Pakistan: Sh. Muhammad Ashraf, 1961.

_______. "The First Written Constitution of the World." *Islamic Review* (1941): 296-303, 334-340, 377-384, 442-449.

_______. "The International Law in Islam: The Laws of War and Peace in Islam." *The Islamic Review* (May 1951): 8-10.

Hannum, Hurst. *Autonomy, Sovereignty, and Self-Determination: The Accommodation of Conflicting Rights*. Philadelphia: University of Pennsylvania Press, 1990.

_______. ed. *Guide to International Human Rights Practice*. Philadelphia: University of Pennsylvania Press, 1984.

Hanson, Paul D. "War and Peace in the Hebrew Bible." *Interpretation* 38:4 (October 1984): 341-362.

Al-Ḥasan, Muḥammad 'Alī. *al-'Alāqāt al-Dawliyya fī al-Qur'ān wal-Sunna*. Amman: Maktabat al-Nahḍa al-Islāmiyya, 1980.

Hashmi, Sohail H. "The Islamic Ethics of War and Peace." Ph. D. diss., Harvard University, 1996.

_______. "Saving and Taking Life in War: Three Modern Muslim Views." *Muslim World* 89:2 (April 1999): 158-180.

Al-Ḥasan, Muḥammad 'Alī. *al-'Alāqāt al-Dawliyya fī al-Qur'ān wal-Sunna*. Amman: Maktabat al-Nahḍa al-Islamiyya, 1980.

Hassan, Farooq. *The Concept of State and Law in Islam*. New York: University Press of America, 1981.

Henkin, Louis. "Force, Intervention, and Neutrality in Contemporary International Law." *Proceeding of the American Society of International Law* (1963): 147-162.

Hillenbrand, Carole. *The Crusades: Islamic Perspectives*. Edinburgh: Edinburgh University Press, 1999.

Holmes, Robert L. "Can War Be Morally Justified? The Just War Theory." In *Just War Theory*, pp. 197-233. Edited by Jean Bethke Elshtain. New York: New York University Press, 1992.

Homoud, Mohammad Ali. *Diplomacy in Islam: Diplomacy During the Period of Prophet Muhammed*. Jaipur, India: Printwell, 1994.

Hosein, Imran N. "Diplomacy in Islam: Treaties and Agreements: An Analysis of the Treaty of Hudaibiyah." *Muslim Education Quarterly* 3:3 (Spring 1986): 67-85.

Hourani, Albert. *A History of the Arab Peoples*. Cambridge, Massachusetts: The Belknap Press of Harvard University Press, 1991.

Hunter, Shireen T. "The Rise of Islamist Movements and the Western Response: Clash of Civilizations or Clash of Interests?" In *The Islamic Dilema: The Political Role of Islamist Movements in the Contemporary Arab World*, pp. 317-350. Edited by Laura Guazzone. Berkshire: Ithaca Press, 1995.

Huntington, Samuel P. "The Clash of Civilizations?" *Foreign Affairs* 72:3 (Summer 1993): 22-49.

Hyde, Charles Cheney. *International Law Chiefly as Interpreted and Applied by the United States*. 3 vols. Boston: Little, Brown and Co., 1945.

Inalcik, Halil. "Ottoman Methods of Conquest." *Studia Islamica* 2 (1953): 103-129.

Iqbal, Afzal. *The Prophet's Diplomacy: The Art of Negotiation as Conceived and Developed by the Prophet of Islam*. Cape Cod, Massachusetts: Claude Stark & Co., 1975.

Islam and Justice: Debating the Future of Human Rights in the Middle East and North Africa. New York: Lawyers Committee for Human Rights, 1997.

Jameelah, Maryam. *A Manifesto of the Islamic Movement*. Lahore, Pakistan: Mohammad Yusuf Khan Publications, 1979.

al-Jamīlī, al-Sayyid. *Manāqib Amīr al-Mu'minīn 'Umar Ibn al-Khaṭṭāb*. Beirut: Dār al-Kitāb al-'Arabī, 1985.

Jansen, Michael. "Terrorism is a Response to Western Hypocrisy." In *Islam: Opposing Viewpoints*, pp. 164-168. Edited by Paul A. Winters, San Diego: Greenhaven Press, Inc., 1995.

Jawad, Haifaa A. *The Rights of Women in Islam: An Authentic Approach*. New York: St. Martin's Press, Inc., 1998.

Jeffrey, Robert. “A Socio-Historical Analysis of Warfare (Jihad and Qital) in Primitive Islam.” Ph. D. diss., Florida State University, 1994.

Johnson, James Turner. *Ideology, Reason and the Limitation of War*. Prinston: Prinston University Press, 1975.

________. *Just War Tradition and the Restraint of War: A Moral and Historical Inquiry*. Princeton, NJ: Princeton University Press, 1981.

Johnson, James Turner and Kelsay, John, eds. *Cross, Crecent and Sword: The Justification and Limitation of War in Western and Islamic Traditions.* Westport, CT: Greenwood Press, 1990.

Kamali, Mohammad H. “Freedom of Expression in Islam: An Analysis of Fitnah.” *American Journal of Islamic Social Sciences* 10:2 (1993): 178-2000.

________. “Fundamental Rights of the Individual: An Analysis of Haqq (right) in Islamic Law.” *American Journal of Islamic Social Sciences* 10:3 (1993): 340-366.

Keen, M. H. *The Laws of War in the Late Middle Ages*. London: Routledge & Kegan Paul, 1965.

Kelsay, John. “Islam and the Distinction between Combatants and Non-combatants.” In *Cross, Crescent, and Sword: The Justification and Limitation of War in Western and Islamic Traditions*, pp. 197-220. Edited by James Turner Johnson and John Kelsay. Westport, CT: Greenwood Press, 1990.

_______. *Islam and War: A Study in Comparative Ethics*. Louisville, Kentucky: Westminster/John Knox Press, 1993.

_______. “Religion, Morality, and the Governance of War: The Case of Classical Islam.” *The Journal of Religious Ethics* 18:2 (Fall 1990): 123-139.

Kelsay, John and Johnson, James Turner, eds. *Just War and Jihad: Historical and Theoretical Perspectives on War and Peace in Western and Islamic Traditions.* Westport, CT: Greenwood Press, 1991.

Kelsen, Hans. *The Law of the United Nations: A Critical Analysis of its Fundamental problems*. New York: F.A. Praeger, 1950.

_______. “The Legal Status of Germany According to the Declaration of Berlin.” *American Journal of International Law* 39 (1945): 518-526.

Kelsen, Hans and Tucker, Robert. *Principles of International Law*. New York: Holt, Reinhart and Winston, 1966

Khadduri, Majid. "Islam and the Modern Law of Nations." *American Journal of International Law* 50 (1956): 358-372.

_______. *The Islamic Concept of Justice*. Baltimore, Maryland: The Johns Hopkins University Press, 1984.

_______. "Islamic Law and International Law." In *The Future of International Law in a Multicultural World*, pp. 157-161. Edited by René-Jean Dupuy. The Hague, The Netherlands: Martinus Nijhoff Publishers, 1984.

_______. "The Islamic Theory of International Relations and Its Contemporary Relevance." In *Islam and International Relations*, pp. 24-39. Edited by J. Harris Proctor. New York: Frederick A. Praeger Publishers, 1965.

_______. *The Islamic Law of Nations: Shaybani's Siyar*. Baltimore, Maryland: The Johns Hopkins University Press, 1966.

_________. *War and Peace in the Law of Islam*. Baltimore, Maryland: The Johns Hopkins University Press, 1955.

Khan, Qamaruddin. *The Political Thought of Ibn Taymiyya*. New Delhi, India: Adam Publishers & Distributors, 1988.

Al-Khattar, Aref M. "Terrorism in the Name of Religion: Perceptions and Attitudes of Religious Leaders from Judiasm, Christianity, and Islam in the United States.""Ph. D. diss., Indiana University of Pennsylvania, 1998.

Kilziyah, 'Abd al-Wahhāb. *al-Shar' al-Dawlī fī 'Ahd al-Rasūl.* Beirut: Dār al-'Ilm lil-Malāyīn, 1984.

Kingsbury, Benedict and Roberts, Adam. "Introduction: Grotian Thought in International Relations." In *Hugo Grotius and International Relations*, pp. 1-65. Edited by hedley Bull, Benedict Kingsbury, and Adam Roberts Oxford: The Clarendon Press, 1990.

Kolocotronis, Jamilah. *Islamic Jihād: An Historical Perspective*. Indianapolis, Indiana: The American Trust Publications, 1990.

Kruse, Hans. "Al-Shaybani on International Instruments." *Journal of the Pakistan Historical Society* 1 (1953): 90-100.

_______. "The Islamic Doctrine of International Treaties." *Islamic Quarterly* (1954): 152-158.

_______. "The Notion of Siyar." *Journal of thhe Pakistan Historical Society* 2 (January 1954): 16-25

Kruse, Hans. "On the Foundation of Islamic International Jurisprudence." *Journal of the Pakistan Historical Society* 3 (October 1955):231-267.

Kunz, Josef L. "Bellum Justum and Bellum Legale." *The American Journal of International Law* 45 (1951): 528-534.

_______. "Individual and Collective Self-Defense in Article 51 of the Charter of the United Nations." *The American Journal of International Law* 41 (1947): 872-879.

Kuper, Leo. "Genocide and Mass Kilings: Illusion and Reality," in *The Right to Life in International Law*, ed. B.G. Ramcharan. Dordrecht, The Netherlands: Martinus Nijhoff Publishers, 1985.

Kuper, Leo. *The Prevention of Genocide*. New Haven, CT: Yale University Press, 1985.

Kurdi, Abdulrahman Abdulkadir. *The Islamic State: A Study Based on the Islamic Holy Constitution.* London:Mansell Publishing Limited, 1984.

Lambton, Ann K. "A Nineteenth Century View of Jihad." *Studia Islamica* 32 (1970):181-192.

Lane-Poole, Stanley. "The first Mohammedan Treaties with Christians" In *Proceedings of the Royal Irish Academy*, pp. 227-256, vol. 24. Dublin: The Royal Irish Academy, 1904.

Lange, C.L. *Histoire de l'internationalisme*. Kristiana: H. Aschenhoug & Co., 1919.

Lapidus, I. M. "The Arab Conquests and the Formation of Islamic Society." In *Studies on the First Century of Islamic Society*, 49-72. Edited by G. H. Juynboll. Carbondale, Ill: Southern Illinois University Press, 1982.

Laurence, Bruce B. *Shattering the Myth: Islam beyond Violence*. Princeton, N. J.: Princeton University Press, 1998.

Laurent, Joseph. *L'Arménie entre Byzance et l'Islam depuis la conquête arabe jusqu'en 886*. Paris: Fontemoing, 1919.

Lauterpacht, Hersch. *International Law and Human Rights*. New York: Garland Publishing, Inc., 1973.

Lauterpacht, Hersch. "The Problem of the Revision of the Law of War." *The British Year Book of International Law* (1952): 360-382.

Lawrence, Bruce. "Holy War (Jihād) in Islamic Religion and Nation-State Ideologies." In *Just War and Jihād: Historical and Theoretical Perspectives on War and Peace in Western and Islamic Traditions*, pp. 141-160. Edited by John Kelsay and James Turner Johnson. New York: Greenwood Press, 1991.

Lawrence, T.J. *The Principles of International Law*. 7th ed. London: Macmillan, 1927.

Little, David et al. *Human Right and the Conflict of Cultures: Western and Islamic Perspectives on Religious Liberty*. Columbia, South Carolina: University of South Carolina, 1988.

Levy, Reuben. *The Social Structure of Islam*. Cambridge, UK: Cambridge University Press, 1979.

Lewis, Bernard. "Licenese to Kill: Usama bin Ladin's Declaration of Jihad." *Foreign Affairs* 77:6 (Nov-Dec. 1998): 14-19.

Lewis, Bernard. "Politics and War," in *The Legacy of Islam*, pp. 156-209. Edited by Joseph Schacht and C.E. Bosworth. London: Oxford University Press, 1974.

_______. *The Political Language of Islam*. Chicago: The University of Chicago Press, 1988.

_______. "The Roots of Muslim Rage." *The Atlantic Monthly* 266 (September 1990): 54-60.

Maher, Colleen. "The Protection of Children in Armed Conflict: A Human Rights Analysis of the Protection Afforded to Children in Warfare." *World Law Journal* 9 (Summer 1989): 297-322.

Mahmassani, Sobhi. "The Principles of International Law in the Light of Islamic Doctrine." *Recueil des cours* 117 (1966): 199-328.

Mahmood, T. "The Grandeur of Womanhood in Islam." *Islamic and Comparative Law* 6:1 (1986): 1-26.

Majumdar, Suhas. *Jihād: The Islamic Doctrine of Permanent War*. New Delhi: Voice of India, 1994.

Malike, S. K. *The Quranic Concept of War*. Lahore, Pakistan: Wajidalis, 1979.

Mallat, C. "Islam and Public Law." *Islamic Law and Society* 2 (1995): 345-348.

Manna', Haytham. *Human Rights in the Arab-Islamic Culture.* Cairo: Cairo Institute for Human Rights Studies, 1997.

Mansour, Aly Aly. "Hudūd Crimes." In *The Islamic Criminal Justice System*, pp. 195-201. Edited by M. Sherif Bassiouni. New York: Oceana Publications, Inc., 1982.

Marrin, Albert. *War and the Christian Conscience: From Augustine to Martin Luther king, Jr*. Chicago: Henry Regnery, 1971.

Martin, Richard. "Religious Violence in Islam: Towards an Understanding of the Discourse on Jihad in Modern Egypt." In *Contemporary Research on Terrorism,* pp. 55-71. Edited by Paul Wilkinson and Alasdair Steward. Aberdeen: Aberdeen University Press, 1989.

Mawdūdī, Abū al-A'lā. *The Islamic Law and Constitution*. Lahore, Pakistan: Islamic Publications Ltd., 1960.

________. *Jihad in Islam*. Damascus: Dār al-Qur'ān lil-Nashr, 1977.

________. *Rights of Non-Muslims in the Islamic State*. Lahore, Pakistan: Islamic Publications, 1961.

_______. *Towards Understanding Islam*. Beirut: The Holy Qur'ān Publishing House, 1980.

Mayer, Ann Elizabeth. *Islamic Law and Human Rights: Tradition and Politics*. 2nd ed. Boulder, Colorado: Westview Press, Inc., 1995.

_______. "Islamic Reservations to Human Rights Conventions: A Critical Assessment." *Recht van de Islam* 15 (1998): 25-45.

_______. "Universal Versus Islamic Human Rights: A Clash of Cultures or a Clash with a Construct?" *Michigan Journal of International Law* 15:2 (Winter 1994): 308-404.

McDougal, Myres Smith. *Law and Minimum World Order: The Legal Regulation and International Coercion*. New Haven: Yale University Press, 1961.

McNair, Lord and Watts, A.D. *The Legal Effects of War*. Cambridge: Cambridge University Press, 1966.

Melzer, Yehuda. *Concepts of Just War*. Leyden, The Netherlands: A.W. Sijthoff International Publishing Company, 1975.

Meron, Theodor. "Application of Humanitarian Law in Non-International Armed Conflict." *American Society of International Law Proceedings* 85 (1991): 83-101.

Miller, Judith. *God has Ninety-Nine Names Reporting from a Militant Middle East.* New York: Simon and Schuster, 1996.

al-Mināwī, Muḥammad 'Abd al-Ra'ūf. *Mukhtaṣar Sharḥ al-Jāmi' al-Ṣaghīr*. 2 vols. Cairo: Dār Iḥyā' al-Kutub al-'Arabiyya, 1954.

Mir, Mustansir. "Jihād in Islām." In *The Jihād and Its Times*, pp. 113-126. Edited by Hadia Dajani-Shakeel. Michigan: The University of Michigan, 1991.

Mohammad, Noor. "The Doctrine of Jihad: An Introduction." *Journal of Law and Religion* 3 (1985): 381-397.

Moinuddin, Hasan. *The Charter of The Islamic Conference and Legal Framework of Economic Co-operation among Its Member States*. Oxford: The Clarendon Press, 1987.

Morabia, Alfred. *Le ğihād dans L'Islam médiéval: Le «combat sacré» des origines au XIIe siécle*. Paris: Albin Michel, 1993.

al-Munajjid, Ṣalāḥ al-Dīn. *Al-Nuẓum al-Diblumāsiyya fī al-Islām*. Beirut: Dār al-Kitāb al-Jadīd, 1983.

Murphy, Thomas Patrick, ed. *The Holy War*. Columbus: Ohio State University Press, 1976.

Nicolson, Harold. *Diplomacy*. London: Oxford University Press, 1969.

Niditch, Suzan. *War in the Hebrew Bible: A Study in the Ethics of Violence*. New York: Oxford University Press, 1993.

"Not Again: A Survey of Islam and the West." *The Economist* (August 6-12, 1994): 3-17.

Nussbaum, A. *A Concise History of the Law of Nations*. New York: Macmillan, 1954.

O'Brien, William V. *The Conduct of Just and Limited War*. New York: Praeger Publishers, 1981.

O'sullivan, D. P. "Al-Islam: An Alternative Approach to the Universal Protection of Human Rights." *Islamic Quarterly* 41:2 (1997): 130-153.

Olayiwola, Abdur Rahman O. "Human Rights in Islam." *The Islamic Quarterly* 36:4 (1992): 262-279.

Palmer, Norman D. and Perkins, Howard C. *International Relations: The World Community in Transition.* New York: Houghton Mifflin Company, 1953.

Partner, Peter. *God of Battles; Holywars of Christianity and Islam*. Prinston: Prinston University, 1998.

Partsch, Karl Josef. "Freedom of Conscience and Expression, and Political Freedoms." In *The International Bill of Rights*, pp. 209-245. Edited by Louis Henkin. New York: Columbia University Press, 1981.

_________. "Fundamental Principles of Human Rights: Self-Determination, Equality and Non-Discrimination." in *The International Dimensions of Human Rights*, 2 vols., ed. Karl Vasak. Westport, Connecticut: Greenwood Press, 1982.

Peters, Rudolph. "Djihad: War of Aggression or Defence?". In *Akten des VII. Kongresses für Arabistik und Islamwissenschaft*, pp. 282-289. Edited by Herausgegeben von and Albert Dietrich. Göttingen: Vandenhoeck & Ruprecht, 1976.

_______. *Islam and Colonialism: The Doctrine of Jihād in Modern History*. The Hague, The Netherlands: Mouton Publishers, 1979.

_______. "Islamic Law and Human Rights: A Contribbution to an Ongoing Debate." *Recht van de Islam* 15 (1998): 7-24.

_______. *Jihād in Classical and Modern Islam*. Princeton N. J.: Markus Wiener Publishers, 1996.

Phillips, Robert L. *War and Justice*. Norman: University of Oklahoma Press, 1984.

Pictet, Jean. *Humanitarian Law and the Protection of War Victims*. Geneva: Henry Dunant Institute, 1975.

Pipes, Daniel. "Political Islam is a Threat to the West." In *Islam: Opposing Viewpoints*, pp. 190-196. Edited by Paul A. Winters. San Diego: Greenhaven Press, Inc., 1995.

Powell-Smith, V. "Settlement of Disputes by Arbitration under Sharī'ah and at Common Law." *Islamic Studies* 34:1 (1995): 5-41.

Proctor, Harris, ed. *Islam and International Relations*. London: Pall Mall Press, 1965.

Provost, René. "Reciprocity in Human Rights and Humanitarian Law." *The British Year Book of International Law* 65 (1994): 383-454.

Qal'ajī, Muḥammad Rawwās and Qunaibī, Ḥāmid Ṣādiq. *Mu'jam Lughat al-Fuqahā'*. Beirut: Dār al-Nafā'is, 1988.

Qar'ūsh, Kāyid Yūsuf Maḥmūd. Ṭuruq Intihā' Wilāyat al-Ḥukkām fī al-Sharī'a al-Islāmiyya wal-Nuẓum al-Dustūriyya. Beirut: Mu'ssasat al-Risāla, 1987.

Qāsim, 'Awn al-Sharīf. *Nash'at al-Dawla al-Islāmiyya 'Alā 'Ahd Rasūl Allāh Ṣallā Allāh 'Alayh Wa-Sallam: Dirāsa fī Wathā'iq al-'Ahd al-Nabawī*. Beirut: Dār al-Kitāb al-Lubnānī, 1981.

Querry, A. *Droit Musulman: Recueil de lois concernant les Musulman schyites*. 2 vols. Paris: Imprimerie Nationale, 1871-1872.

Qutb, Sayyed. *Islam and Universal Peace*. Indianapolis, Indiana: American Trust Publications, 1983.

Ralston, jackson H. *International Arbitration from Athens to Locarno*. Stanford, California: Stanford University press, 1929.

Ramcharan, B.G. "Equality and Non-discrimination." In *The International Bill of Rights*, pp. 246-269. Edited by Louis Henkin. New York: Columbia University Press, 1981.

Ramcharan, B.G. *The Right to Life in International Law*. Dordrecht, The Netherlands: Martinus Nijhoff Publishers, 1985.

Ramsey, Paul. "The Just War According to St. Augustine." In *Just War Theory*, pp. 8-22. Edited by Jean Bethke Elshtain. New York: New York University Press, 1992.

Ramsey, Paul. *The Just War: Force and Political Responsibility*. New York: Charles Scribner's Sons, 1968.

Rashid, Ahmed and Lawrence, Susan V. "Joining Foreign Jihad." *Far Eastern Economic Review* 163:36 (Sept. 7, 2000): 24.

al-Raysūnī, Aḥmad. *Naẓariyyat al-Maqāṣid 'ind al-Imām al-Shāṭibī*. Beirut: al-Mu'ssasa al-Jāmi'iyya lil-Dirāsāt wal-Nashr wal-Tawzī', 1992.

Rechid, Ahmed. "L'Islam et le droit des gens." *Recueil des cours* 60 (1937): 402-502.

Renard, John. "Al-Jihad al-Akbar: Notes on the Theme in Islamic Spirituality." *Muslim World* 78 (July-Oct. 1988): 225-242.

"The Retreat from fundametalism." *Economist* 351:8117 (May 1, 1999): 42.

Reuter, Paul. *Droit international public*. Paris: Presses Universitaires de France, 1958.

Roberts, Adam. "What is a Military Occupation?" *The British Year Book of International Law* 55 (1984): 249-305.

Roberts, Adam and Guelff, Richard, eds. *Documents on the Laws of War*. Oxford: The Clarendon Press, 1982.

Romahi, S. El-Wadi. *Diplomacy in Classical Islam*. Tokyo: Chuo University Press, 1989.

Russel, Frederick H. *The Just War in the Middle Ages*. Cambridge: Cambridge University Press, 1975.

Said, Eduard W. *Orientalism*. New York: Random House, 1979.

al-Sanhūrī, 'Abd al-Razzāq. *Maṣādir al-Ḥaqq fī al-Fiqh al-Isāmī*. 6 vols. Beirut: al-Majma' al-'Ilmī al-'Arabī al-Islāmī, n.d.

Salinger, Gerard George. "The 'Kitab al-Jihad' from Qadi Nu'man's 'Da'ā'im al-Islam': Translated with Introduction and Notes." Ph. D. diss., Columbia University, 1953.

Salmi, Ralph H. et. *al. Islam and Conflict Resolutions: Theories and Practices.* Lanham, Maryland: University Press of America, Inc., 1998.

Sanderson, Judith. "War, Peace, and Justice in the Hebrew Bible: A Representative Bibliography." In *Holy War in Ancient Israel.* Edited by Gerhard von Rad. Grand Rapids, Mich.: Eerdmans, 1991.

al-Sayyid, Ridwan. "Contemporary Muslim Thought and Human Rights." *Islamochristiana* 21 (1995): 27-41.

Schleifer, S. Abdullah. "Jihad and Traditional Islamic Consciousness." *I. C.* 27:4 (1983): 173-203.

Schleifer, S. Abdullah. "Understanding Jihad: Definition and Methodology." *Islamic Quarterly* 27:3 (1983): 118-131.

_______. "Jihad: Modernist Apologists, Modern Apologetics." *I. C.* 28 (1984): 25-46.

Schroeder, Ralph. *Max Weber and the Sociology of Culture*. London: Sage Publications, 1992.

Schwartz, David Aaron. "International Terrorism and Islamic Law." *Columbia Journal of Transnational Law* 29 (1991): 629-652.

Scott, J. B. *Classics of International Law*. New York: Oceana Publications, 1939.

Sen, B. *A Diplomat's Handbook of International Law and Practice*. The Hague, The Netherlands: Martinus Nijhoff Publishers, 1965.

Serjeant, R. B. "The 'Constitution' of Medina." *Islamic Quarterly* 8 (1964): 3-16.

Shalabī, Aḥmad. *Mawsū'at al-Tārīkh al-Islāmī*. 10 vols. Cairo: Maktabat al-Nahḍa al-Miṣriyya, 1984.

Sherwani, Haroon Khan. *Studies in Muslim Political Thought and administration*. Lahore, Pakistan: Sh. Muhammad Ashraf, 1945.

Shihata, Ibrahim. "Islamic Law and the World Community." *The Harvard International Law Club Journal* 4 (December 1962): 101-113.

Siddiqi, Aslam. "Jihad: An Instrument of Islamic Revolution." *Islamic Studies* 2 (1963): 383-398.

Sivan, Emmanuel. "The Holy War Tradition in Islam." *Orbis* 42:2 (Spring 1998): 171-194.

Solf, Waldemar A. "Protection of Civilians against the Effects of Hostilities under Customary International Law and Under Protocol I." *The American University Journal of International Law and Policy* 1 (Summer 1986): 117-135.

Sonn, Tamara. "Irregular Warfare and Terrorism in Islam: Asking the Right Questions." In *Cross, Crescent, and Sword: The Justification and Limitation of War in West and Islamic Tradition*, pp. 129-147. Edited by James Turner Johnson and John Kelsay. Westport, CT: Greenwood Press, 1990.

Stadter, I. Licher. "The Distinctive Dress of Non-Muslims in Islamic Countries." *Historia Judaica* 5 (1943): 33-52

Starke, J.G. *An Introduction to International Law*. London: Butterworths, 1977.

_______. "The Concept of Open Cities in International Humanitarian Law." *Australian Law Journal* 56:11 (November 1982): 593-597.

Stern, Jessica. "Pakistan's Jihad Culture." *Foreign Affairs* 79:6 (Nov-Dec 2000): 115-126.

Strawson, J. "A Western Question to the Middle East: Is there a Human Rights Discourse in Islam?" *Arab Studies Quarterly* 19:1 (1997): 31-58.

al-Tābi'ī, Muḥammad. *Al-Safārāt fī al-Islām.* Cairo: Maktabat Madbūlī, 1988.

Swidler, Leonard. "Human Rights and Religious Liberty: From the Past to the Future," in *Religious Liberties and Human Rights in Nations and in Religions*, ed. Leonard Swidler. Philadelphia and New York: Ecumenical Press and Hippocrene Books, 1986.

Talbi, Mohammed. "Religious Liberty: A Muslim Perspective." In *Religious Liberty and Human Rights in Nations and Religions*, pp. 175-187. Edited by Leonard Swidler. Philadelphia: Ecumenical Press, 1986.

Thomas, T. S. " Prisoners of War in Islam: A Legal Inquiry." *Muslim World* 87:1 (1997): 44-53.

Thornberry, Patrick. "Self-determination, Minorities, Human Rights: A Review of International Instruments." *International and Comparative Law Quarterly* 38 (October 1989): 867-889.

Thompson, Henry. *World Religions in War and Peace.* Jefferson, N. C.: McFarland, 1988.

Tibi, Bassam. *The Challenge of the Fundamentalism: Political Islam and the New World Disorder.* Berkeley, California: University of California Press, 1998.

Tillema, Herbert K. *International Armed Conflict Since 1945: A Bibliographic Handbook of Wars and Military Interventions.* London: Westview Press, 1991.

Tooke, Joan D. *The Just War in Aquinas and Grotius*. London: S.P.C.K., 1965.

Toope, Stephen J. *Cultural Diversity and Human Rights.* Montreal: McGill University Libraries, 1988.

_______. *Public International Law.* Montreal: McGill University, 1992.

Trend, J.B. "Spain and Portugal." In *The Legacy of Islam*, pp. 1-39. Edited by Thomas Arnold and Alered Guillaume. London: Oxford University Press, 1931.

Trimingham, J. Spencer. *Islam in the Sudan*. London: F. Cass, 1965.

Trowbridge, Stephen Van Rensselaer. "Mohammed's View of Religious War." *The Moslem World* 3 (1913): 290-305.

Tucker, Robert W. "The Interpretation of War." *The International Law Quarterly* 4:1 (1951): 11-38.

Turner, Bryan S. *Weber and Islam: A Critical Study*. London: Routledge & Kegan Paul, 1974.

al-'Ubaydī, Ḥammādī. *al-Shāṭibī wa Maqāṣid al-Sharī'a*. Tripoli, Libya: Manshūrāt Kulliyyat al-Da'wa al-Islāmiyya, 1992.

Vanderpol, A. *La doctrine scolastique du droit de la guerre*. Paris: A Pendone, 1925.

Von Rad, Gerhard. *Holy War in Ancient Israel*. Marval J. Dawn, trans. Grand Rapids, Mich.: Eerdmans, 1991.

Vreeland, Hamilton. *Hugo Grotius: The Father of the Modern Science of International Law*. New York: Oxford University Press, 1917.

Walters, LeRoy. "The Just War and the Crusade: Antitheses or Analogies?" *Monist* 57 (1973): 584-594.

Walzer, Michael. *Just and Unjust Wars: A Moral Argument with Historical Illustrations*. New York: Basic Books, Inc., Publishers, 1977.

Watt, Montgomery W. *The Influence of Islam on Medieval Europe*. Edinburgh: The University Press, 1972.

Watt, Montgomery W. *Islamic Political Thought: The Basic Concepts*. Edinburgh: Edinburgh University Press, 1968.

_______. "The Significance of the Theory of Jihad." In *Akten des VII. Kongresses fü Arabistik und Islamwissenschaft*, pp. 390-394. Edited by Herausgeben von and Albert Dietrich. Göttingen: Vandenhoeck & Ruprecht, 1976.

Weber, Max. *Economy and Society: An Outline of Interpretive Sociology*. 3 vols. New York: Bedminster Press, 1968.

Weeramantry, C.G. *Islamic Jurisprudence: An International Perspective*. London: Macmillan, 1988.

Wei, Su. "The Application of Rules Protecting Combatants and Civilians against the Effects of the Employment of Certain Means and Methods of Warfare." In *Implementation of International Humanitarian Law*, pp. 375-393. Edited by Frits Kalshoven and Yves Sandoz. Dordrecht, The Netherlands: Martinus Nijhoff Publishers, 1989.

Weinfeld, Moshe. "Divine Intervention in War in Ancient Israel and in the Ancient Near East." In *History, Historiography, and Interpretation: Studies in Biblical and Cuneiform Literatures.* Jerusalem: Magnes, 1983.

Wellhausen, Julius. "Muhammad's Constitution of Medina." In *Muhammad and the Jews of Medina,* pp. 128-138. Edited by A. J. Wensinck. Berlin: Adiyok, 1982.

Westbrook, David A. "Islamic International Law and Public International Law: Separate Expressions of World Ordet." *Virginia Journal of International Law* 33 (1993): 819-897.

Williams, John Alden. *Themes of Islamic Civilization.* Berkeley, California: University of California Press, 1971.

Williams, Robert Jeffrey. "A Socio-historicaal Analysis of Warfare (Jihad and Qital) in Primitive Islam (Arabia)." Ph. D., diss., The Florida State University, 1994.

Wright, Quincy. *A Study of War.* 2nd ed. Chicago: University of Chicago Press, 1965.

_______. "The Meaning of the Pact of Paris." *American Journal of International Law* 27 (1933): 39-61.

Wyman, Ann Crusa. "Christian and Islamic Medieval Understandings of Just War: Grounds for Comparison with Post-Persian Gulf War." Ph. D., diss., University of Maryland College Park, 1995.

Yamani, Ahmed Zaki. "Humanitarian International Law in Islam: A General Outlook." *Michigan Yearbook of International Legal Studies* 7 (1985): 189-215.

Youssef, Michael. "Al-Jihad: An Islamic Social Movement." Ph. D. diss., Emory University, 1984.

Youssef, Michael. *Revolt Against Modernity: Muslim Zealots and the West*. Leiden, The Netherlands: E.J. Brill, 1985.

Zawati, Hilmi. *Rights of the Palestinian People between Theoritical Position and Practical Application in the Occupied Territories*. Beirut: Assanabil Cultural Est., 1979.

Zemmali, Ameur. *Combattants et prisonniers de querre en droit international humanitaire*. Paris: Pedone, 1997.

al-Zuḥaylī, Wahba. al-'Alāqāt al-Dawliyya fī al-Islām Muqārana bil-Qānūn al-Dawlī al-Ḥadīth. Beirut: Mu'ssasat al-Risāla, 1981.

_______. *Āthār al-Ḥarb fī al-Fiqh al-Islāmī: Dirāsa Muqārana*. Damascus: Dār al-Fikr, 1992.

III. Cases

Copt v. Ibn 'Amr Ibn al-'Ās. Tārīkh al-Tabarī, vol. 2, p. 364.

Khālid Ibn al-Walīd v.Ḍirār Ibn al-Azwar. al-Sunan al-Kubrā, vol. 9, p.104.

Peoples of Smarkand v. Qutayba Ibn Muslim al-Bāhilī. Tārīkh al-Ṭabarī, vol. 3, p. 532.

IV. Legislations

Agreement for the Prosecution and Punishment of the Major War Criminals of the European Axis Powers and Charter of the International Military Tribunal, August 8, 1945, 82 U.N.T.S. 279, 59 Stat. 1544, E.A.S. No. 472.

Cairo Declaration on Human Rights in Islam. (A/CONF. 157/PC/62/Add. 18) Annex to Res. No. 49/19-P, 9 June 1993.

Charter of International Military Tribunal for the Far East, January 19, 1946, April 26, 1946, T.I.A.S. No. 1589, 4 Bevans 20.

Convention on the Prevention and Punishment of the Crime of Genocide. G.A. Res. 260A (III), 3(1) U.N. GAOR at 174, U.N. Doc. A/810, 1948.

Declaration on the Elimination of All Forms of Intolerence and of Discrimination Based on Religion or Belief. G.A. Res. 36/55, 36 U.N. GAOR, Supp. (No. 51) 171, U.N. Doc. A/36/51, 1981.

Declaration on the Protection of Women and Children in Emergency and Armed Conflict. G.A. Res. 3318 (XXIX), 29 U.N. GAOR, Supp. (No. 31) at 146, U.N. Doc. A/9631, 1974.

Declaration on the Rights of Persons Belonging to National or Ethnic, Religious and Linguistic Minorities. G.A. E/1992/22, Chap. II, Section A.

Geneva Convention I for the Amelioration of the Condition of the Wounded and Sick in Armed Forces in the Field, of August 12, 1949, 75 U.N.T.S. (1950) 31-83.

Geneva Convention III Relative to the Treatment of Prisoners of War, of August 12, 1949, 75 U.N.T.S. (1950) 135-285.

Geneva Convention IV Relative to the Protection of Civilian Persons in Time of War, of August 12, 1949, 75 U.N.T.S. (1950) 287-417.

Hague Convention IV Respecting the Laws and Customs of War on Land, of 1907, UKTS 9 (1910), Cd. 5030.

Hague Convention V Respecting the Rights and Duties of Neutral Powers and Persons in Case of Wars on Land, of 1907, 2 AJIL (1908) Supplement 117-127.

Hague Convention VIII Relative to the Laying of Automatic Submarine Contact Mines, of 1907, UKTS 12 (1910), Cd. 5116.

International Convention on the Elimination of All Forms of Racial Discrimination. G.A. Res. 2106 A (XX) 20 U.N. GAOR, Supp. (No. 14) at 47, U.N. Doc. A/6014, 1965.

International Covenant on Civil and Political Rights. G.A. Res. 2200 (XXI), 21 U.N. GAOR, Supp. (No. 16) at 52, U.N. Doc. A/6316, 1966.

Protocol I Additional to the Geneva Convention of 12 August 1949, and Relating to the Protection of Victims of International Law, 1977, UK Misc. 19 (1977), Cmnd. 6927.

Protocol II Additional to the Geneva Conventions, of August 12, 1949, and Relating to the Protection of Victims on Non-International Armed Conflicts, 1125 U.N.T.S. 609.

United Nations Charter, signed at San Francisco, 26 June 1945.

Universal Declaration of Human Rights. G.A. Res. 217 A(III), 3(1) U.N. GAOR Resolutions 71, U.N. Doc. A/810, 1948.

Universal Islamic Declaration of Human Rights, 1981, Human Rights Sourcebook (1987), 917-926.

Vienna Declaration and Programme of Action on Human Rights, Doc. A/CONF, 157/24 (Part 1), 13 Oct. 1993.

Index

www.ingramcontent.com/pod-product-compliance
Lightning Source LLC
LaVergne TN
LVHW090354210926
848480LV00002B/335